DENIS WAITLEY

TIMING IS EVERYTHING

Turning Your Seasons of Success into Maximum Opportunities

OLIVER
NELSON

THOMAS NELSON PUBLISHERS
Nashville

Published in Nashville, Tennessee, by Oliver-Nelson Books, a division of Thomas Nelson, Inc., Publishers, and distributed in Canada by Lawson Falle, Ltd., Cambridge, Ontario.

The Bible versions used in this publication are THE NEW KING JAMES VERSION, copyright © 1979, 1980, 1982, Thomas Nelson, Inc., Publishers, and the King James Version of the Holy Bible.

Sam Deep/Lyle Sussman, *Smart Moves*, © 1990, by Sam Deep/Lyle Sussman. Reprinted by permission of Addison-Wesley Publishing Company.

Printed in the United States of America.

Library of Congress Cataloging-in-Publication Data
Waitley, Denis.
    Timing is everything / Denis Waitley.
      p.   cm.
    ISBN 0-8407-9163-1 (hard)
    1. Success—Psychological aspects. 2. Time management.
  I. Title.
  BF637.S8W275   1992
  158′.1—dc20   92-22981
                                    CIP

1 2 3 4 5 6 — 97 96 95 94 93 92

TO

Susan,
the woman for all of my seasons

Contents

Habits; Block the Prime Time of Your Life; Twenty Ways to Live in Prime Time; Balance the Short View and the Long View; If Your First Plan Fails . . . Try Again!

SPRING

SUMMER

My Thanks and Gratitude

To Victor Oliver, my publisher, whose unbounded faith, integrity, energy, and creative brilliance have set a standard of excellence difficult to measure up to;

To Jan Dargatz, whose research, theme development, and writing skills propel an author like me to the next higher level of genuine quality;

To Sam Moore, and all the team members at Thomas Nelson, who are simply the finest and most respectable publishers in the world;

To Lila Empson, my senior editor, who has had to put up with my unique style on more than one occasion and whose talent and patience I would like to franchise;

To a loving God, who has blessed me with my family and a time to share.

To everything there is a season,
A time for every purpose under heaven . . .
A time to plant,
And a time to pluck what is planted.

—*Ecclesiastes 3:1,2*

1

Are You Waiting for Success?

♣

Are you waiting for success?
If you are, it will never arrive.
Success is who you are and what you do during each day and night.
It is not a reward or destination.
Success is a way of traveling, tilling, and gardening.
In my opinion, there are no successful people—only people who enjoy successful moments in time.
We hear about them every day.

· "He was at the right place at the right time."
· "Her timing was perfect."
· "It was an idea whose time had come."
· "She knows what she wants and goes after it with a passion."

For the most part, these statements apply to others. Rarely do we direct them toward ourselves. But what if we could say proudly and honestly,

· "I placed myself at the right place at the right time."
· "My timing was perfect."

· "It was my idea whose time had come."
· "I know what I want and go after it with a passion."

Why not?

I believe the major reason is that we are "out of sync," like the engine of a car distributing the spark to the wrong energy chambers at the wrong time. Or like an amateur farmer in a hurry to harvest what has not been properly planted and cultivated during specific growing seasons.

Timing may not be everything in life, but when it comes to success, it's difficult to think of another single factor that makes or breaks more people's lives. Everything ultimately happens at a point in time, and when the convergence of factors in time is positive . . . success is unavoidable!

Again and again as I travel throughout the world, observing, lecturing, and learning, I meet individuals who have experienced phenomenal successes (and a few who have experienced phenomenal failures), and they tell me that *timing* was the number one factor in their success or failure.

Mastering time—not only the minutes and hours of each day but the "times" of one's life—is essential to turning dreams into reality and to achieving the goals you set for yourself.

Literature and everyday conversation are both filled with references to the seasons of a person's life. The seasons are not mere literary devices or metaphors; they are very real. Life has phases, passages. It has periods clearly delineated by beginnings and endings. Most important, these periods come in *sequence*. They occur and recur. They imprint our lives with a pattern of growth and rest that is simultaneously cosmic and intensely personal.

This book is about the seasons of success in your life. It is about being at the right place at the right time with the right plan . . . by choice rather than by chance.

It's about understanding the seasons and using them to maximum advantage for professional, personal, family, and financial fulfillment. It's about living the maximum life with minimum strife.

What time is it . . .

what season is it . . .

in your *life?*

If you're successful in your business and personal lives, if you want to stay committed and on track, and if you desire to gain even more enrichment than you are presently enjoying, this book is designed with you in mind.

If you have had success before and are facing challenges today in renewing and recapturing that success, this book is also designed for you.

And if you are highly effective most of the time but sometimes find it difficult to stay focused and keep moving up, this book can make a real difference in the way you approach your goals in the future.

We're about to enter a new century of human growth and development. We need to reexamine and reevaluate the way we think and the way we choose our actions and responses to life's daily experiences in this era of unprecedented change.

We need a fresh, enduring strategy for viewing our potential and mapping out our goals—goals that are truly worthwhile, believable, and achievable. What will make this happen? Informing ourselves and others about how to find the right way at the right time.

This is especially critical in today's global neighborhood in which the game of life is unbelievably complex. The players are more knowledgeable and sophisticated, the pace is much faster, the stakes are higher, and the playing field is anything but level.

This book will help you uncover the fertile soil for growth within yourself and in your global playing field, giving you the right tools to prosper.

It is about planting the right kinds of seeds and watering them, cultivating them, fertilizing them, and pruning them after they bloom to bear the most abundant fruit.

This book is about the joy of reaping harvests of inner and outer wealth and of sharing these harvests with others in a great celebration of thanksgiving.

It is about making *now* your season, your time, your turn . . .
                                                    . . . to WIN!

2

Timing Is Everything!

Ever since childhood I've been convinced that real success in life has no apparent relationship to a gifted birth, special talent, or intelligence quotient. How can we account for identical twins born and raised in a ghetto by a single parent—one stays in the ghetto and becomes a mirror of the environment, and the other becomes a national youth leader? Or how can we account for two children raised by educated, nurturing parents in a fine neighborhood—one becomes a circuit court judge, and the other goes to prison for drug peddling?

My boyhood environment was a roller coaster of confusion and conflicting input: love, divorce, picnics, World War II, nourishment, insecurity. Emerging from those groping, struggling, and frequently frustrating youth years, I entered into twenty years of career that were marked by only fleeting success.

In many ways, I did not grow in those years beyond the understanding I had as a boy of nine working alongside my grandmother in a Victory garden we planted. I learned from our garden of homegrown vegetables and fruits that what we put in the soil had a direct relationship to the harvest we reaped. Carrot seeds yielded carrots. Weeding helped. Watering was vital. What didn't sink in, however, was that the growing time for each crop is different. Not all crops grow as quickly as beans and radishes.

I came to expect from life the immediacy of that summer garden, and my career was marked by impatience. As soon as I planted the seeds of a worthwhile project, I expected immediate gratification, and I lost interest quickly in anything that didn't bear instantaneous, visible results. Even into my thirties, I was like a little boy playing farmer, digging up my planted seeds every few days to see how they were doing.

I also fell into the trap experienced by nearly all adolescents and young adults. I believed I was physically immortal. Therefore, I had no sense of planning for the long run of my health.

In all, the picture of the first four decades of my life is distinctly different in quality from the life I lead today.

I am now winning across the board. My career has mushroomed. My personal and family lives are exceptionally rewarding. My wife and I love and respect each other and truly like being around each other. Our six children are on their own, most having found a gratifying profession after graduating from college, and two having decided to gain more education to become teachers. I harbor no hostility or resentment to anyone. I enjoy good health and have learned to convert the stress I used to endure into productive energy for achievement and service to others. I relish life with a passion and stand in awe of God's craftsmanship as I explore the wonders of the natural world.

What happened? How did I turn my life around from one of frustration to one of celebration? Very simply, I took a deep breath, stepped back from the landscape of my life, applied my research and the principles of this book to my life—and began to allocate my *time* as if my life and health depended on it.

Of all the wisdom I have gained, the knowledge that time and health are taken for granted until they are depleted has caused me to reorder my daily priorities. As with health, time is the raw material of life. Many people spend their time at nothing more than hurrying around, getting ready to live, yet never arriving anywhere. We can bide our time, but we can't save it for another day. We can waste and kill time, but by killing time, we also are mortally wounding our opportunities.

Time is the ruler in each person's life. Each human being has exactly 168 hours a week and so many finite hours and minutes each day. Think about it! Scientists can't invent more minutes.

Superrich people can't buy more hours. Queen Elizabeth I of England—the richest, most powerful woman on earth of her era—whispered these final words on her deathbed: "All my possessions for a moment of time!"

We worry about things we want to do but can't instead of doing things we can do but don't. It is not the experience of today that causes us the greatest stress. It is the regret for something we did or didn't do yesterday, and the apprehension of what tomorrow may bring.

For me, the moment of truth came in 1972, at the age of thirty-nine. I looked in the mirror and saw a stranger in a hurry, going nowhere. To that point, my life had been a kaleidoscope of experience. I had flown supersonic jets as a navy pilot, given simulation seminars to Apollo astronauts, enrolled in a doctoral program in human behavior, traveled the world, skied Vail and Aspen with my wife and children, hobnobbed with entertainment and sports heroes, made the rounds on Wall Street and Madison Avenue, and devoted several years to raising money in behalf of Dr. Jonas Salk at the Salk Institute for Biological Studies in La Jolla, California.

My house, perched on a cliff high above the ocean, had an unobstructed view of the entire southern California coastline from La Jolla to Laguna Beach. I literally had the view from the top, but I had no inner perspective or vision. I appeared to be in a rich harvest season materially, but in other areas of my life, I had barely begun to plant.

I had everything going for me . . . and nothing coming together. It was as if life was a race to get through as fast as possible. I had the house but not the home life. I had the family, the photo albums, and the videotaped memories but not the spiritual foundation so vital to relationships. Like everything else, religion, at that time, was a ritual wedged into an overloaded calendar.

That isn't to say I didn't care about my family, my community, my church, my fellow citizens, and a life of service. I did! My problem was one of motivation and prioritizing my goals. In many ways, I was expecting harvests for which I hadn't yet planted seeds. I was out of sync and going against the seasons. I did the urgent but put off the important. I was having a lot of fun but wasn't really happy. I was doing the right things *at the wrong time*.

No single event caused me to change my approach to life. Rather, several experiences came together to leave me with a sense of wasted minutes and squandered time. My twentieth high-school reunion had been a disaster. I saw tired middle-aged people who claimed to be my classmates. We had to wear name badges so we could put faces with names!

That same week, my pastor and I went flying. At ten thousand feet he turned off the gas pump and refused to turn it back on until I made a commitment to live my religion instead of giving it lip service and a weekly ten-dollar offering. He really knew how to get my full attention!

The next week after attending church, my wife and I piled the family in the station wagon and headed for the La Jolla Beach and Tennis Club to watch our sons compete in a local swim meet. In between events, I took a stroll down the beach by myself to do some soul-searching. Walking north beyond the pier of the Scripps Institution of Oceanography, I paused among the tidal pools. If you have ever spent time observing these miniature universes, you know they are teeming with life.

As I watched the anemones, tiny sculpin, and skittering crabs, I asked myself some questions:

· How would I like a parent like me if I were my children?
· How would I like to be married to me?
· How would I like an employee like me if I were my employer?
· How would I like a manager like me if I were my employee?
· If it weren't for time, money, or circumstance, what would I do with my life?
· Why, with all my creative ability, education, experience, and drive, am I not really building any lasting success?

The answers to the first four hard questions came easily: "Sort of but not really." The answer to question five also came easily: If it weren't for time, money, or circumstance, I would write books and give lectures on the very topic with which I was struggling—"Life Management."

The answer to the last question came to me after many more hours of reflection, self-assessment, and prayer. I wasn't building any authentic, lasting success because I was substituting spur-of-the-moment ideas and frantic action for thoughtful planning and planting. And I was confusing procrastination and laziness with patience. Like a frustrated scientist who finally stumbles onto the solution that has been hiding in front of his eyes all along, I discovered that . . . **timing is everything!**

I learned that while we all say we don't have enough time in this rapidly changing world, each of us has all there is. I also learned that none of us really has a time management problem. We really have a *time-sequence* problem and a *priority management* opportunity.

It would take several books for me to tell you what happened during the ensuing years to confirm my belief that timing is everything and that, for the most part, you create your own timing by choice, not by chance.

Perhaps the most critical concept to internalize from this book is that there is a *sequence of success* for each project and for each area of your life. These sequences frequently overlap from one area to the next.

Let me share an example from my experience. At the time I was in the final stage of earning my doctoral degree in human behavior, I was in the field-testing phase of my public speaking career. At that same time, I was in the research and planning phase of my first book. In the terminology with which you'll become familiar in this book, I was in

- the *autumn* season of my academic life.
- the *early summer* season of my public speaking career.
- the *winter* season of my career as an author.

Simultaneously.

The summer of 1972 also became the winter, or dreaming time, for my research into high-performance healthy behavior. I was in the final stages of writing my doctoral dissertation entitled "The Psychology of Winning."

I took a portion of my academic harvest—my dissertation—and used it as the seed for a new nonfiction book and audio program upon which I planned to base my entry into the self-improvement industry.

From 1972 to 1977 I focused my professional efforts—my research, my associations, my reading and listening—on preparing the very best program possible on ten common denominators exhibited by winning human beings. That five-year period became the spring, or planting time, of my effort toward success as an author and lecturer.

And as I researched, dug, and planted the ideas on paper and in my mind, I internalized the concepts and began to practice what I preached. I began to appear at local service clubs as an after-dinner speaker. Gradually, the invitations to speak increased and became more varied.

With a new career entering a summer stage of growth, I embarked on a winter, or planning season, in my personal life. I weeded out the unimportant posturing and escaping and concentrated on building a new marriage and a family life that could endure any circumstance. Cocktail parties were replaced with fireside chats with loved ones. Sports stars and show business acquaintances were superseded by educators, scientists, thinkers, and role models who set an outstanding example in their service to others.

Instead of caring about how good I looked or sounded to others, I embarked on a program of seeking a healthy life-style and inner joy.

And I made a concerted effort to keep my priorities in sequence and in season, regardless of difficulties, temptations, or problems encountered along the way. I did my homework. I planned each project. I put in the effort and built a network of relationships to give my projects roots. And I persisted patiently.

In 1978, I reaped a major career harvest. Earl Nightingale and Lloyd Conant, founders of Nightingale-Conant Corporation, the pioneers of audio programs for personal and professional growth, published *The Psychology of Winning.*

The timing was perfect for the harvest—but it was no accident. I had completed my doctoral studies and a significant amount of research so that my book and tape bore both the credentials of academia and the depth of substance. I had put in literally thousands of hours of public speaking to audiences across the nation. Furthermore, my personal life was on an even forward-moving keel so that my family and I could take the career harvest in stride.

The Psychology of Winning, in audio form, has become the most listened to personal growth program in the world. One out of every twenty Americans has listened to the tapes or read the book. It has been published in seventeen languages. It was the seedbed for my writing and speaking career. I found myself at the right place at the right time with the right stuff. Like me, hundreds of thousands of individuals were eager to put their lives together as a total person in learning that success is a way of traveling, not a destination.

The harvest of *The Psychology of Winning,* of course, was not the end of the story. That book and tape effort became the seed-bed for future projects—including the ones I enjoy today.

The Seven Principles of Timing in Your Life

What I learned through these life-transforming years of moving from sporadic success to pervasive success . . . from career-only success to total life success . . . from immediate happen-stance success to planned, well-executed success . . . were seven vital principles that relate to timing. Let me share them with you. . . .

Principle 1: View your success from the long view of time.

Success is a process, not a status. I don't believe success is something to be possessed. Rather, it is the lifelong process of becoming all we can and should be. Real success has little to do with money, although there is nothing wrong with being a rich success. Some rich people are extremely successful; others are not.

Too often we narrow our ideas about success to fit the popular mold. We spend a great deal of time, effort, and money trying to display how successful we are—or wish we were—with material possessions, rituals, and styles to impress others. If we measure our success only by what we produce or purchase, we are doomed to eternal dissatisfaction. There is always someone who can produce or purchase more, faster, or better. There is always someone new who is prettier, more popular, smarter, or stronger.

If you base success on who you know, where you go, and what you've got to show, you've got what I call the Edifice Complex, which is the need to build monuments to your own progress for posterity.

The truth is, we can't buy success or happiness, nor can we wear it, drive it, live in it, or travel to it. Success and happiness are rooted in the inner life, the being and living through the sea-sons—not in the outer trappings, the items we own and acquire, the positions and honors we achieve and receive.

What good are fortune and fame if we miss the truly valuable things in life, such as love, health, respect, family, and friends, to name only a few?

Success is the collection of your memories, the employment and enjoyment of your present moments, and the anticipation of the coming seasons. To say, "I am a success," is to attach some kind of permanence to the word as if nothing will ever change or as if things will always be the way they are now. But things don't stay the same. Everything changes—above all, success. Success is fickle and fleeting, but *living successfully is always possible.*

All enduring success must be grown from the inside out. A feeling of inner success is much more difficult to acquire than material success. It requires questioning what we really want out of life. It demands self-honesty and the realization that success is not a constant. It must be continually renewed through the seasons.

Success is looking in the mirror, at any given moment in time, and seeing someone of value you respect as a role model.

Principle 2: View your failures from the short view of time.

Failure is delay, not defeat. It is a temporary detour, not a dead-end street. Regard it as a short-term phenomenon.

Choose to use failure as the fertilizer of your success. Farmers use manure, decomposed plants, mulch, and other substances to fertilize their crops. In much the same way, your failures and disappointments can be used to enrich the soil of your mind for planting the seeds of success.

Some people say that failure should be avoided at all costs. But if you think it through, that cost is too high. The only way to avoid failure at all costs is to do nothing. Although you avoid failure and defeat by doing nothing, you also avoid success and fulfillment.

The way to turn failure into fertilizer is to use your errors and mistakes as a way to learn and then to dismiss those errors and mistakes from your mind. Use failures and disappointments only as corrective feedback to get you on target again. It has been said that failure should be our teacher, not our undertaker.

One of my mentors, Dr. Jonas Salk—who developed the polio vaccine and who is now engaged in research to find a vaccine for the HIV virus associated with AIDS—has said that he spends 98 percent of his time documenting things that don't work in his pursuit of things that do.

The board game we all play, Monopoly, was created by Charles

Darrow, an unemployed heating engineer. Darrow took his first version of the game to a toy company in 1935. That company originally rejected the game for containing fifty-two fundamental errors. Darrow wasn't defeated, however. He used that temporary failure to refine his success! Today, the game is so popular that its maker, Parker Brothers, prints more Monopoly money every year than the amount of real money printed annually by the U.S. Bureau of Engraving and Printing.

Only one danger can arise from adversity—to mistake the failure as yourself rather than as an event. Contemporary psychologists agree that setbacks and failures mean little in themselves. The meaning of any failure—or any success, for that matter—is in how we take it and what we make of it.

Principle 3: Dreams and goals must be charted in time to be realized.

A dream is your creative vision for your life in the future. It is what you would like life to become. A goal is what, specifically, you intend to make happen. Dreams and goals should be just out of your present reach but not out of sight. Two great tragedies in life are never to have had great dreams and goals for yourself *and* to have fully reached them so that tomorrow holds no eager anticipation of challenge.

Many individuals become spectators, resigned to experience success vicariously through others' accomplishments. They can see success for others, but they can't imagine it for themselves.

Dreams and goals are previews of coming attractions in your life.

In all of my studies of high-performance, happy individuals during the past twenty-five years, I have found several common denominators that make the critical difference between those who are successful achievers and those who are part of the vast unsuccessful majority. Here are three of them:

- *Successful people believe in their dreams,* even if dreams are all they have to go on.
- *Successful people shape their dreams* into specific goals and action plans. They have a sense of direction. They know where they are headed. Furthermore, they project dreams and goals into time.
- *Successful people work their plans.* They exert effort, adapt,

and persevere until their goals are reached. They develop the skills needed for planting, replanting, and cultivating until they reap the harvest they desire. They put in the time required.

Your dreams and goals are vital to your success, but they will never yield success until you place them in time.

Perhaps the greatest torture that could be devised would be for us to be forced, in our later years, to watch a continuously repeating videotape of the lives we could have led had we dared to believe in and pursue the dreams and goals that were available and attainable in our lifetimes.

Principle 4: Your purpose in life will determine how you choose to segment and prioritize your time.

Purpose is the engine that powers our lives. Without it, we toil in a job but never build a career. Without purpose, work becomes a necessary interruption between weekends. Weekends, to many people, are an escape from a weekly prison of purposelessness.

The success of an effort depends not so much on the outcome of the effort but on the motive for making the effort in the first place. The motive makes the difference. The greatest companies, the greatest men and women in all walks of life, have achieved their greatness out of a desire to express something within themselves that had to be expressed, a desire to solve a problem using their skills and creativity as best they could. This is not to say that many of these individuals have not earned a great deal of money and prestige for what they have accomplished. Many have. But the key to their success is to be found in the fact that they were motivated more by providing excellence in a product or service to fill a need than by thinking of profit.

All of your real value and worth is built in by design. You received it as a precious present when God gave you the gift of life. That gift—all of what's in you—is really all the value you'll ever need. It isn't a matter of finding value, earning value, or proving value. It's a matter of living up to the value built in at the beginning.

Truly successful individuals look to contribute, not to receive. The employees who love their mission and their work get the raises and promotions more often than the employees who care the most about getting the raises and promotions.

Real winners don't look for achievements that will bring them the most with the least amount of effort. They look for the challenges that will mean the most to overcome. They do not seek get-rich-quick schemes, lottery jackpots, or pyramid fads. They look for something difficult—some problem to solve—the accomplishment of which will give them great personal satisfaction.

Many people have confided in me that they don't have the vaguest idea about their purpose in life. They lack a spiritual connection and are not open to looking beyond their mortality for meaning. For them, I simply offer the idea that they can begin to discover their purpose by learning the most, experiencing the most, and sharing the most value they possibly can *with other human beings.* To make life breathe easier for one person every day is to make a worthwhile start toward a destination that we can never fully reach but will be a process that gives meaning to our existence. There is always another opportunity to learn, to grow, and to extend our reach to someone groping for our strength.

Principle 5: Your sense of responsibility and your integrity keep you concerned with time.

Why are American industries suffering from foreign competition? Why are companies downsizing? Why are future generations likely to enjoy less prosperity than their parents have? Why is the American dream fading? Who is to blame?

The real problem is that everyone is pointing the finger at someone else.

A verse in the New Testament talks about sowing and reaping. Whatever we sow, we reap, says Galatians 6:7. God's unfailing boomerang is that we cause our own effects in life by our choices and actions. Who you are goes full circle, and that is exactly what a boomerang is designed to do.

The person of integrity does not blame others for his failure—or expect others to provide his success. He shoulders his own destiny.

If there's one quality above all others that I want my children to epitomize, it is this: personal responsibility. I take 100 percent of the responsibility for my choices and actions in life. Every choice has a corresponding reward or consequence based on the integrity of that choice.

A little quote above my desk guides me through the seasons:

"Life is like a field of newly fallen snow. Where I choose to walk, every step will show."

Principle 6: Perseverance maintains you through the passing of time.

Much of what you will read in the pages ahead has to do with perseverance, or staying power. The lack of persistence is the major reason most people fail to attain their goals.

Perseverance means doing the tough things first and looking downstream for gratification and rewards. It means being dedicated to gaining more knowledge and making more progress. It means making more calls, going more miles, establishing more contacts, challenging more of your own time-grown assumptions, getting up earlier, and always being on the lookout for a better way of doing what you're doing.

Perseverance is sticking with it when the odds stack up against you. It is very often taking the road least traveled by your friends and peers. Perseverance is not complaining but sustaining.

Patience is the subtle side of persistence. Patience cautions us to focus our efforts on what we can change and accept what we cannot. When external circumstance rains on our parade, patience is our umbrella. Instead of blaming what we cannot control, patience gives us pause for reflection so we can dry off and start looking for a new way.

Everything, over time, is either ongoing or offgoing. We achieve our goals, we abandon them, or we . . .

Hang in there! You see, when a goal is distant and difficult to reach, patience is our ally. Time changes everything, but with patience, we can keep our desires relatively constant. If we can just hang on long enough, we know that time will finally create for us the conditions in which we can succeed.

How does patience relate to the deep desire to find a destiny worthy of ourselves? It is absolutely indispensable. No one can attain the fullness of his or her whole life early in life or according to a timetable. No one can find a destiny worthy of a full life without living that full life conscientiously, passionately, and organically in the natural order in which it comes. When we plant a flower or a tree, we need to have the patience to let it grow, and the same is true of ourselves.

As long as we are persistent in our pursuit of our deepest destiny, we will continue to grow. We cannot choose the day or time when we will bloom fully. It will happen in its own time. The secret of success is to live wholeheartedly, honestly, and steadfastly in each season as it comes.

Principle 7: Success is SEQUENCED in time.

Most everything in life can be broken down into phases. We do that with our lives. Even though we live our lives as a seamless day-to-day-to-day flow, we speak about infancy, childhood, teenage years, college days, young adult years, middle age, and golden years as if they were specific stages or phases through which we all pass.

The same holds true for the seasons—or the "phases"—of our success management. The seasons of our success are stages, segments, time frames. The good news is that unlike the seasons of the year or the seasons of your life, you can control the seasons of your success. You make time work for you!

In your success . . .

It's not a matter of being in the right place at the right time nearly as much as it is a matter of taking the time to determine what the right place and time ought to be!

The next chapter tells you more about how the seasons work and can work for you.

3

What Season Is It?

Successful people are at the right place at the right time to a great extent because they have learned how to take certain action steps in proper sequence. They have learned that scriptural truth, "To everything there is a season,/A time for every purpose under heaven." They know that everything they desire has an appropriate place and time for accomplishment, and toward that end, they set their priorities in certain orders, prepare themselves in certain ways, and refuse to give in to discouragement or failures along the way.

What about those who are unsuccessful?

Some fail because they lack dreams or they don't believe in the possibility of their dreams becoming reality. Some fail to reach their full potential of a rewarding harvest in life because they have not turned their dreams into specific goals and plans of action for reaching those goals. Many others fail, however, because they are out of sync with time and place:

- They planted or fertilized their goals in the wrong season.
- They planted before they fully planned.
- They attempted to harvest a goal before it was fully developed.

Such failures arise not from a lack of determination or willingness to keep trying but from efforts that are out of proper sequence. The result is that those who fail because of their improper alignment of time and place soon become frustrated, begin to believe that it's impossible for them to achieve anything significant, or allow their disappointments to develop into a failure-anticipating mind-set.

If that is the case in your life . . . I have good news for you! You can become a success-experiencing winner in every area of your life. It is possible to "grow" a rewarding harvest. But first, you must learn the secrets to . . .

Mastering the Seasons

We are confronted at every turn with seasons—football season, baseball season, basketball season, hunting season, the opera or concert season, the holiday season. Let's note several key characteristics about seasons as they relate to your success.

Number One: The seasons of success do NOT tie in directly with the natural seasons.

We are using the natural growing seasons—winter, spring, summer, and autumn—only as an analogy in this book because they are something to which we all can relate at some level. Even if we have never set foot on a farm, we have some understanding of what it takes to plan, plant, till, and harvest a crop.

I've found that the dentist in Denver, the salesperson in Seattle, the minister in Miami, the entrepreneur in Elgin, the supervisor in San Diego, and the foreman in Fort Worth all seem to understand the principle of natural growth and natural seasons. The seasons are a common denominator for us.

In this book, we'll deal with the seasons in this way:

· WINTER is the season for DREAMING and PLANNING.
· SPRING is the season for PLANTING.
· SUMMER is the season for GROWING and CULTIVATING.
· AUTUMN is the season for HARVESTING and DISPERSING.

Therefore . . .
The thermometer outside your kitchen window may say 105°

as you plan. Even though the weather is scorching, you'll be in the winter season, the planning season, of your success.

The snow may be coming down at a blizzard pace as you work through the long, hard months of your success summer. Even though the calendar says winter, on the success cycle you're between planting and harvesting.

Number Two: The seasons are NOT necessarily all the same length.

The planning (winter) season for one area of your life may last a couple of weeks. The planting (spring) season may last years.

Conversely, the planning season may take longer than the planting season. The winter season may very well be the most time-intensive season you experience.

In fact, at the end of this book, the entire cycle of success is compressed into a 90-day time frame so that you may walk through, step-by-step, the processes involved and experience a short-range harvest.

Number Three: A season has a beginning and an ending.

Each season has a starting and stopping point. This is true especially in the cultural and athletic seasons—the first game, the final four, the World Series, the Super Bowl, the last concert, the final package unwrapped. The seasons have a less precise starting and stopping point in nature; even so, we have an awareness that seasons come and go. We mark their arrival on our calendars with specific dates, of course. Winter begins "officially" on December 21, spring on March 20, summer on June 20, autumn on September 22—at midnight!

On a more practical level, we mark the change of seasons by the way we dress and the way we decorate our homes, and we even alter our eating patterns from ice cream to hot stew. We note the changes in season as a part of daily conversations: "Autumn is finally in the air"; "Spring has sprung"; "Winter has hit"; "Summer has arrived." The seasons are always in forward progress, each one moving us ever closer to the next one in a steady march of days.

The same holds true for the seasons of success. Each has a beginning and an ending. The time comes to shift gears and to enter the next phase of our growth—to do all that we can do in one season and then move to the next.

Number Four: The seasons ALWAYS come in sequence.

Spring always follows winter. Autumn always comes after summer. We have no control over the order in which the seasons occur.

The same is true for the seasons of success. One cannot "harvest" life's rewards without first planting seeds.

The seasons are a tool for us to use in grappling with the idea of time sequencing and priority management. The seasons of success follow each other. Furthermore, one season in the success sequence makes possible the next. Without a successful planning time, you have no focus for planting your efforts. Without a successful planting, you'll have nothing to till and cultivate. Without proper management of your growing season, you'll never reap the harvest you desire.

Number Five: "Crops" of success may have different growing periods, but all follow the same sequence of seasons.

In the natural world, beans can be planted, sprout, and grow to maturity in a matter of a few weeks. A grapevine, on the other hand, takes several years of cultivation and growth before it reaches the point of peak production. The beans must be planted and harvested annually. A grapevine may live and continue to produce in a seasonal pattern for several decades. Both types of plants, however, are subject to the same principles of growth: A time to plant, a time to cultivate, a time to harvest.

And along the way . . . a proper time to prepare the soil, to prune away unfruitful branches, and to train the vines.

Some of your successes will fall into place quickly. Others will take years. One area of your life may experience slow growth; another, more rapid growth. The overriding concept to keep in mind is this: The growing sequence for success remains the same regardless of the area of your life or the speed with which certain goals are reached.

Number Six: "Success crops" may be cultivated in several areas of your life simultaneously.

Beans and grapes—strawberries and almonds, cotton and alfalfa—can be grown side by side, as is so frequently seen in the valleys of California where I make my home. One crop is harvested even as another is sprouting. The same principle applies to your success in various areas.

You may be in one season in your personal, social, or family life —and in quite a different one in your career or business. You may face one set of seasonal challenges as you seek to develop a new skill or to complete a degree program—even as you face quite a different set of seasonal challenges in your effort to become more physically fit or healthy.

The activities and arenas of life overlap. Many types of success may be at various stages of growth in our lives *simultaneously*. However . . . each activity or arena follows the same sequencing of seasons toward a successful harvesttime.

Number Seven: The seasons come again next year.

We never fully arrive as life-farmers. We do not have the luxury of living in a harvest season forever. Chances are, we wouldn't want to do so even if it were possible! We always have before us the potential of tomorrow, no matter how bright or how grim today may seem.

A farmer never relies on the yield of the present harvest to last him for the rest of his life. He reaps and immediately begins to prepare for a new and greater harvest next year.

The successful person also never relaxes very long in the glow of current accomplishments. He or she always anticipates more. The wise person celebrates success rather than tries to capture it forever.

More may not be defined in quantitative as much as qualitative terms. It may not be counted in terms of number of square feet, number of dollars, number of employees, number of executive toys. It may be counted in terms of greater fulfillment, greater meaning, greater joy, greater depth of relationships that count. Still, the anticipation is there in the successful person that life holds more.

· Have you accomplished a goal? Set a new one!
· Have you seen a long-held dream become a reality? Dream a new dream!
· Have you experienced a new plateau of achievement? Look up to a still higher plane!
· Have you entered a new phase of inner joy? Be aware that even greater joy lies ahead!

The successful person is always seeking out the next area for growth, mapping out the next plan, working on the next idea, pursuing the next opportunity, looking for the next challenge, aiming at the next target.

Our work as life-farmers is never completed. On a personal level, we find there's always more nurturing, more adapting, more changing, more setting of priorities, more weeding out of bad habits, more coping with, and more adapting that we can do.

The successful garden of life—just as the successful flower or vegetable garden—is always in transition. It is always in process. It is always subject to the rhythms and cycles of life that are much broader and all-encompassing than the will of the farmer.

We are always facing new challenges and attempting to overcome new obstacles as we confront the workings of external unforeseen forces. Although the garden never reaches a state of perfection or conclusion, the cycle of growing and harvesting yields fulfillment, meaning, fruit, livelihood. The purpose for the growing is culminated in harvest. In a broader sense, the harvest is ongoing; purpose is found in participating fully in all that gives order, meaning, total perspective, and synergy to our lives *during* the process of growing and changing, sowing and reaping.

Number Eight: EVERY person is capable of managing the seasons of success.

Each of us is given seeds.

Each of us is subject to the patterns of life's weather, pestilences, and the twists, turns, and tugs of nature.

Each of us bears fruit—a yield—very often in direct relationship to our ability to till, to plant, to nurture, and to reap.

I have always looked upon life as a magnificent fertile garden plot that has been given to me as a gift. It is my responsibility—as it is yours—to tend my plot and to tend it in a way that brings the greatest productivity and satisfaction.

Our goal must be like that of every farmer . . .

> *Seek and expect the*
> *greatest*
> *harvest possible.*

To the 95 percent of the international population that is less fortunate than you or I, success is having a bit of land to farm, a job that pays enough to cover the most basic bills, and a way to provide enough food and medicine for one's children to grow to adulthood.

To you and me—who live in a veritable Garden of Eden compared to most of the rest of the world—success also includes the satisfactory manifestation of our personal goals and dreams. We have already achieved a way of satisfying our basic needs for food, water, shelter, clothing, warmth, and personal protection. Our goals now have become ones related to quality, to meaning, to having a purpose in life.

Success to you and me means more than survival and mere security. It is taking the talents we were born with and the skills we have developed and using them fully toward a purpose that makes us feel worthwhile. Happiness is the natural fruit of living a worthwhile life—regardless of one's status, material possessions, or external appearance. *Our* success must include bringing benefit to others. A current level of success is never adequate if you catch a glimpse of the needs around you. Once you capture an awareness and feel a responsibility for helping others, you'll aim at an even higher level of success.

Therefore, no matter what you experience today or experienced in the past . . .

Expect a better year!

No matter what your past might have held, no matter the results of this year's harvest—good or bad—anticipate a better harvest ahead!

No matter where you are in life, in terms of status, age, or personal development, you have an opportunity before you to grow a bigger and better success.

The successful person doesn't lean back on his laurels. He leans forward in anticipation of a new race to be run . . . and won.

Furthermore, he faces that challenge with hope. I have yet to meet a farmer—a true-to-the-bone, heartfelt, wouldn't-be-anything-else-but-a farmer—who doesn't have a perpetual belief that next year will be an even better year. No matter the yield of one crop or one year's worth of crops, a farmer always sets the goal of besting his best the next go-round. He invests in better fertilizers and pesticides, more advanced equipment, and new and improved strains of seed. He bones up on the latest information—whether he gets it from agricultural magazines or shoptalk around the tables at the local cafe. He conducts a personal study of the weather and of marketing trends. And always he has an eye on the *next* harvest, which he is sure will be his *best* harvest.

Expect the NEXT
to be the BEST.

That's the attitude of hope we must have as we tackle the seasons of success. That's the attitude that will keep us motivated toward a harvest.

That unseen attitude of hope is ultimately the reason a farmer continues to produce year after year . . . and a life continues to be productive decade after decade. Take away a farmer's hope, and he'll walk away. When he does, the land dries up or becomes overgrown with unfruitful foliage. Take away forward momentum and hope in life, and life withers.

Kindle your hope today. Look for a harvest ahead!

The opportunity for success *is* yours. Believe it. Regardless of what you experienced in your past, the future can hold success for you. No matter how bleak you may feel right now, you can know the joy of a harvest.

And now . . .

Begin your cultivation of success today by choosing to experience the WINTER SEASON to its fullest.

Getting Ready for Winter

 Do you have a dream for your life?

 Do you have identifiable, concrete, written goals for your life?

 Do you have a plan for turning your goals into action and for engineering your action into time?

Unless your answer is yes to each of these questions, you need to begin your quest for success in WINTER.

Winter

THE SEASON FORECAST

To the unsuccessful person: Winter is a bleak time. The ground lies frozen, the earth unproductive. The trees are bare and seem lifeless. Cold paralyzes. Snow and ice slow us down, hem us in, and cover our potential for growth. This is the time to hole up, hibernate, wait out life, drudge on, and expect little.

To the successful person: Winter is alive with dreaming. Visions arise from the red-hot glow of the fireplace. Conversations are lively. This is the time for anticipating the coming year's harvest season. Goals are set. Plans are made. Growth is anticipated . . . all with an attitude of celebration and expectation.

To the successful person,
winter is the first season
of a wonderful future success.

4

The Season for Dreaming

Giant oaks DO grow from little acorns.
But first, you must have an acorn.

Consider the great oak tree. It grows from a tiny acorn. Let's stop for a moment to consider the processes involved.

When an acorn falls to the ground in the autumn, it has two potential fates: to get into the ground during the winter months, or not to get into the ground (and perchance be carried away by an eager squirrel or crunched underfoot by a human hunter or a grazing animal). The acorn's only chance for survival—and per-petuation—is to get firmly covered over by earth where it can be warmed a few weeks later by spring sunshine radiating through the topsoil and eventually germinate, sprout, and send out two shoots: an upward stem and a downward rootlet.

When that happens, the acorn is no longer a nut—or a seed. It's a tree in the making! The more the seed soaks up the moisture and nutrients of the soil by osmosis, the more its tender roots wind their way through the soil in search of still more nutrients. The higher the seedling stem pushes upward and forms leaves, the more the sun forms chlorophyll in the plant through photo-synthesis, and the more the leaves generate nutrients to sustain the plant's life. The pores in the leaves take in carbon dioxide gas from the air and give off oxygen. As the tree feeds itself, the roots grow deeper and deeper to anchor the stem as it grows higher and higher. The stronger the anchor, the greater the stability of the young sapling tree against the ravages of wind and animals.

Oak trees grow slowly, and they continue to grow as long as they live, which can be up to three hundred years. If proper growth conditions are not met through the seasons, the tree will develop problems, and its growth will be limited. Inadequate root space or lack of water will stunt its growth. Insufficient sunlight will limit the development of leaves and, in turn, the availability of nutrients for growth.

Much about the oak tree can be related to our personal lives, the goals we set, and the projects we develop.

Consider this key question . . .

Are You an Oak Tree or a Potted Plant?

To become healthy, self-actualized adults, we need to have a solid root structure of values and positive beliefs that become anchored in commitment and persistence so that they will remain strong and resilient even in the face of ravaging winds of adversity or change. We need the sunlight of dreams to warm us and to compel us to grow upward and outward through what we plan, learn, do, and achieve. And just like the leaves of the oak tree, we must breathe in the nourishing encouragement offered by others —our colleagues, the members of a support group or parish, or a teacher, mentor, or role model—and give back our optimism and enthusiasm to help others remain motivated and optimistic about their growth and development.

Many people are like an oak tree planted in an indoor flowerpot. They never grow to their true potential. The roots of their self-esteem are cramped, and the development of their values is stunted. Their goals have a low ceiling. They live in an environment void of others who give encouragement, motivating ideas, or inspirational advice.

People with such limitations on all sides tend to list the reasons why dreams can't come true rather than look for ways to turn them into reality. They continue to stunt their growth by failing to seek personal, educational, family-building, or career-enhancing opportunities. Frequently, they spend more time day-dreaming than setting goals. They watch their heroes and heroines making money and enjoying life—on television. They read about people who have dreams fulfilled—in novels. They sit on the sidelines or look through the windows to watch other oak trees growing taller and broader with each passing year.

Projects, too, are like oak trees. The largest corporations in this country have one thing in common. Each began with the seed of an idea—planted in good soil, cultivated properly, with a portion of each harvest reinvested into the nurture and growth of the company.

Now, not all acorns will grow into oak trees. Neither will every idea or dream turn into a fulfilling, satisfying, rewarding harvest of benefit.

Conversely, no oak tree can grow unless one first has an acorn!

Great companies, careers, projects, relationships, children, health, and inner growth don't happen by chance. Neither do they rain down from heaven or spring forth into reality from the depths of a dark abyss. No! Everything we regard as successful, or success-reinforcing, comes first from an idea . . . a dream . . . a "seed notion" that arises from the heart and mind of a human being.

The person *without* a dream can never reap a satisfying, fulfilling harvest of success. Stated another way . . .

You must BEGIN your success with a dream.

Many of us will say, "Oh, I have my dreams." Too often, they are casually conceived, for-the-moment, temporary whims. We call dreams those things that we "wish" we could have as the result of seeing the first star at night.

I call those whims. Nice ideas. Daydreams.

A real true LIFE-DREAM is something that you envision for your total life, all your life.

> A life-dream is the way you want to live,
>   not just the things you want to own.
> A life-dream is the person you want to be,
>   not just the title you want to see under your name on
>   the door.
> A life-dream is the mind-set that you have,
>   not the degrees you earn.

A life-dream is the worldview that you claim as your
    own,
    not the collection of stamps in your passport.

What is *your* life-dream today?
How is it that *you* want to live . . . to think . . . to work . . .
to play . . . to grow . . . to love . . . to worship . . . to create
. . . to spend your hours and days and years on this earth?

What Do You Want to Be
When You Grow Up?

As children, we had fantasies about what we wanted to be
when we reached adulthood . . . astronaut . . . scientist . . .
entertainer . . . soldier . . . teacher . . . doctor . . . parent
. . . world leader . . . farmer . . . fire fighter . . . nurse . . .
business owner. We tried on numerous roles during our play-filled
days of childhood and our dream-filled days of adolescence. Each
role, job, or successful accomplishment seemed equally possible
to us and equally real in our imaginations.

As we grew older, we began to narrow the possibilities. Some
careers seemed beyond our reach. We were advised—or ill-
advised, as the case might be—by teachers, parents, other adults,
or even our peers that we couldn't be, shouldn't be, or wouldn't
be an expert, leader, or successful worker in this profession or
that. Too often, our possibilities were narrowed, by ourselves or
by our choice to believe the limiting opinions of others, to the
point of our living in stifling rigidity with a tightly compressed
self-image. The vast fertile fields of our lives began to shrink in
our mind's eye until we saw our future plot of success as being
"flowerpot" in size. Suddenly, most of the world seemed impossible or inaccessible to us . . . in our imaginations.

The critical point to recognize, of course, is that both the unlimited potential of childhood and the tight constraints of adulthood originate and reside primarily in the imagination.

If you *believe* you can . . . you probably can.

If you *believe* you can't . . . you most assuredly won't.

It's time to reset the dream machine and to adjust the dials in
favor of success.

Turn on the Dream Machine

Many of us have gazed into roaring fires, long into the night, nearly mesmerized by the flames as they dance and eventually collapse into blazing embers. We know how our imaginations can soar in the relaxed atmosphere of a cozy hearth on a cold winter's night. Yes, winter seems to be the natural season for dreaming!

The winter season of success need not take place, however, during the natural winter months. It can occur anytime you find yourself in a position where you need to recapture old dreams or create new ones.

Think of your imagination as a skill rather than an ability. A universal law teaches us: "If you don't use a skill, you lose it." Those of you who have ever worn a cast will recall that the muscles under it were very weak when the cast was removed and that you needed several weeks of regular exercise to bring full strength back to those muscles. If that is a result of lack of use for six weeks, think what would happen if you didn't use those muscles for several months or years. Like all other skills, imagination is a skill you must exercise.

Here are a few exercises to stimulate the power of your creative imagination:

1. Starting now, become acutely aware of your senses. Take in as many sights, sounds, smells, textures, and tastes as you can. Feel the texture of wet sand or cool grass or plush carpet between your toes. Smell the countryside, the sea breeze, the fragrance of trees and flowers, the aromas of a restaurant or bakery. Notice all the shapes and colors as you walk from one business appointment to another or relax on a weekend. Be more curious and aware about everything in the environment.
2. At business and social meetings, as you listen to someone talk, try to form a mental image of the situation he or she describes. Allow the words to form images, feelings, and sensations.
3. When you speak, use words rich in visual imagery. Describe events and plans in detail and with enthusiasm. You'll enjoy a side benefit of becoming a better conversationalist and public speaker if you do.

4. Sit comfortably in a chair. Relax for a few seconds. Look at the objects around you. Now close your eyes. With your eyes closed, try to recall as many objects from the room as you can. You'll be surprised how many objects you'll be able to recall. Continue this exercise as often as you can. As you recall an object, try to remember its color, shape, texture, and size. The key is to recall the object by its image, not its name.

5. Close your eyes and hold an object in your hand. Feel the object as you move it from one hand to the other. Trace the shape of the object with your fingers, and picture its shape at the same time in your mind.

6. In addition to reading books like this one, purchase a book on tape in which the narration has accompanying sound effects and is dramatized with actors and actresses. Put yourself in the plot as you listen. I do this when I read fiction and when I listen to drama on the radio.

7. Try relating to television with your eyes closed. It may sound silly, but it's the best way to exercise your imagination with that medium. Television is one of the foremost reasons why creativity is stifled so early in our children's lives. Television gives them no or little interaction and opportunity to stimulate their own power of imagination; all the images are provided.

8. Write down your thoughts on a regular basis. The best way is to buy a bound book with lined pages at a stationery store. You don't need to view it as a diary because most people have a stereotyped response to diaries. If you have a diary, many people think you are *(a)* writing your autobiography, *(b)* falling in love, *(c)* rebounding from a lost love, or *(d)* gathering evidence for a lawsuit!

I carry a notebook in my briefcase and fill it with brainstorming ideas while I wait in the lounges at airports. Along with the ideas, I make notes about nearly everything and everyone I see during those so-called idle times.

With a little effort you can enhance and sharpen your imaginative skills and place yourself among the top 5 percent in the world who use their thoughts as a video and software library of rich memories, and as a weather satellite to map and forecast a bright future.

Set an atmosphere for yourself that is conducive to identifying life-dreams. From my experience, I've found several steps to be highly beneficial in this area.

Get by yourself. I go to the loft in my barn in the mountains, take a long drive by the ocean, walk in the woods, or sit by myself in front of the fire. When I am alone, with no distractions, my thoughts soar, and my imagination comes to life.

Set the mood for dreaming. I turn on soft, slow relaxing music. I love Bach, Handel, and Vivaldi and have an affinity for strings. I also love epic movie theme music, preferably *Out of Africa, Somewhere in Time,* and *Love Story.* I begin by reflecting on all the happiest, most magnificent memories of my past. As I remember, I allow myself to travel back in time and relive those rich experiences.

Focus on your future. I design a day in my life five years from now. Where am I? Where do I go? What am I doing, saying, feeling, thinking? Who are the people around me? What do my house and office look like? What is different about my life? What is the status of my health? Am I fit and trim? Have I written a new book? On what subject? What do I do during my free time? I picture myself meeting with my financial advisers. What does my financial picture look like? What is the status of my savings and retirement account? After all, it is five years from now!

Make some notes for your reference. Can you isolate in a few words the main hallmarks of your ideal life? Remember that these notes are classified for your eyes only.

Think and write in concrete terms. Don't simply write down, "I want to be rich and famous." Write down what service you will provide that will solve many people's problems and, as a result, keep you busy filling the orders.

Some of my notes include the following: write self-esteem textbook for children . . . translate audiotapes into languages of developing countries . . . develop services that can be provided without traveling in person to the client . . . establish a preventive and predictive wellness program and change life-style accordingly to add years and years to life . . . develop video and audio series for senior citizens called *The Golden Years: Getting Older, Getting Better* . . . take more time for spiritual growth alone and with family.

Revisit Your Childhood Dreams

What did you really want to be as a child? In many cases, childhood dreams hold the key to a person's true cache of talents, abilities, and motivation.

An awkward, funny-looking girl in New York, she was totally obsessed with becoming a professional entertainer . . .

Barbra Streisand

A lonely boy in the Midwest, he grew up in foster homes, treating everyone with love and respect, which he wanted most, dreaming of serving others and not being dependent on others . . .

Tom Monaghan
founder of Domino's Pizza

"Ever since I was twelve, I dreamed I would do something important in aviation! . . ."

Neal Armstrong
first man on the moon

As a child in England, he spent hours and hours creating cardboard sets and elaborate staging for the puppet shows and miniature stage shows he would produce to entertain his family . . .

Andrew Lloyd Webber
creative genius behind *Evita*
and *Phantom of the Opera*

Three young brothers were fascinated by anatomical pictures and descriptions in the *World Book Encyclopedia* . . .

The Salk brothers
one a leading veterinarian; one a
leading child psychiatrist;
and one a leading immunologist,
Dr. Jonas Salk

When he was eleven years old, he attended a banquet honoring the legendary NFL running back Jim Brown. "I'll break every record you have set," the scrawny undernourished youngster promised Brown . . .

O. J. Simpson

From her grammar school days, she dreamed of helping the less fortunate . . .

Margaret Thatcher

At fourteen, visiting state capitals with her family during summer vacations, she contemplated a future as a lawmaker . . .

Sandra Day O'Connor
Supreme Court Justice

His love of woodworking and violin music began in childhood . . .

Antonio Stradivari

Cut from a basketball team as a youngster, he still dreamed that he would play someday . . .

Michael "Air" Jordan

A series of remarkable studies conducted by British behavioral scientists over a twenty-eight-year period confirmed that what we love and do well at as children continues to be our latent or real talent as adults. The lives of fifty individuals were tracked; evaluations began at age seven, and reevaluations took place every seven years until each reached the age of thirty-five.

Incredibly, nearly all of the subjects eventually ended up engaged in a professional pursuit related to their interests during the age span of seven through fourteen. Although most of them had discarded or strayed from those interests from ages fifteen to twenty-one and beyond, virtually all found their way back to recapture their early childhood dreams by the age of thirty-five, even if only as a hobby or an avocation.

- · What happened to your childhood dream?
- · Who stole it from you?
- · What convinced you to lay it aside?
- · Why haven't you pursued that one thing you always wanted to be when you grew up?

If You Could Live Life Over

In my goal-setting seminars, I include the dream session "If I Could Live My Life Again." It is designed to allow us to consider why and how we should think about achieving some of our dreams. I encourage you to ask yourself that question during your winter season of success. What would you do differently if you could go back in time and rechart your course in life? Why?

Then explore the idea of taking that path now.

I recently met a man in his late thirties. He is in his senior year of medical school, after having pursued a career in engineering for more than ten years. His children are now teens. One day as he and his wife were dreaming about their life together, she asked him, "Would you do anything differently if you could go back to college and choose another major?"

He said to me, "I answered her even before I gave it a thought. I said, 'Sure.' "

"What would you choose?" she asked.

"By this time," he confessed, "I was in too deep to get out of the conversation gracefully so I said what I genuinely felt, 'I'd choose to be a physician.' "

"What kept you from making that decision when you were twenty-one?" his wife asked.

He answered her, "I didn't know if I could make the grade. It seemed like a long, hard course that not only took a lot of years but cost a lot of money. I wanted to get out of school and start making money, get married, have a family.

"And then," this man concluded in telling me his story, "my wife said, 'Well, you have made money and built up a savings account, you are married, you've raised a family, you've proven yourself in your field . . . so what keeps you from becoming a physician now?' I couldn't think of anything to say. All through the night, I thought of very little else other than what it would take to get into medical school and pursue that dream of my youth. I decided to go for it. I've got one year left. My grades are good. The tuition money is earned. My wife is supportive. And I've never felt more fulfilled in my life."

All of us seek our destinies and desire to spend our lives in unique ways. Most of us find ourselves in the same dilemma as this man, however. We want our long-term goal. But we also want to realize some of our immediate goals. Often they are not compatible.

If you have detoured from the path of a long-term goal you once held close to your heart, explore what it would take to pursue that goal at this point in your life. It may not be impossible to get back on track!

Ask yourself as you dream,

- In which areas of my life have I failed to dream? Have I been selling myself short in one or more areas? Is there more I could be "living" in one part of my life? Am I living up to my potential?
- What has been my attitude about dreaming dreams, setting goals, making plans? Is it an attitude that has led me to greater success?
- Do I have a keen awareness of the future? Or am I so busy struggling through the day-to-day grind that I rarely think about what lies ahead?

Living by Default or Design?

We have to make a decision.

Are we going to live by default? Will we, without any effort on our part, allow circumstances and others to dictate to us the major decisions of our lives and thus determine who we are and what we will become? Will we let others define—and limit—our level of success? Will we go with the flow, as regulated and channeled by others, unconcerned about where we are going?

Or are we living by design? Are we letting our imaginations roam freely across the terrain of all possibilities, resting lightly on those that might become probabilities, and eventually choosing those that we desire to pursue into reality—all the while never shutting ourselves off from the full vista of opportunities around us? Are we allowing ourselves to think bigger today than we did ten years ago? Are we challenging ourselves to rise above our circumstances and see our world from a new, higher-up perspective?

When asked, "How are you doing?" so many people say, "I'm doing fine—under the circumstances."

Get out from under the circumstances! That's a terribly uncomfortable position that leads to a terrible way to live with a terrible view! Get above the circumstances, and choose a new dream to pursue.

If you don't have a dream, you won't develop goals. In fact, you'll have no need for them.

If you don't have goals, you'll have no need for mapping out plans for reaching them. You'll have no need for strategies or timetables related to them. You'll have no need for additional training or experience to accomplish them nor will you discipline yourself to acquire new habits necessary for attaining them.

People who live in the "default setting" tend to be people whose automatic wired-in putterings waste minutes into weeks, and weeks into months, and months into years. Their minds tend to run on a treadmill, replaying the same scenarios, worries, and ideas. Their conversations tend to dwindle down to a mundane concern for things, rumors, or gossip. They choose activities to relieve tension rather than stimulate ideas. They are going no place . . . sometimes very quickly.

On the other hand, people who live in the "design setting" are open to new ideas, new situations, and new challenges. Their conversations and thoughts tend to involve ideas—theories, opinions, and creative ponderings. Their world is ever growing and ever evolving. They are seeking to go someplace and are determined to enjoy all of the beauty, drama, and joy that they can along the way!

Questions for Dreamers

Ask yourself several questions today as you begin to dream anew about your life.

How big is my world? Have I confined my interests and the possibilities for my life to this house? This building or block? This neighborhood? This city? This state? This nation? This hemisphere?

Think expansively as you let your mind reach out by completing these sentences.

· If I had a great deal of money, I would . . .
· One thing I'd really like to experience in my life would be . . .
· I would like to be the kind of person that everybody describes as . . .

· A place I would like to visit someday is . . .
· My life would be better if . . .
· I wish I knew how to . . .
· If I could just get up my nerve, I'd like to . . .
· If I just had the time, I would . . .
· If I could start over, I would . . .

What would I like to do but DON'T believe I can do? Make a list. In fact, take a moment to write down six things you *don't* believe you can do but you'd like to do.

1. _____

2. _____

3. _____

4. _____

5. _____

6. _____

Now take a look at your list again, this time as objectively as possible. Who told you that you couldn't do these things? Did you believe you could do them as a child? Do you still have a desire to do them?

Delve a little deeper in your thinking. What stands in your way of doing the things that you once dreamed of doing or being?

Do you not have the money you think it takes to pursue your dream? How might you get the money? Have you ever seriously mapped out a plan and given it a budget? Is it possible that at least a portion of your dream might become a reality?

Are you in a relationship with someone who would disapprove of your acting on your long-lost desire to fulfill a life's dream? Are you certain the person would stand in your way? Have you talked with the person about it? You may be surprised!

Are you out of shape physically, or have you perhaps gained too much weight to engage in a life-dream activity? Can you get back in shape? Go for it!

Granted, certain illnesses, injuries, and various mental, emotional, physical, or family factors can put certain limitations on our abilities. They very rarely, however, eliminate a person from the activity entirely!

One-legged teenagers participate in Special Olympics slalom races at speeds that astound me.

Paraplegics engage in bicycle races at speeds that many men could never match.

The fully paralyzed have written books . . . painted with oils . . . and dictated masterful political speeches.

What would I like to do and believe I CAN do? Again, make a list.

1. _____

2. _____

3. _____

4. _____

5. _____

6. _____

My secret hope is that your list is a repeat, at least in part, of the one you just made for the previous question. As you reappraised your first list, did you find yourself beginning to believe— perhaps with just a twinge of possibility—that you might be able to follow through on that life-dream? Can you see at least a glimmer of a way in which your dream might still live?

Have you lost a dream today because you feel as if you dropped the "magic" you once had in life? It isn't "magic" at all that enables a person to grow a harvest of success. Don't wait for the lottery to hit, the long-lost millionaire uncle to die, or the treasure of a lifetime to emerge in an earth-shattering quake. Take hold of your dream again. Dream it one more time. Hold it close and cherish it. Don't crush it with self-doubt or self-imposed superstitions.

True Dreams Rarely Die

A genuine heartfelt dream rarely dies. It only goes underground —buried deep within the recesses of your mind—where it often smolders into deep disappointment, resentment, and/or frustration and may erupt at some point as a volcano of violent anger or cause a cave-in of heavy depression.

Furthermore, most dreams shouldn't die. Dreams are rarely ones of destruction, violence, harm, or loss. Most dreams are ones in which we envision a better future, a happier day-to-day life, more fulfilling work, more fulfilling relationships, and deeper, lasting joy. Most dreams are ones in which health, optimism, laughter, friends and close relationships, a feeling of satisfaction, and hope abound—and fear, worry, and stress are nowhere to be found. Most dreams are worth the dreaming!

A true dream is one that you dream month after month, year after year. It's one that you come back to again and again in quiet, reflective moments.

Most dreams are worth pursuing, at least to the goal-setting stage.

Live with Your Dream A While

Try on your dream a while. Explore the downside of your dream as well as the upside. If you were financially wealthy, for example, would you be prepared for the dozens of requests you would receive for donations from worthwhile organizations? How would you handle the requests from your family and friends for money? What are the dangers of being overextended financially? Would wealth impose additional demands on your time—including time away from your family? Are you willing to make that sacrifice? If you were famous, would you eventually resent the loss of privacy? Would you tire of people thinking that they know you when they truly know only what they read in the tabloids?

This is not to say that an appraisal of your dream is intended to puncture it! The real value of a life-dream is that it is the dream of your soul about how you would truly like to live your life. If you base goals on dreams that aren't clearly in focus, you're likely to end up with something that you hadn't really desired in the first place—you just didn't know that you didn't want it when you first dreamed about it!

Factor in others.

Take some time to qualify and focus on your dreams for your life. Weigh your relationships and the place they play in your dreamscape.

See in your mind's eye the way in which your life-dream impacts, includes, or intersects with other people. It's one thing to dream of a life alone on a desert island in which you can do anything you want to do. It's quite another thing to envision a life involving others, including their dreams!

Root your dreams in your values.

Bear in mind that a true life-dream is firmly rooted in, not separated from, your values and beliefs. Don't allow yourself to fantasize about something that you know would ultimately make you miserable because it would be completely cross-grain to your values.

Don't lace your dreams with worry.

Consider the stress feelings you may have about your dreams. Your dreams should be big enough to stretch you but not stress you. Don't attach worrisome obligations to your life as you dream. Forge your dreams in such a way that you dream them stress-FREE. If you feel clenching pangs of tightness as you dream, consider dreaming a different dream!

Dream until you dream in positive detail.

Many people have difficulty visualizing themselves actually achieving real goals. They can see a new and better life for others, but they frequently can't see it for themselves. Many times they've conditioned themselves over the years to live in the rut of the average.

Can you imagine yourself living a more successful life? Can you close your eyes and see it?

What you see is what you get. The same holds true for dreams. What you see in your mind's eye—what you envision for your life —preestablishes what you will get out of life.

If you see a life that is negative, downtrodden, impoverished (in every way, not only money), and unimportant . . . that's probably what you'll get!

Dream in color. See things vividly. Set the scene in motion.

Be curious about and keenly aware of everything in your dream environment.

The more you detail your dream environment, the more you'll enjoy visiting there and elaborating on the life you lead in your dreamworld. Nearly everyone who envisions a dream place envisions a place of relaxation for the body and stimulation for the mind. What are the chairs and other pieces of furniture like in your dream place? What are the colors on the walls? What is the view? What sounds do you hear? Is water nearby? What about living plants and flowers?

What stimulated your mind? Does your dream place include access to new stimuli, opinions, and information? Does your dream life include encounters with new people and an open, generous hospitality?

Return to your dreams as often as necessary.

You may need to return to your dreamworld several times to fully define and clearly focus your dreams for your life. Feel free to do so! Just as we rarely have only one fire in the fireplace during a natural winter season, so our dreams rarely emerge full-blown during just one dream session in the winter season of our success.

Like all other skills, the ability to dream develops with practice. I've found it useful to let my mind take a vacation every day for about ten or fifteen minutes. I relax without interruption and travel, in my imagination, to a place I've been or a place to which I'd like to go. I frequently recall pleasant times and places that I've visited during vacations with my family. I close my eyes and let my attention drift to particular scenes, recalling the feelings of the time as vividly as possible. By linking feelings and images, I'm able to recall both better. I focus on one especially memorable part of an experience and survey it in my mind—recalling how it looked, what I heard, how I felt, and what I did.

I've discovered over the months and years of my doing this that several things have happened.

First, my present experiences are enhanced. I tend to look for important and pleasurable cues in everyday life—ones that might lend themselves to a revisit later. I'm more acutely aware of moments that are meaningful, conversations that are memorable, and scenes that are beautiful. In fact, I seek out such experiences and then relish them more than I once did!

Second, my memory is enhanced. By linking emotions and images as I recall my past, I have developed a tendency to link images and emotions more readily in the present, which makes these new mental impressions all the more easy to recall.

Third, my ability to imagine my dream life of the future is enhanced. I have a much better ability to see, touch, feel, taste, and otherwise envision the way I desire my life to grow and to be. Because of this, I can "try on" new dreams more easily and more quickly and readily discard aspects of a dream that aren't satisfying.

The Power of Your Dreams

Woodrow Wilson summed up his belief in the power of dreams like this:

> We grow great by dreams. All big successes are big dreamers. They see things in the red fire of a long winter's evening, or through the mist of a rainy day. Some of us let these great dreams die, but others nourish and protect them, nurse them through the bad days 'til they bring them to the sunshine and light, which come always to those who sincerely believe that their dreams will come true.

Solid achievements first begin in someone's imagination.

- The wheel was invented when a cave dweller imagined that it might be easier to roll an object than to drag it.
- Gutenberg imagined a machine that would mechanically turn out many printed pages at one time.
- The great cathedrals of Europe were built because people imagined buildings soaring into the heavens.

Dreams are for your benefit. Use them constructively to construct your future and success!

Enjoy the Process

Above all . . . enjoy the process of engaging in life-dreaming. Dreaming shouldn't be work to you. It should be a great delight for you to envision a better, more joyful, more exhilarating, more fulfilling journey through life!

Have fun with your dreams. Value them. Embrace them. Enjoy them. Believe in them.

As you do, you will find them becoming ever clearer and more real to you.

Once your dreams are vividly in focus, the time has arrived for you to move forward in your winter season of success toward molding your dreams into goals.

5

The Season for Setting Goals

To get somewhere, you must know where you're going.

Sounds logical, doesn't it? Yet I've encountered countless un-happy, unsatisfied people who have as their number one goal just to get through the day. They float along in their daily lives like driftwood in the ocean—taking whatever job falls their way, ex-erting the least amount of energy possible, and putting most of their focus on lunch breaks, the five o'clock whistle, and payday.

If your goal is merely to get through the day so you can spend your evening with a beer and the tube, that's probably what you'll achieve in life—a beer and the tube . . . even though you may secretly dream about something better. The main reason is that you do not truly have goals.

Winter is the season for setting goals—specifically, for turning dreams into goals.

Goals Provide Guidance

The human mind can be compared to the guidance system of a missile on automatic pilot. I watched, as I'm sure you did, as the Patriot missiles were fired from Israel and Saudi Arabia during the Gulf War. Aimed at an incoming Scud missile, the Patriot had a self-adjusting computerized system that constantly monitored the course of its own navigation, making whatever corrections were necessary to stay on target and eventually to intercept the Scud successfully. If the missiles had not been programmed properly or if the target had been too far out of range, the missiles would have wandered erratically until their propulsion systems failed or they self-destructed.

A human being behaves in a similar manner when the mind is targeted on a worthy goal. Once a goal is set with conviction, the mind will constantly monitor self-talk and environmental feedback—both positive and negative—to make adjustments along the way in order to hit its target. However, when the mind is programmed with expectations that are too vague, or if the goal that is set is beyond the range of the person, the individual is likely to wander aimlessly until he gives up in fatigue or frustration (or self-destructs with liquor, drugs, or other sources of sensual gratification that mask the sense of failure).

Goals must be reachable.

Goals should be just beyond one's present grasp but not out of sight.

A person may dream of marrying a prince (or princess) and then living happily ever after in a kingdom that has no problems and in which all material needs are met without an ounce of effort or a single shed tear. Such a dream is not only out of sight, it's totally out of the realm of possibility!

Don't set a dream for yourself that can't be put into concrete terms of an immediate goal—one that is achievable not only over a lifetime but in the next few months or years.

At the same time . . . aim high. Setting reachable goals may seem like a contradiction to aiming high—but it really isn't. For example, if you are an average American citizen living in Arizona, it is unrealistic for you to set a goal of being the leader of Argentina. It is not, however, unrealistic for you to set a goal of being governor of Arizona!

I recently watched a television interview with Ann Richards, the governor of Texas. She told the reporter who was interviewing her, "I woke up one day and said, 'What is it that I want on my tombstone?' I decided I surely didn't want it to be, 'She kept a clean house.' " Party officials in her city asked her to run for public office, and that was the beginning of a series of goals she set for herself that eventually led to the Texas statehouse. While there's nothing wrong with keeping a clean house, Governor Richards didn't set that as a goal for herself. She wanted something else! At the same time, she didn't aim at becoming the Queen of England. Her goal was a realistic one, yet a high one.

Perhaps the foremost challenge you face as you set goals for your life is to be realistic and yet aim high enough. I've discovered over the years that people tend to err on the side of aiming low (rather than aiming at goals that are unrealistic). Set high goals for yourself! You may not reach the summit of your dream, but in aiming high, you will accomplish much more than if you aim low.

Goals should be motivating.

Aimless work yields little joy. In fact, aimless work is debilitating. It results in negative attitudes, poor self-esteem, and a failure mind-set. Effort without a goal is just that: effort.

On the other hand, virtually nothing on earth can stop a person who is pursuing a goal clearly in sight.

The Greek philosopher Aristotle once devised a formula for success and happiness. "First," he wrote, "have a definite, clear, practical idea—a goal, an objective." Second, he recommended attaining it by whatever means available, whether "wisdom, money, materials, or methods. Third, adjust all your means to that end."

Goals can be creative.

Many people resist the idea of goal setting because they assume that it results in a formula-driven, highly uncreative life. The exact opposite can be true. Those who assume that everything will work out in the end—and therefore choose to hang loose, believe in *que sera sera* (whatever will be will be)—very often lead lives that they do not "create."

Setting goals is actually a more creative approach to living; it's fashioning or "creating" the life of your choice. It's taking your life, as a lump of clay on the potter's wheel, and turning it into an item of beauty and utility that gives pleasure to you, its creator, and to others. To turn the wheel of life and *not* to fashion something with the clay is to send the clay splattering in every direction!

In my experience the most creative goals are fashioned to pass the Double Win Test. A double win is when you win and every other person around you also wins—simultaneously. Ask yourself as you set goals, What will be the effect of my realized goal on the lives of others with whom I am in relationship? If someone you know and love will be hurt by your reaching your goal, reevaluate it!

Goals should be flexible.

Some people seem to resist goal setting because they believe it to be a rigid process. Not so! A goal may be likened to the rudder of a ship. Though small and inflexible, the rudder can turn the ship in any direction that the ship's captain chooses to go! In that, there's a great deal of flexibility.

Once you set a goal for yourself, you can change it, adjust it, modify it, alter it. It's your goal!

A Goal Is More than a Dream

What is the difference between a dream and a goal? Many definitions are possible, but I like this one because it is succinct:

> *A dream is what you would LIKE*
> *for life to be and hold,*
> *but*
> *a goal is what you*
> *INTEND to make happen.*

Many people dream of an ideal life that they would like to have someday. They even go so far as to dream the potential future life with a great many concrete details. They do not, however, move forward to set specific goals for one main reason: They never really INTEND to pursue their dream and to turn it into a reality.

Goals are intentional. They are rooted in commitment and a desire to do whatever it takes to make a dream come true.

A goal is not a whim. It is a true, lasting, worthwhile dream taken one step further to the point that you are willing to put numbers, places, facts, and details to it—always with an eye toward *reaching* the goal you've set.

Ask yourself a simple question: How will I know when I am living my life-dream? Your answer will dictate the specific goals connected with your dream.

Personalize Your Goals

The best goals are those that are your own. In fact, they are the only ones worth pursuing because they are the only ones that you are likely to reach and to maintain with a sense of satisfaction or personal fulfillment.

Many people attempt to live up to other people's goals for their lives. They pursue college degrees, invest their money in certain possessions, enter into relationships, and make career moves based on what someone else thinks or believes they should do, be, or have. If you are in that position, I suggest that you take time during a winter season to reevaluate where you are going in life and why. You may very well achieve all that others think you should achieve, but you still have a hollow feeling in the pit of your soul. Ultimately, the only goals that truly will be satisfying to you—mentally, spiritually, physically, and relationally—will be those that *you* want to achieve. They are the only goals that will give you a deep sense of personal fulfillment and meaning in life.

Personalized goals aren't necessarily selfish.

I believe strongly in the idea of the double win, as defined above and restated here: "If I help you win, I win, too."

This philosophy of life goes against the grain of many people. They've been taught to look out for number one . . . to win by intimidation . . . to seek to have it all . . . and to get theirs no matter what others get and to do it to others before they can do it to you.

Such people see life in win-or-lose terms. I see a different world. I believe it's possible to dream dreams, set goals, and achieve success *without* stomping on other people. I believe that a person can be all that he or she can be without destroying someone else in the process.

During the past decade, I served as Chairman of Psychology on the U.S. Olympic Committee Sports Medicine Council. Our job on the council is to enhance the performance of our Olympic athletes, and we spend long hours working with skiers, skaters, sprinters, leapers, jumpers, and throwers of all kinds. If you ever imagined an enterprise in which only one winner takes home the gold, it may well be the Olympics. The original purpose behind the establishment of the Olympic Games, however, was twofold: to develop individual ability and give it proper merit and recognition and, at the same time, to build an enterprise with esprit de corps in which each team member learned to have a collective responsibility for all other team members.

The true Olympic concept is one not of individual effort but of team effort—with team members rooting for and assisting other team members for a total team victory. I believe strongly in that concept for all areas of life. Life doesn't have one winner; it holds the capacity for every person to be a "winner" in his or her chosen field of endeavor.

Strive to set personal goals in which you achieve all that you can achieve, without detriment to others. Make it one of your goals to achieve personal success within the context of group success.

Your group may be your family. It may be your place of business or your company. It may be your church or synagogue. It may be your community.

As with goals and dreams, your group is what *you* define it to be. Evaluate your personal goals in the context of your group.

Virtually every person I know has a dream of making a positive difference with his or her life. I want my life to "count" in some way. I suspect that you feel the same about yours. You want to make a mark on the world. Can you state that dream as a goal?

A personal goal statement may be: "I want to be able to give $10,000 a year to the charity of my choice." Or "I want to give at least twenty hours a month to community service." Or "I want to serve my nation through some form of public service"—and then name a specific avenue for giving that service (such as elected official, volunteer, government appointment).

Your personal goal statements will only be as self-centered as you are.

Set a Destination Point

Goals clearly delineate where you intend to arrive. They focus on a destination point.

Do you dream of making a lot of money? That's a dream of many people, and above all, it's important to realize that "making a lot of money" is a dream statement—not a goal. A goal statement will answer this question: How *much* money do you want to have? A goal statement may be: "I want to make $80,000 a year, net, within three years after I open my own consulting firm." (You set the numbers!)

A dream statement may be: "I want to be the boss." A goal statement, on the other hand, will answer the question: Boss of what? Do you want to be the supervisor of your current department, the chief sales representative, the top account executive, the vice president of your division, or the president of the company? Or, perhaps, do you want to begin your own business?

"I would like to spend more time with my family" is a dream statement, one voiced by just about every young executive I meet, male or female. How might you state that dream as a goal? Consider this: "I want to spend at least two full hours a day doing nothing but talking, playing, and doing home-style chores and errands with my spouse and children." Or "I want to spend at least a half hour a day with each of my children in direct one-to-one communication." Or "I want to be home from the office no later than 7:00 P.M." Or "I want to devote all of Sunday to being with my family."

"I want to enjoy my retirement" is another dream statement I hear frequently. It is not, however, a goal. A goal statement may be: "I want to retire at sixty with sufficient income to be able to travel at least sixty days a year." Or "I want to retire to a home on the lake where I can go fishing four times a week." Or "I want to move into a retirement complex when I am sixty-five so that I no longer need to cook three meals a day or do my own laundry."

You, and only you, can define your dream into specific goal statements. Each person's idea of a good income, good family dynamic, good retirement, or good job will differ. The critical factor is to be as specific as possible and then to ask yourself, Am I *really* willing to do what it takes to make this dream come true?

You may dream of making $100,000—or $200,000 or $500,000— a year. But are you really willing to make the effort of doing so? Are you willing to make other sacrifices in your life to put in the time and energy necessary for building up a business or a career to that level of earning power?

You may dream of retiring at age sixty, but are you *really* willing to do what it takes now for the achievement of that goal? Are you willing to set aside the extra money each month to place into long-range investments so that you will have the money you need? Are you willing to forgo the pleasures of today so you can enjoy life the way you want to enjoy it ten, twenty, or thirty years down the line?

You may dream of a happy family life, but are you *really* willing to put in the extra hours and make the compromises, turn down the opportunities, or avoid the temptations necessary for achieving one?

Always, always, always remember:

> *Goals are your personal statements of what*
> *you are truly WILLING TO DO to achieve*
> *what you really want to achieve.*

Put Your Goals in Writing

Commit your goals to writing. Attorneys know the wisdom of a written contract. It requires that a situation be put in very clear, specific terms, with all conditions, dollar amounts, and time frames carefully detailed. Make a contract with yourself—that you will enter into a successful relationship with yourself!

Take time during your winter season of success to list your goals. Your goals should reflect your wants, needs, and desires, not those that others have set for you.

Make the list as long and as grand as possible. Enjoy making it! Pull out all stops. Aim high. Be specific in stating your goals.

If you are like most people, you'll find your goals clustering in eight major areas of life. I've provided a few key words for you to consider in each area as you begin to set goals.

- **Physical:** weight, level of fitness, nutrition plan, new sports skills, exercise schedule, facial, make-over, dermatology, dentist, annual physical exam, ophthalmologist, wardrobe improvements
- **Family:** relationship with spouse, relationship with parents, relationship with children, relationship with other relatives, family priorities, family activities, changes in family routine or habits
- **Financial:** income, retirement fund, savings, investments, property, business capital, special funds, charitable giving
- **Professional:** promotion, participation in professional society, license or certification, continuing education, professional development activities, relationship with colleagues,

relationship with superiors, relationship with subordinates, relationship with clients, relationship with vendors, equipment purchases
· **Community:** volunteer work, civic clubs, political involvement, fund-raising activities, relationship with neighbors, community improvement activities
· **Mental:** nonfiction reading, fiction reading, self-education study, vocabulary building exercises, enrollment in courses, regular reading habits, cassette tape courses
· **Social:** improve friendships, make new friends, club activities, new recreational pursuits
· **Spiritual:** church attendance, inspirational reading and study, contemplation and prayer time, service to others, relationship with clergy

Take a few minutes to note several of your personal goals related to each area.

Now, study your list. Ponder each item. What does it mean to you personally? Clearly imagine achieving each goal. Consider the consequences of each goal. How will it affect your life?

Categorize Your Goals

A goal is not a goal unless it has a deadline. In my seminars, I frequently describe three kinds of goals:

1. *Primary goals.* They can be achieved within the next three to six months.
2. *Intermediate goals.* They require six months to three years. They may include completing a college degree or vocational training program, reaching the middle management level in your firm, or purchasing a new home.
3. *Life goals.* They take longer than three years. They include long-term career plans as well as things that you desire to do or be in future years for which you need to prepare *now* (for example, retirement).

For some people, deadlines aren't enough. You need to put deadlines on your deadlines. Map out the progress you need to make, and set deadlines for completing each stage. For example, stating, "I'll write my next book by May 1," is not enough of a deadline. I do better when I say, "Section 1, with two chapters, will be finished by January 1. I'll set aside one week for rewriting and then begin Section 2, completed by March 25, and so on, until the entire manuscript is completed on schedule by May 1." Arrange your goals onto the "Goal Categorization Grid."

GOAL CATEGORIZATION GRID

Goals	Primary	Intermediate	Life
Physical			
Family			
Financial			
Professional			
Community			
Mental			
Social			
Spiritual			

Delineate and
Prioritize Your Goals

Your next step is to outline your goals in each of the grid segments. Strive to have no fewer than three goals and no more than ten in each box of the grid. Through the seminars I've conducted over the years, I've found that few people can mentally handle the challenge of more than ten goals in any area.

Now, arrange those three to ten items in each grid in terms of their importance. Keep rearranging them until you have them in the order of priority.

Take as long as you need for this process. This isn't something to do in an hour. Leave your list for a few days and return to it. Study it again. Rearrange items as you need to. (A few weeks is not too long for you to take in setting life goals if you've never attempted to set them before.)

You may find, as a very practical matter, that you would like to create this grid on a bulletin board, using index cards, each with a goal. Using cards makes the process of arranging and prioritizing a snap.

When you have your goals in order, zero in on the number one priority in the "Primary" category for each area. Write out each goal fully, using a separate card for each one. (You may choose, instead, to write them into your daily planner or to write them on the back of business-size cards that you can put in your wallet.)

Guidelines for Making
Priority Goal Cards

As you state each goal, use one sentence. Keep your statement brief, concrete, and to the point. Begin the sentence with "I am . . ." and be very specific about your level of achievement. By stating your goal in terms of "I am," you are asserting your goal as if you have already achieved it! Add a date to your goal. For example . . .

You may identify your top-priority physical goal as "lose weight." Your specific goal statement on your index card should read something like this: "I weigh 170 pounds on December 1." (The exact weight and date, of course, would be of your designation.)

You may identify your top-priority mental goal as "read three books that will help me reach my professional goal." Your specific goal statement on your card should be something along this line: "I am reading one book every four weeks."

Your goal may be the development or maintenance of a new habit. For example, your top-priority physical goal may be "maintain my weight loss." Set forth your specific goal statement in terms that include success affirmations. Here are some examples: physical goal (female)—"I enjoy weighing 120 pounds and looking slim in my new bathing suit"; physical goal (male)—"I weigh a trim, athletic 165 pounds and enjoy exercising every day"; mental goal—"I enjoy encountering new ideas and information as I read one hour a day at least five days a week."

In stating your goals precisely, be sure to . . .

- use the pronoun *I*.
- use action modifiers whenever appropriate, such as *easily, regularly, readily, naturally*.
- use words that convey emotion, such as *enthusiastically* or *happily*.
- choose terms that imply you have already reached your goals.

Using Your Goal Cards

Take these TOP-PRIORITY GOAL CARDS with you everywhere you go. Refer to them often. When faced with a decision, ask yourself whether your choice would help or hinder you in achieving one of your paramount life goals. In so doing, you will . . .

- reinforce your goals in your mind, literally developing a "goal mind."
- keep your goals as priorities despite distractions or obstacles that you may encounter.
- align your daily activities and schedules to help you achieve your goals.

From this point forward, choose to do only the things that bring you closer to achieving your goals!

Your grid of goals is essential as you map out a plan for accomplishing your goals.

But first . . . you need to survey the field in which you will plant your success.

6

The Season for Surveying the Challenge Ahead

Apart from your dreams and goals, you, as a life-farmer, must have a field in which to plant. You must recognize at the outset of your venture toward success that you are inherently gifted and specifically trained and prepared to pursue a specific type of farming, to grow a specific type of crop.

The type of farmer you are created to be . . . and the type of field in which you plant . . . are two critical factors underlying any success you will ever achieve.

Appraise Yourself as a Life-Farmer

One of your winter-season challenges is to appraise your personal abilities as a farmer.

· What kind of farmer are you innately?
· What type of work do you enjoy doing?
· What crops give you pleasure?
· How strong are your skills and traits for farming?

Begin your answers to these questions by identifying your personal traits. Focus on things in which you know you are strong.

Conduct a personal inventory of your assets during the winter season. List them. Don't be bashful! As with all of winter's dreams, goals, and plans, your personal inventory of assets is FYEO: For Your Eyes Only.

Conduct a Personal Inventory

First, identify your personal character strengths.

Are you honest? Trustworthy? Do you have good communication skills? Are you joyful? Do people enjoy being around you? Do you have a natural ability to lead? Are you curious about the world around you? Are you willing to lend a helping hand? Do you handle money and possessions in a responsible manner? Are you free of chemical addictions? Are you enthusiastic? Optimistic? Do you have a realistic understanding of your limitations and those of others? List at least five personal traits that you perceive as strengths.

Second, identify your natural abilities and traits— emphasizing what you feel you were born with or have exhibited throughout your life.

Do you have a strong physical constitution? Do you have the capability to endure hard physical work? Can you sing? Are you good with words? Are you especially coordinated physically? Are you highly intuitive? Do you see trends easily? Are you mentally quick? Are you alert to changes and quick to perceive details? Do you have good mechanical, reasoning, or mathematical ability? Are you exceptionally creative? List several of your natural abilities and traits.

Third, list your educational or training experiences that have resulted in skills or information pertinent to the goals you are setting for yourself.

Do you have a degree in the field in which you are about to start a business? Have you read all of the information you can put your hands on about how to succeed in this venture ahead of you? Have you worked alongside a parent in a similar business for years? Have you completed an apprenticeship? What related skills do you have?

Be sure to include areas of self-study. Not all education happens within the confines of a classroom or a degree program.

Focus on your formal and informal training—as related to your goals—and list what you consider to be the areas in which you have gained the most information and skills training.

Fourth, identify experiences that closely mirror the challenges represented by your new goal.

Have you already put in ten years of work in a particular field? Have you extensive volunteer experience in an area in which you are now seeking employment? Do you have a hobby in which you have experience and in a field that you would like now to pursue as a career? List the experiences that relate specifically to the goals you identified in the previous chapter.

Fifth, name individuals who may be helpful as you attempt to reach your goal.

List people who may supply you with information or advice. Identify those who give you the greatest amount of encouragement and who are truly your fans. Name those who may be able to help you in practical ways—such as helping you secure financing, writing letters of recommendation or introduction on your behalf, providing hands-on help (such as helping you move furniture, stuff envelopes, or ZIP-sort a mailing), or giving you gratis professional assistance (such as legal, public relations, computer, or office-decorating services).

Take a few minutes now to complete the "Personal Inventory."

PERSONAL INVENTORY

Personal Character Strengths	
Natural Abilities and Talents	

Acquired Skills and Education	
Valuable Related Experiences	
Helpful Associations and Relationships (already in place)	

Identify Areas of Weakness

As you conducted your personal inventory, you might have encountered items that you wish you could have put down as strengths but were unable to. Face up to those areas as ones that are weak in your life, and seek to make them strong.

Bear in mind that these weaknesses are to be evaluated in light of your personal goals. You may not be able to stand on your head (literally), but your goals in life may not require that you be able to do so! You may not be able to sing like an opera star, but your goals may not require that you sing a note.

On the other hand, you must be able to face up to the weaknesses related to your goals. As long as they remain, they will keep you from maximum success. Take a moment to identify five things about yourself that you believe you need to strengthen to maximize your success and to reach your goals in record time with a high level of quality achievement.

Identify these areas of weakness, and add them as your "Personal Inventory Postscript." Note to yourself that you will be actively seeking growth, development, or change in these areas. Therefore, they will not be a part of your permanent personal inventory. They are temporary items that you are hoping to eliminate as negatives and add as positives within a matter of weeks or months.

Consider matters of health . . . of physical fitness . . . of information . . . of association . . . of experience . . . of personality . . . of addictions.

PERSONAL INVENTORY POSTSCRIPT

Areas to Be Strengthened	

Next to each weakness, record the means by which you anticipate turning it into a strength.

Don't expect to convert all of your weaknesses into strengths before you begin to implement your goals. If we all waited to become perfect people before we set out to accomplish goals, none of us would ever get started on the road to success!

Do expect, however, to work on your weaknesses as you pursue success. Make their remedy a goal in and of itself.

What If You Don't Know Yourself?

The old adage "Know thyself and to thine own self be true" doesn't work unless you have a basic understanding of your natural abilities and gifts. Some people don't. If that sounds like you, use this winter season to take an aptitude test.

Being successful is not strictly a matter of attitude and perception; it is also a matter of natural talent or aptitude. You can dream for years about accomplishing something—and even set specific goals and begin to make plans that will lead you in that direction—and yet if you do not have aptitude in that field, you are likely to fall short of your dream and be extremely frustrated along the way without knowing why.

In my previous books and audio programs, I have mentioned the value of tests offered by the Johnson O'Connor Research Foundation, headquartered in New York with a number of Human Engineering Laboratories in major cities across the country.

In studying the work of the Johnson O'Connor Foundation, which has been conducting research for more than half a century, I discovered that each of us is given several marvelous natural talents at the time of birth. Some of these aptitudes are passed on to us by the parent of the opposite sex. The ability to visualize solids and think in three dimensions—vital to surgeons, engineers, and architects—seems to be inherited by sons from their mothers only. Daughters can inherit this trait from either parent, however. Furthermore, many skills we assume are learned actually have an inherited attribute associated with them. For example, the ability to learn a foreign language with ease is an inborn trait, not just the result of practice.

It is amazing (even pathetic) how little parents know about their own children's natural abilities. Parents and counselors, and children themselves, tend to make college and career decisions based upon report cards and a few hours of discussion plus a lot of peer pressure. Frequently, these decisions don't line up with the child's natural aptitudes.

I imagined my oldest daughter, Debbie, might become a professional actress. Today, she has a Ph.D. and is a management development consultant for a Fortune 500 financial services company.

I pictured my next daughter, Dayna, as a veterinarian. She loved to care for animals when she was a young girl. She holds a Ph.D. in psychology and is a nationally recognized platform speaker.

My older son, Denis, played football with Herschel Walker on Georgia's national championship team. I pegged him as a professional athlete. He is a public relations and sales executive.

My younger son, Darren, is a little shy and introspective. I thought he would become a quiet researcher. He is doing radio commercials and has his own video production service.

My next daughter, Kimberlyn, is the ideal homemaker in my eyes. She merchandises upscale children's clothes and designs computer-based programs.

My youngest daughter, Lisa, was a summer camp counselor; therefore, I thought she was destined to become a social worker. She recently completed her linguistic training in Mandarin Chinese in Beijing, is bilingual in Spanish, and is considering a career in international business.

Each of my children has been tested for natural gifts, and they all scored very high in the areas they eventually discovered as their career paths.

I believe children should be tested for their natural abilities as they enter high school so they can become aware of their aptitudes early enough to select courses and skills training to shape these talents into stimulating careers or avocations.

Few people tested by the Johnson O'Connor Foundation have more than seven aptitudes. The usual number is three to five. The tests confirmed to me what I now know about myself. How I wish I could have taken the tests in high school!

Had I taken the natural gifts tests as a teenager, I would have discovered that the more appropriate course for my life would have been to go to a university to pursue studies in English, foreign language, music, the fine arts, writing, and speaking—which would have yielded information and helped me develop the very skills I use and enjoy using today.

Instead, I went to the U.S. Naval Academy at Annapolis, where strong emphasis was put on marine engineering, electrical engineering, navigation, ordnance, and gunnery. I struggled through those studies and went on to flight school where I struggled further with subjects for which I wasn't naturally gifted.

As a carrier-based attack pilot, I held my own due mostly to quick reflexes, determination, and an excellent memory. From a mechanical and engineering standpoint, I had no idea how my multimillion-dollar high-performance aircraft operated. I just flew it by the seat of my pants.

In my discussions with the experts at the Johnson O'Connor Foundation, I learned that many people are pursuing careers for which they are not naturally suited, and in so doing, they are limiting their fulfillment.

The late Ray Kroc, my former neighbor who founded McDonald's restaurants, stressed the importance of people doing a good job, not just for the money, but for the inner satisfaction it brings. He told the business school at the University of Southern California that the first thing a business executive needs is an idea he or she loves. "If you don't love it, drop it" was his advice. "If you're going to prostitute yourself at an early age and look for a job where the money is, you'll be working for money all your life. To love your work is very important, particularly for young people. If they lose that love, they'll rarely be able to recapture it."

In her study of top achievers, as reported in her book *Megatraits,* Dr. Doris Lee McCoy notes that the number one problem in not maintaining the necessary motivation for success is *a career not suited for your talents.*

Many people choose a convenient career, one in which they merely put in their hours and then go home to try to pursue what they really enjoy. Achievers, however, choose three courses of action:

1. They find out what career is most rewarding and interesting to pursue in order to use their full potential.
2. They sometimes find it necessary to go through several job changes and, in the process, test and discover new talents.
3. They use their jobs to develop their talents and potential.

You should assess carefully the areas in your life that are most enjoyable and in which you are most talented. You may feel today that you aren't where you need to be—that you are out of step with others who seem to be enjoying their careers and who seem to have natural abilities to succeed in your job arena. You may be right! Use your winter season to explore more of your aptitudes.

If you feel locked in to your present job, recognize that other options exist. See a career counselor. Take a natural gifts test. Also, consider taking a behavioral assessment test. Talent tests like those offered by the Johnson O'Connor Foundation must be conducted in the organization's offices. However, behavioral tests, such as the excellent ones offered by the Winslow Research Institute in Redwood City, California, can be sent for, completed at home, and turned in by mail; the results are returned in a comprehensive written and graphic report.

Take time to analyze your interests and talents. Totally forget, during this process, any thoughts about making money. Think only about what gives you the most satisfaction. What activities excite you? What brings you the most praise?

Get rid of the idea that your career and work should *not* be enjoyable. The more you like your career, the more productive you will be. And chances are, the more money you will earn in the long run as a result.

Don't be dismayed that you might have been pursuing a career not ideally suited to your talents. Be encouraged that you're discovering the fact now so that you can make a midcourse correction in your life. Many parents raise their children to pursue professions they perceive as being successful rather than raise their children to become successful in the area of their natural gifts. Others of us are guilty, even as adults, of continuing to pursue doggedly a career for which we aren't suited because we believe that things will get better if we just "hang in there" and "work harder."

To get your dreams sharply in focus and your goals and plans in line for maximum success, you must first make certain that your dreams are in keeping with who you *are*.

Use your winter season to discover your natural gifts!

Face Your Inner
Field Objectively

As you stare at the field of your success, ask yourself,

· What rocks need to be pulled from my life?
· What trees need to be felled?
· What brush needs to be cleared away?

Early frontier settlers did not encounter the rich farmlands of the Midwest in the condition we find them today. Virtually every acre needed to be cleared with painstaking, backbreaking effort. The ground needed to be made level. Rocks needed to be removed from the soil.

The field of your potential may also need to be cleared and made level.

Clear your personal field of self-doubt.

You not only *can* cultivate and harvest rewards from a field of success . . . you *should!* For many people, the greatest obstacle to success is their perception of themselves. Three principles are vital as you clear your field.

Principle 1: You are worthy of success. Many people do not believe they are worthy of success. Therefore, they do not dream of it. Are you one of these people?

If so, take time during the winter season to reevaluate your level of self-esteem. Ask yourself such questions as these . . .

· Do I accept myself for who I am?
· Would I rather be somebody else? If so, why?
· Do I internalize criticism—that is, take things personally— rather than seek to learn from criticism?
· Do I feel guilty when I indulge in a "selfish" activity?
· Am I comfortable when others praise or compliment me?
· Do I ridicule myself before others, or do I speak about myself with respect?

- Is the exterior of my life-style more important to me than my inner values?
- Is making a good impression on others more important than being true to myself?
- Do I constantly have to prove my worth by my outer achievements?

If you conclude that your self-esteem is low, I heartily recommend that you set as your number one goal "develop better self-esteem." Make it a priority in your life.

Recognize, first of all, that you are a masterpiece of creation. Although I may never be an artist of the caliber of Renoir, I have painted the interior and exterior of several of our homes through the years, and I take pride in my painting. Although I may never be the king or queen of a royal court or lead a nation, I do enjoy the special privileges of my own birthright and the opportunity I have to be part of a closely knit family. No matter who you are or what your family background, you are special, unique, and irreplaceable. Engage in activities that will help you recognize your individual talents, abilities, and opportunities for success. Associate with people who will encourage you toward and then applaud your accomplishments.

Don't confuse narcissism with self-esteem.

Narcissism is concerned with self-gratification and self-indulgence. The word comes to us from ancient Greek mythology and the story of Narcissus, who fell in love with his own image as he saw it reflected in a pool of water. He was the original "me first and whatever pleasures me is OK" guru.

Narcissism is very different from healthy self-esteem. The word *esteem* means "to appreciate the value of." You can value yourself without reducing the value of others. You can appreciate yourself as a person capable of beauty, honesty, sound values, achievements, healthy relationships, and truthfulness—without worshiping yourself or causing yourself to be placed at the center of your universe.

Self-esteem also need not imply that you consider yourself to be at the center of anyone else's universe! Self-esteem is not an exercise in vying to be Number One.

Don't confuse having high self-esteem with being egocentric.

Esteem and ego are worlds apart.

ESTEEM	I'm valuable.
EGO	I'm the only person who's valuable.
ESTEEM	What I say is important.
EGO	Only what I say is important.
ESTEEM	I can look at others and value them because I value myself.
EGO	Others must look at me and value me.
ESTEEM	I am a creation of God and am truly wonderful and unique.
EGO	God should have stopped after He created me.

Having healthy esteem and keeping your ego within bounds are both possible!

It is better to set internal standards for success rather than to live by comparison. When you compare yourself with others less successful than yourself, you run the risk of an overly inflated ego, which requires a lot of time and energy to maintain. If you compare yourself unfavorably with others, you may become frustrated. Executives often belittle their efforts by comparing their accomplishments to the giants in the field who have done better than they.

Make a list of every talent you have, however small, and every goal you have accomplished that has been important to you. Go back to your childhood, teen, and early adult years. You will likely discover that some of your greatest reasons for self-esteem are buried in past experience.

Surround yourself with positive, supportive, nurturing people. Remember that one way to feel good about yourself is to be helpful and supportive of others, even as they encourage you.

No matter what you do or what position you occupy, give it your best effort *because you are worth your best effort.*

Don't be like the man who says, "This job is not worthy of me. I'm too good to be doing this." In his contempt for his current means of employment, he refuses to do his best. He is dissatisfied, restless, and unhappy. And he lets everyone know about it! Ultimately, he'll lose his job. Understand this: He didn't fail his job. The job is still there and is being done by someone else. He failed himself.

I saw a woman on welfare being interviewed on a network news program. She said the only job she could find paid $1,000 a month, but she was receiving $1,200 a month for not working. Therefore, she saw no reason to work because it wasn't worth the effort. With that attitude, she will always depend on the system, and she will never grow beyond the level the system dictates to her.

There is no job too unworthy to do well. As they say in show business, "There are no small parts, only small actors."

Lisa G. is an example of a great actress in a small part. She went to New York City fresh out of college, looking for a job in publishing. No one was hiring. Finally, economic necessity made her take a job as a waitress in a coffee shop.

Undaunted, she did her best. She acted professionally, always greeting each person with a smile and providing excellent service. Several months later, a regular customer said to her, "I bet you aren't a waitress all the time. What else do you do?"

"Well," she replied, "I'd like to become an editor. I work evenings here and go on job interviews during the day."

As it turned out, the man was a prominent literary agent who needed a bright young assistant. He arranged for her to have an interview, and she got the position. She was on her way.

Lisa put into practice the principle of doing your best wherever you are. She instinctively knew that her position as a waitress was not a stumbling block but a stepping-stone. In that case, it was a far more direct stepping-stone than she had imagined.

God never puts anyone in a place too small to grow. We do that to ourselves. Wherever you may be—in an office, at a teacher's desk, on a sales route, behind a luncheonette counter, in a kitchen, in front of a word processor, on a utility pole with tools on your belt, or on an assembly line—do your job to the best of your abilities. You'll expand your talents by using them. It's not so much what the job gives you. It's what you give to the job.

Others may accept us and make us feel we belong. Others may be lavish in their praise of who and what we are, but if we have violated our conscience or sense of value, we will not feel worthy.

The principle of feeling worthy of quality, worthy of success, worthy of excellence, is one of the basic corporate missions across America. In a global market, with increasing competition from Asia, Europe, and other developing regions, it is imperative for each member of the work force to believe that he or she is a "quality" individual, expressing that quality in excellent production and service. With increasing pressure on profits and the need to do more with fewer people and less resources, we must raise the value of the employees' stock in themselves when we cannot, in a volatile economy, give them more stock in the company or more money as an incentive to do their best.

Principle 2: You can overcome the problems standing in your way of success. What problem do you think is keeping you from success? Some obstacles that appear repeatedly in the seminars I conduct are in the "Obstacle Checklist." Use this checklist, but don't limit yourself to the obstacles on it. Expand it to include your personal recognition of shortcomings.

OBSTACLES CHECKLIST

☐	Insufficient education	☐	Negative childhood
☐	In with wrong crowd	☐	Abusive environment
☐	Insufficient capital	☐	Chose wrong profession
☐	Vietnam veteran	☐	Accepted wrong job
☐	Bad economic times	☐	Too many dependents
☐	Bad credit rating	☐	Unresponsive boss
☐	Inflation	☐	Discrimination
☐	Federal government	☐	Economic recession
☐	Chemical addiction	☐	National debt
☐	Alcohol dependency	☐	Chose obsolete industry
☐	Uncooperative spouse	☐	Restrictive company policies
☐	Wrong horoscope	☐	Born at wrong time

Take a look at the items you checked. Virtually every item on this list can be turned into a positive with a little effort and re-training, rethinking, or regrouping of your resources.

Remember:

- Helen Keller graduated magna cum laude although she had been deaf and blind since infancy.
- Franklin Delano Roosevelt was president of the United States, even though he had been crippled by polio.
- Modern artist Henri Matisse created some of his best work when he was aged, bedridden, and nearly blind.
- Patti Catalano, one of the top women marathon runners in recent history, overcame the self-destructive habits of over-eating and chain-smoking to become a world-class runner.

Thomas Edison's father called him a dunce. His headmaster at school told him he would never make a success of anything.

Henry Ford barely made it through high school.

Edwin Land, the father of the Polaroid camera, failed at developing instant movies. He described his attempts as trying to use an impossible chemistry and a nonexistent technology to make an unmanufacturable product for which there was no discernible demand. That, in his opinion, created the optimum working conditions for the creative mind.

Principle 3: You CAN make a difference. You may feel as if any success you achieve won't make a difference in your life or that of others. Miss Lawson, a seventh-grade teacher, may have felt that way. Joe Sorrentino, author of the powerful books *Up From Never* and *The Concrete Cradle,* credits his success in life largely to Miss Lawson. He writes, "As a result of her concern and confidence, I applied myself to learning and eventually achieved the highest grade average in junior high school." High-school peer pressure tripped up Sorrentino for a while, but he says, "When I returned to night high school at the age of twenty, I had the memory of Miss Lawson and the academic aptitude she had nurtured in me."

Sorrentino went on to graduate magna cum laude from the University of California. To clear a bad military record, he reenlisted in the Marine Corps and became the first person in history to receive an honorable discharge after having been previously discharged under less than honorable conditions. He became a student leader at the Harvard Law School, and an outstanding juvenile court judge in Los Angeles. He taught law and lectured at the University of Southern California and has been one of the most sought-after speakers in America. Thank you, Miss Lawson.

- Frank Sinatra learned his superb breath control from band leader Tommy Dorsey.
- Plato learned from Socrates.
- Jesse Owens credited his winning of the 1936 long jump to a tip given him by his German competitor, Luz Long.
- Olympic champion Carl Lewis had his father and Jesse Owens as his role models.
- Mary Lou Retton had Bela Karolyi, the former Romanian gymnastics coach, as her mentor.
- Anne Sullivan made the difference in Helen Keller's life.

Loving and valuing yourself are prerequisites to loving and giving value to others.

It is impossible for you to esteem others unless you first have self-esteem, just as it is impossible for you truly to love others unless you first love yourself. Accept yourself today—just as you are—and believe that you are worthy of changing, growing, and becoming a success.

Your healthy self-esteem is vital to your ability to dream of success. If you do not see yourself as worthy of success, you'll never pursue it.

Twelve Steps for Building Self-Esteem as a Life-Farmer

In building your self-esteem, consider taking some of these steps immediately . . .

1. Greet others with a smile, and look them directly in the eye. A smile and direct eye contact convey confidence born of self-respect. Others will treat you with greater courtesy and respect, further reinforcing a positive way for you to perceive yourself.
2. Answer the phone pleasantly, whether at work or at home. In placing calls to others, give your name before asking to

speak to the party you've called. Leading with your name underscores that a person of value is making the call.

3. Listen to inspirational radio or cassette tape programs as you drive. Arrive at your destination with an uplifted spirit.

4. Invest in your knowledge and skill development. Build up your capacities and abilities.

5. Always say, "Thank you," when you are given a compliment. Don't downplay or sidestep a compliment. The ability to accept, or receive, is the universal mark of an individual with solid self-esteem.

6. Don't brag. People who trumpet their own exploits or demand special favors or service are desperate for attention. In fact, they are likely to be people of low esteem who are attempting to build themselves up in the eyes of others because they don't perceive themselves as already worthy of respect.

7. When you make a mistake, are ridiculed, or are rejected, choose to view your errors as an opportunity to learn. View a failure as the conclusion of one performance, not the end of your entire career! Don't make excuses. Own up to your failures, and at the same time, refuse to see yourself as a failure. A failure is something you have done, not necessarily something you will do, and definitely not something you are!

8. Spend this coming Saturday doing something you really want to do. Indulge yourself. It's OK to spend an entire day of the week on yourself! Choose to enjoy every hour of "your day."

9. Seek out successful role models. When you meet a mastermind, choose to become a "master mime" of that person—learning everything you can about him or her, and imitating the person as closely as you can. We all learn by miming others until we are confident enough to step into our own style.

10. Don't make your problems the centerpiece of your conversations. Talk affirmatively about positive aspects of your life and the forward progress you are trying to make.

11. Become aware of your negative thinking. Notice how often you complain. When you hear yourself criticize something or someone (including self-criticism), say to yourself, "Bad seeds! That's not like you!" And find a way to be helpful instead of critical.

12. Increase your productive activity level. During bad times and depressing moments when self-esteem is hurting, we tend to sit around and engage in "analysis to paralysis." The late Malcolm Forbes said, "Vehicles in motion use their generators to charge their own batteries. You can't recharge your battery when you're parked in the garage, unless you are a golf cart!"

Get out of your chair and get into an activity that, at least, requires physical movement. Forget about watching television and reading the daily newspaper. Take on a specific project, do it well, complete it, and get the accompanying reward for having been successful.

Forbes believed the important thing is never to say die until you're dead, and he lived that example to the hilt. Life is, as we realize suddenly when we attend our fortieth high-school reunion, a short journey. It is also difficult to be depressed and active at the same time!

Consider the Soil into Which You Will Be Planting Your Efforts, Ideas, and Hopes

High alkaline percentage?
Sandy loam?
Clay?
Different types of soil produce different crops. Every farmer knows that for a harvest to have a high yield, the soil must be right for producing the crop with which it is seeded.

As a life-farmer, you may be ideally suited to farm a particular type of crop, but you may be planting your seeds in the wrong kind of soil.

Take time during the winter season of your success to appraise the field into which you will be planting. Ask yourself questions such as these . . .

- What can I offer that others aren't offering?
- What needs aren't being met by others?
- What niche hasn't yet been developed?
- How can I add value to the service or product I now provide?
- Is there a way to produce a product more efficiently?
- Can the product be manufactured less expensively?

- What would people pay for that isn't available now?
- What trends are going to alter the way a service or product is used and rendered?
- Is the need for this service or product lasting (or is it just a fad)?
- What more can I do to help my clients (or distributors, franchisers, retailers) in their jobs?

Will you own the field or farm in someone else's field?

Many people limit their sights to employment in someone else's field. Though there's nothing wrong with being a hired hand working in someone else's field, make certain that you have made a conscious decision to be an employee rather than an employer. If you choose to be an employee, rise as high as you can for as great a benefit and opportunity for influence as you can. To choose to be an *employee*, however, you must first rule out the possibility of being the plantation owner.

Certainly not everyone can be self-employed or start a company. Still, many people can. America is the only nation on earth with such an abundance of opportunities to do just that. America is the best place to be if you want to open a new business, invent a new product, or offer a new service.

More and more people are working independently as self-employed "offices of one." They are offering consulting services, training, writing and editing services, graphic arts services, CPA and bookkeeping services, legal advice, and a wide variety of support services for companies that choose to pay by the project rather than add to their work force.

Still others are going into home-based manufacturing—providing piecework manufacturing, distribution, or telemarketing services for others, or starting their own manufacturing ventures.

Don't overlook those opportunities. Don't discount them without exploring them fully . . . during the winter season of your dreaming and setting goals.

Don't be dismayed if the farmer before you failed in cultivating the field.

Your field—your chosen area in which to plant for your future success—may be a field that someone else considers a failure.

It may be the corner lot on which three previous used-car businesses have come and gone. Still, the corner hasn't seen your used-car business! The field of failure for someone else may be your field of success.

It may be the job within the organization that no one else wants or will take on. What others have avoided as a potential swamp may actually be highly fertile ground for your energy, ideas, and abilities.

It may be a field that others see as overcrowded. I read about a real estate agent who lived in a community in which one out of twenty houses was on the market. What her town didn't need was one more house for sale and one more real estate agent vying for buyers. Or so everyone else thought. It turned out that her city did need one more agent—this young woman, who made a barter with her brother that she would give him a portion of her commission if he would help her move furniture in and out of vacant houses. She had a knack for decorating and a vision for showing people the true potential of a well-decorated house. She went after the top-appraised value for each house for maximum commission. Together, she and her brother turned vacant houses into model homes with dramatic sales results. All it took was an idea and some extra muscle power.

Not all fields are destined for failure. They might simply have had bad farmers at work in them prior to your arrival!

Be Willing to Transform the Landscape Before You

Deserts can bloom.

Barren plains can yield life-giving produce.

First . . . you must be willing to change the landscape before you.

When I was doing the research for my book *The Psychology of Winning,* I came across a study of a native tribe in South America. The people in the tribe had been dying prematurely from a strange illness for many generations. Scientists finally discovered that the disease was carried by an insect that lived in the walls of their adobe homes. The natives faced several possible solutions. They could destroy the insects with a pesticide. They could tear down and rebuild their homes. They could move to another location where the insects weren't found. Or they could do nothing and continue to die young, just as they had for generations. What did they choose to do? Incredibly to me, they have chosen to remain as they are. They have taken the path of least resistance and no change.

Many people I meet have a similar attitude about achieving personal success. They realize that if they do certain things, they can succeed. The things require change, however, and they resist the change. They allow themselves to stay as they are and, in many cases, to die without ever really living.

To be a successful farmer with the high yield of goals realized and life-dreams turned into reality, you must be willing to change the way things are now. If you have no success to which you can point, you must be willing to move toward success. If you have some success, you must be willing to pursue greater success!

Face down the fear of taking a risk to improve your life.

Recognize at the outset of your winter planning and dreaming that luck has little relationship to success. The fear of taking a risk is far more responsible for keeping people from failure than getting a dose of bad luck.

I have my own definitions of fear and luck. *Fear* is

> **F**alse
> **E**ducation
> **A**ppearing
> **R**eal

Fear is always related to the unknown. As you gain knowledge about a subject, situation, circumstance, or person, fear tends to dissipate.

And *luck* is

> **L**aboring
> **U**nder
> **C**orrect
> **K**nowledge

If you work with accurate information, you'll be prepared for opportunities that will arise as you work. Another word for *luck* may very well be *effort*.

Consider two people you probably know well . . .

Gambling Gary. Do you know a person who says, "I try and try, but nothing ever seems to work out for me"? Such a person has probably never stopped to learn from previous mistakes. The person who repeatedly fails to achieve goals has likely never confronted the levels of information, experience, or ability necessary for achieving them.

Perhaps the person has the goal of making a million dollars. Unless that person confronts the fact that it takes a certain amount of savvy about money, the economy, and "doing business" to make that amount of money, he or she is likely to spend (and lose) a great deal of money at betting games or in casinos, always hoping for the big win . . . to make snap decisions about investments without first investigating them and gathering as much information about them as possible . . . or to launch into projects without counting all of the costs in terms of time, money, and effort. Such people seem to have permanent potential—they are always looking for a score on the long shot and never succeeding at the step-by-step building process that leads to true success. They exhibit what I term the *lottery syndrome*. The seasons of success aren't based on long odds. They are based on taking a long hard look at the future, investing lots of long hours and hard work, and reaping rewards that are long-lasting!

Security Sally. At the opposite end of the scale from the person who lives with the lottery syndrome is the person with the *no-risk-total-security syndrome.*

What are the characteristics of such people? First, they increasingly narrow their path as they grow older. They take fewer and fewer risks, narrow their opportunities, limit their horizons, reduce the flow of fresh viewpoints and new ideas into their lives. They stop their education and freeze their knowledge at whatever level they had when they last "graduated" from some type of school or course. They predetermine, to some extent, how far they will go in their careers. They form friendships and then close their circle of friends. They tend to seek out a comfort zone, preferring not to move unless they absolutely must. They abhor change, and when forced to change, they change as little as possible. When faced with a challenge or opportunity, they'll avoid it if possible. When confronted, they'll take the easy way out. When given choices, they'll choose the path of least resistance.

The no-risk-total-security person rarely tests his potential. She is seldom concerned about personal or career growth. He tends to see his career as a job and to define his free time as a means of escaping from that job. She hates taking chances. She prefers not to know when something goes wrong. Such a person may not know what it takes to succeed, but he usually knows how to avoid failure.

Total security is a myth.

In fact, it's one of the greatest myths you can ever believe. Virtually everybody I meet talks about wanting security. People want a world without disruptions, negative circumstances, problems, or risks. Furthermore, they think such a world is possible. Most people envision a successful life as a secure one.

Toward that end, they seek a financially secure future by investing in savings plans, IRA's, and insurance. They seek to make their homes secure with locks and elaborate alarm systems.

The truth is that security is never possible with a 100 percent money-back guarantee. Nothing and no one can assure you of security. No person has ever lived an entire life totally secure from start to finish. The only truly secure person is one lying horizontally, lily in hand, six feet underground.

Life is inherently risky. Birth is a risk. The place most of us instinctively envision as the safest place we've ever been is our mother's womb. Our mother's womb was actually a place of great potential danger should we have decided to linger there a few weeks past the proper time for our birth. If a baby doesn't leave its mother's womb, it will die there.

Crossing the street is a risk.

Entering a relationship is a risk.

Starting a company is a risk.

Beginning a new job is a risk.

Planting is a risk.

The biggest risk is one you should avoid, however. That's the risk of doing nothing. Doing nothing sets you up for entropy, a lack of forward motion. Entropy leads to barnacles, moss, and the attachment of other creatures and minerals that slow you down. Entropy leads to atrophied muscles, which are more easily injured and strained, and tissues without a sufficient supply of oxygen (which comes from blood coursing through vessels, which is the consequence of exertion and activity). Entropy leads to death.

To do nothing eventually leads to something: your demise.

Risk taking is a part of life, and people who seek a risk-free life actually spend a great deal of energy avoiding risks. That same amount of energy could likely be channeled into taking calculated risks that would bring greater success, less frustration and self-doubt, and greater fulfillment and joy in life!

A person cannot live in a pie-in-the-sky, hope-my-number-comes-up mind-set and experience success. Such a person will lose his lottery winnings faster than he ever imagined winning them because he never truly dreamed of what life would be like managing such success. He only dreamed of receiving a check!

It's impossible to set reachable goals if you live with either the Gambling Gary or the Security Sally syndrome. Life isn't a lottery with instant winners. Neither is life ever risk free.

You must take the shackles off your apathy and choose to take a risk to experience success.

- Success means asserting the option to grow—and seeking out controlled growth.
- Success means taking risks—and taking them after responsible appraisal.
- Success means being willing to change—and making certain that the changes are for the better.

And now is the time for PLANNING it.

7

The Season for Making Plans

It's ironic—no, tragic—that many people take more time to plan vacations than they do the major parts of their lives. They become deeply involved in selecting a destination, setting a date, choosing a method of travel, mapping out a budget, preparing for the life-style they'll lead upon arrival at their destination, and arranging all of the details for a trip (from dog kennels to plant-watering house sitters)—yet rarely do they approach life's bigger agenda with this same degree of planning and preparation.

On New Year's Eve, instead of going out in search of a hang-over, our family members congregate around the fireplace to reflect on the events that made the past year memorable. We have our own Oscar presentations at the Academy Awards Ceremonies for Goals. Each of us opens a sealed envelope in which we placed our written goals on December 31 of the previous year. Then, using those written goals as an outline, we proceed to share our blessings and accomplishments, admitting, too, the areas in which we have missed the targets or fallen short of a goal.

Winter is your season for making a self-development plan.

Planning Is "Engineering" Your Goals

The Aluminum Company of America, more commonly known as ALCOA, coined a wonderful word: *imagineering*. Imagineering has two phases: letting your imagination soar, and then engineering your dreams to make them happen. Planning is the engineering process for your goals.

Several steps are involved in this engineering process.

First, segment your goals into a plan with small doable steps. Research has shown again and again that when people go after one big goal at once, they invariably fail. It's as if you tried to swallow a twelve-ounce steak with one gulp. You'd choke. To eat a twelve-ounce steak, you must first cut it into small pieces and eat one bite at a time.

So it is with planning. Each life goal must be broken down into bite-sized pieces. Each small task or requirement on the way to an ultimate goal becomes a minigoal.

Study the example that follows each step of the breaking down process.

First, choose one of your top three goals, and write it at the top of a sheet of paper in bold letters.

> Goal: Lose forty pounds in the next five months (for an average of two pounds a week).

Then, below the goal, break your goal into a series of subgoals or minigoals. Add as many steps as possible.

> See a physician.
> Decide on a diet plan.
> Choose and add a moderate exercise program to the diet plan.
> Increase level of exercise.
> Increase level of exercise a second time.
> Avail self of a motivational program to maintain psychoemotional momentum.
> Choose and establish a maintenance program.
> Lose first ten pounds.
> Lose second ten pounds.
> Lose third ten pounds.
> Lose last ten pounds.

Keep breaking down your goals into smaller and smaller components until each component seems accomplishable in one sitting or within a few days.

> Lose five pounds.
> Lose a total of ten pounds.
> Lose a total of fifteen pounds.
> Lose a total of twenty pounds.
> Lose a total of twenty-five pounds.
> Lose a total of thirty pounds.
> Lose a total of thirty-five pounds.
> Lose a total of forty pounds.

Now, number and letter (as with an outline) these subgoals in the order in which they should be accomplished.

1. See a physician.
2. Decide on a diet plan.
4. Choose and add a moderate exercise program to the diet plan.
6. Increase level of exercise.
9. Increase level of exercise a second time.
7. Avail self of a motivational program to maintain psychoemotional momentum.
11. Choose and establish a maintenance program.
3. Lose first ten pounds.
5. Lose second ten pounds.
8. Lose third ten pounds.
10. Lose last ten pounds.
3a. Lose five pounds.
3b. Lose a total of ten pounds.
5a. Lose a total of fifteen pounds.
5b. Lose a total of twenty pounds.
8a. Lose a total of twenty-five pounds.
8b. Lose a total of thirty pounds.
10a. Lose a total of thirty-five pounds.
10b. Lose a total of forty pounds.

Now list your goal and subgoals in order on a new sheet of paper. As you make your list of subgoals, don't think about obstacles or hurdles. Assume that you will be able to complete each step successfully.

1. See a physician.
2. Decide on a diet plan.
3. Lose first ten pounds.
   a. Lose five pounds.
   b. Lose a total of ten pounds.
4. Choose and add a moderate exercise program to the diet plan.
5. Lose second ten pounds.
   a. Lose a total of fifteen pounds.
   b. Lose a total of twenty pounds.
6. Increase level of exercise.
7. Avail self of a motivational program to maintain psychoemotional momentum.
8. Lose third ten pounds.
   a. Lose a total of twenty-five pounds.
   b. Lose a total of thirty pounds.
9. Increase level of exercise a second time.
10. Lose last ten pounds.
    a. Lose a total of thirty-five pounds.
    b. Lose a total of forty pounds.
11. Choose and establish a maintenance program.

Notice that steps 2, 4, 7, and 11 require the acquisition of additional information. As these steps are approached and begin to take shape, you may need or want to establish further subgoals.

Break down your goals into component goals.

Let me give you two more samples of goal listing, breaking down maxi-goals into minicomponents.

Example 1: The Professional Goal of Acquiring More Advanced Computer Skills

1. Determine the skills needed.
   a) Discuss the need for additional skills with supervisor.
   b) Read about trends in field and anticipated need for selected skills.
   c) Check Sunday newspaper want ads for skills being required for positions similar to the one I presently have; note skills required for positions higher up the pay scale than mine.

      d) Consult computer publications about new industry trends in software.

2. Find a course of study that offers these skills for the best possible price in the least amount of time.

      a) Make call to local junior college or vocational training center.

      b) Consult knowledgeable computer software salesperson about self-instructional programs.

3. Enroll in course.

4. Complete course.

5. Seek immediate opportunities to implement new skills (for maximum reinforcement of learning).

Example 2: The Family Goal of Planning a Traditional Five-Year Family Thanksgiving Reunion

1. Set date and place—six months in advance of reunion.

      a) Make preliminary call to key family members about availability on three choices of weekends and locations.

      b) Get additional addresses (and updated addresses).

      c) Call key family members with dates that work for everybody.

2. Reserve location.

3. Plan event.

      a) Select menu.

      b) Find entertainment.

      c) Determine special activities for children.

      d) Choose decorations, if desired.

4. Send "mark your calendar" postcard to all family members—four months in advance of the reunion.

5. Send letter detailing location, time, activities, food, reservations information—eight weeks before reunion.

Do you see how a goal can—and needs to—be broken into subgoals?

Build Your Plan with These Questions in Mind

In breaking down your goals into their component tasks, you might have recognized a need for additional input. Keep these three questions at the forefront of your mind as you frame your plan. . . .

Question 1: What do I need to know?

We've all heard the statement: "When all else fails, read the instructions!" I'm continually amazed, however, at how frequently well-intentioned dreamers and goal setters map out plans without first getting the facts and information they need.

When I was in college, my professors taught me to use the library to check the primary sources. I can no longer count the number of times that I've spent an afternoon digging through card files and microfiche records, and walking up and down aisles of books seeking to verify facts or quotes. Most of the time, I discover that even the "reputable sources" have misquoted a person or misinterpreted a statistic.

For years, I held onto and even repeated misinformation about Albert Einstein. I, like many others, had read at one time that Einstein failed his early math and science classes as a young boy. I made a sweeping generalization in my lectures that implied Einstein had been something of a dunce while in grade school, but he had climbed out of his intellectual ghetto to achieve greatness. I even thought I remembered "reading somewhere" how he had failed his college entrance requirements but then had gone on to develop the theory of relativity. I used him as a prime example, of course, of a person who had tapped into his inner capabilities and turned himself around on the road from failure eventually to achieve great success.

Had Einstein really failed those math and science classes? My check of primary sources revealed that Einstein had always scored very well in math and science! Historians had noted that Einstein's top grade of six (on a scale of one to six with six being high) had dropped to a level of one from one year to the next. They had assumed he had started to flunk those courses. The truth of the matter was, however, that the school had reversed its grading system to make the highest grade a one instead of a six.

Don't assume that what you always held to be true still is. New discoveries might have been made since you last checked your references. Be an open-minded skeptic about what you know and what you hear.

In approaching any new position, challenge, project, business, or investment, you need to avail yourself of information in at least these five areas.

1. What is the jargon spoken, and what are the basic concepts underlying those terms? Every enterprise has its own shoptalk. If you are moving from the assembly line to the front office, you'll encounter a completely new vocabulary. If you are embarking on a new degree program or area of vocational study, you'll probably be overwhelmed by new words. It's no accident that a foundational course for medical school is anatomy, a great part of which is a thorough introduction to the names of every bone, muscle, and tissue substance of the body! If you are in the computer field, you know that the jargon changes from month to month. If you are new to the stock market or to one particular kind of investment or financial vehicle, you'll need to learn the set of terms appropriate for that enterprise.

Count on taking vocabulary lessons when you enter a new field or attempt to grow to a new level of success. Anticipate learning a new set of terms and the concepts underlying them. Make certain that you verify your understanding of the concepts. Can you cite examples? Can you also point to examples of behavior to be avoided, faulty products, failures in reasoning, miscalculations, or misapplications? Very often the identification of bad examples is as important as that of good ones. Do you know how concepts relate to one another? Can you use the terms and concepts appropriately in discussions?

2. What is the TRUE organizational chart? Every enterprise is structured in a particular way. Frequently, the stated organizational chart—the one posted on the wall or published in the annual report—is only an approximation of the way things truly work within a company. Learning who's who and how authority is structured is vital to your survival within an organization. Equally important is the power structure of a community should you be seeking political office or the appeals process if you are involved in litigation. On a more personal level, you may have as a goal the achievement of a greater degree of physical fitness. Who at your gym has the authority to open the doors a half hour earlier or to give you permission to invite a guest?

3. What are the foremost issues or problems challenging the success of an enterprise? Every project has built-in obstacles or hurdles that must be surmounted before success can be achieved. How can these obstacles be circumvented or diminished in their impact? How can the hurdles best be crossed? If you are planning on starting your own business venture or introducing a new product line, you face the challenge of mapping out the marketplace and determining where the strengths and weaknesses lie in the larger economy for your product. If you are planning to strengthen your family ties, you need to take into consideration all of the factors that might work against you—conflicting schedules, differing priorities, the influence of outside forces (such as peers, club obligations, or school requirements).

4. How does the information flow? Every enterprise has a distinctive grapevine for information—usually a formal set of information channels and an informal one. Ask, Who has access to the most current, reliable, and useful information? Do you know where your stockbroker gets his tips? Do you know where the trainer at the spa gets her information on health matters? Do you know where your boss gets the information on which he bases his decisions and opinions?

Once you have determined the people most reliably "in the know," seek to discover their sources of information and then avail yourself of them. Read what your boss reads. Beyond that, read what the president of the company reads! Keep current with trends, data, and new inventions, processes, and theories.

5. What is the accepted protocol for introducing ideas or making changes? Every enterprise has built-in rules for how things should happen. The protocol may refer to the way in which changes are made within your corporation; the way new members are initiated into the club; the proper promotional strategy for most effectively announcing a new product line. Explore how an industry works and what steps are usually undertaken in making changes. You may be able to gain this information from the organization itself—from personnel handbooks or previously published manuals about procedures. You may need to consult textbooks related to the field.

One of the most common disclaimers associated with virtually every exercise or nutrition program is this: "Consult your physician before undertaking an exercise program or going on a diet." Why? There's a protocol for making safe changes in your physiology. The same holds true for any personal changes you seek to make in your life. There's a right way and a wrong way to go about the process of growing, changing, learning, developing. Find out what the experts agree on. Follow their advice.

Good information is critical to the planning process. Where do *you* go to get the knowledge that you need for planning?

Unfortunately, many people rely only on their parents, friends, spouses, coworkers, and a smattering of television programs for information about their futures. I urge you to spend a few hours in your winter season of success closely examining the sources from which you have gained, or are gaining, insights into your life—and especially information and insights directly related to achieving your goals.

My personal approach to developing an information base related to my goals is to scan my local newspaper for community events that might affect my family. I look for things that we can do together and programs that will enhance our communication and relationships as a family.

I scan the *Wall Street Journal* and the *New York Times* for national, international, and business information that may influence my day or my week.

I scan *USA Today* for human interest stories and a general awareness of future trends.

Every Monday I scan the new issues of *Time* and *U.S. News & World Report* magazines to pick up what I might have missed in my cursory newspaper speed reading.

Every month I read *Omni, Discover, Consumer Reports,* and *Reader's Digest.* The first three keep me on the cutting edge of future breakthroughs. *Reader's Digest* gives me a needed boost of inspiration as well as an opportunity to continue to increase my vocabulary. (By the way, did you know that a broad vocabulary, as a result of good reading habits, is the single most commonly identifiable trait in successful people, regardless of their occupations? Interesting, isn't it?)

In addition to reading, I listen to educational cassette tapes and, occasionally, a novel on tape. Numerous self-enriching, motivational, and instructional audiocassettes and videotapes are available on the market. (Consult your local Waldenbooks and B. Dalton Booksellers outlets.) You may want to get a catalog of items available from Nightingale-Conant, Thomas Nelson, or other firms specializing in such materials.

You can listen to these tapes as you walk, ride your bike, jog, do housework, commute in your automobile, or travel by bus, train, or plane. Convert some of your downtime into a moving university without walls!

Don't overlook the information available through instructional computer software and free computer networks. Your personal computer modem and phone line are your means of accessing vast data banks and a national library of information on just about any subject you can name.

Consult your local library for informative materials. Libraries stock numerous videocassettes that can help you move forward to your personal and professional goals. They also have trade magazines in numerous fields as well as the tried-and-true reference books and source books. I rarely leave a library without a stack of photocopies of articles related to goals I'm seeking to achieve. I look upon my goals as something of a term paper with an urgent due date!

On what do you base your definitions of *truth?* If the information were to be challenged, on what basis would you defend it as accurate or wise?

You may be amazed at how frequently you ingest information from your environment—which includes people—that is little more than speculation based on biased opinion. In many cases, you aren't getting facts—you're getting hype.

In sum . . .

- Allow your search for knowledge to take you to the library, to lectures, to seminars, to workshops. (Always review carefully the credentials of every potential teacher—whether speaker or author.)
- Never rely on secondary sources of hearsay evidence.
- Listen to a variety of opinions and sources. Be open to hearing what they have to say and skeptical enough to check them for accuracy and relevancy to your particular needs.

Question 2: Who do I need to know?

Take a few moments to identify four key people to whom you turn for advice about how to reach one (or more) of your top three life goals.

Did you list persons who have a track record of success? (I'm continually amazed at the percentage of people who turn to unsuccessful people for information and encouragement about how they might personally become more successful!)

What are the credentials of the people you consult?

Role models give you an example of a plan that is working. When the term *role model* is used, many of us automatically think of a person that children can look up to.

Parents are supposed to be good role models for children. So are teachers, professional athletes, coaches, Scout leaders, pastors, and others in leadership or authority roles. While it's true that children need good role models, it's equally true that people of all ages need role models.

Not only do we need role models to show us how to "do" and to "be" various aspects of life, but we have role models whether or not we recognize them as such. We have people to whom we look and say, "I want to be like that."

I advise you *not* to look to most of commercial television for your role models. The characters of prime-time television frequently do not portray the characteristics that we would like to see emulated by our children or that we hope to display in our own lives. Television may bring celebrity status to people and name-brand recognition to characters, but television also presents a fairly warped image of our world. Few successful people will encounter the violence or sexual relationships portrayed as the norm on prime-time television, and fewer still will want to experience these activities and relationships in their lives.

Choose role models who have overcome what you face. One of the greatest career boosts you can ever experience is to find a mentor who represents what you want to both be and do. The best role model is the person who most nearly approximates who you are—has a similar background or career path, has been where you've been, and is already where you want to go. Don't choose a celebrity as a role model—that is, someone you worship from afar. Choose someone you can know up close and personal. Choose someone with whom you can spend time and with whom you enjoy having conversations and exploring ideas.

Of course, you can have favorite authors, teachers, or leaders as role models or mentors. You can learn a great deal from persons whose work is published and whose ideas are available in print, audio, or video form. If you discover authors or speakers with whom you feel a special affinity, make the effort to get your hands on everything they've ever written or said. Really become a *student* of their work and of their lives. Don't just admire them; learn from them.

Choose role models who are winners in all areas of their lives. In seeking out role models and mentors, seek out those who are not only winners—those who have achieved success in the field you are in—but those whose lives apart from their careers are worthy of emulation.

Rarely can we separate a person's achievements from character. One facet of a person's life will invariably affect all other facets. Reject role models who prove by the conduct of their lives that they aren't worth imitating.

Sam Walton was one of the finest role models in our nation. Not only because his financial value as cofounder and chief executive officer of the one thousand Wal-Mart and Sam's outlets consistently placed him at or near the top of the Forbes "richest people in America" list—but because of the way he chose to live with his wealth. He drove the back roads near his Bentonville, Arkansas, home (population 9,901) in a 1979 red-and-white Ford pickup and had his bird dogs at his side during quail season. Even when he was retirement age, he was anything but retired. He sometimes piloted one of the company planes that took him to visit his stores and to open new stores. He wasn't above hopping onto a chair to lead everyone in a Wal-Mart cheer: "Give me a *W* . . . give me an *A* . . . give me an *L* . . ." and so forth.

He unashamedly believed in being loyal, working hard, getting ideas into the system from the bottom up, treating people right, cutting prices and margins to the bone, and sleeping well at night. If you had happened to drive down their street, you would have seen a mailbox marked "Sam and Helen Walton" next to the drive leading to a rustic, modestly furnished ranch-style home set back in the woods. He didn't marinate in hype or his own press clippings.

When Sam went into his stores to purchase items, he waited in line with the other customers. One day, when he went to his barber of twenty-five years, John Mayhall, for a haircut, he realized he had forgotten his wallet. Mayhall said, "Forget it. Just take care of it next time." Walton replied, "No, I'll get it." He went home, got his wallet, and came back to pay his bill.

Yes, Sam Walton was a rich man. His money really has little to do with it. Less than a month before he died, Sam Walton was awarded the Presidential Medal of Freedom, the nation's highest civilian honor.

Lord Chesterfield said it well: "We are more than half of what we are by imitation. The great point is to choose good models and to study them with care."

Have encouragers backing you up. In addition to good role models, we need encouragers—personal cheerleaders or personal fan-club presidents. They are the people who will try to help you rather than impress you. They give you time when you come to them with questions, opinions, or ideas. They'll ask you questions rather than tell you their life stories. They'll help you find the road that's best suited for you rather than try to sell you on their idea or plan for your life. They have your best interests at heart. Encouragers want to see *you* succeed.

You can't always choose the people with whom you work on a day-to-day basis, but you do have some control over the people with whom you choose to spend your spare time. Avoid those who fall into any of these categories:

- Pity party-goers
- Gripers
- Chronic complainers
- Doomsdayers
- Pessimists
- Naysayers
- Excuse makers

Choose to spend your time with people who want to be successful, who are growing positively, who are seeking to enact positive change in our world, and who are uplifting and encouraging.

We are more than half of what we are by imitating. Ask yourself today,

- Who am I imitating?
- Who are my role models?
- Who are my mentors?
- Who are my encouragers?

If you are young and relatively inexperienced, network with more mature, seasoned entrepreneurs. Your enthusiasm and desire, combined with their richness in experience, can be a very powerful combination. If you are a veteran executive, seek out a young entrepreneur who may be more open to new ways to achieve your goals and who hasn't learned the meaning of frustration and defeat.

Question 3: What experience do I need to have?

Learning about something is a far cry from actually doing something by yourself.

One of the best ways to prepare for success is to plan for simulation activities as a part of your self-development program.

The word *simulate* means "to assume the character of or to imitate." Simulation is a process we have come to identify closely with pilots and astronauts as well as with athletes. Many times we'll note on television the small-type disclaimers at the bottom of a commercial: "Simulation only." Keep in mind always that watching a simulation on TV or on a videocassette is one thing. *Doing* the activity yourself is another.

The best simulations are those that call upon your body to react to stimuli. The more stimuli and the more physical reactions evoked, the better the simulation. For example, the simulator used by American Airlines in Dallas, Texas, has the same complete cockpit instrumentation found in various types of aircraft flown by American's pilots. Through the use of audiovisual technology, pilots can "fly" the simulator through various types of weather conditions and equipment emergencies. They taxi from the ramp, take off, fly to a city, and land—never leaving the ground, of course, but feeling in their bodies the pull of various forces, hearing all of the sound effects, and seeing the sights as if making the trip in real life.

Another form of simulation is the type that I recall experiencing in navy flight training. It might well be labeled dress rehearsal. The task we were learning was low-altitude, high-speed bombing. The simulation took place at 20,000 feet in real aircraft. Our instructions were to begin a high-speed run at the target, then pull up steadily in a four-G climb, lofting the bomb toward the target at a precise moment. We were then to continue climbing, go into a loop, and at the top of the loop perform an Immelmann, a sort of barrel roll, as we escaped the shock blast from the payload. The challenge was to engineer the roll precisely so that the plane was on course back to our aircraft carrier and below enemy radar. The maneuver wasn't easy.

On my first effort, I exited the roll and found myself climbing straight up. My air speed fell to zero, I stalled, and I took all of

15,000 feet to regain control of the aircraft. On my second try, I overcompensated and exited the roll heading straight down. I nearly blacked out from the excessive G force, felt the wings shudder under the strain, and again used about 15,000 feet to pull my aircraft back into position.

The other members of my training group, however, had greater success than I had. In fact, we performed so well as a group that we were told in the debriefing room that the next day we were going to do the bombing run for real. Our high-speed run would be 50 feet above the desert floor. I managed to squeak out a question: "Sir, at the highest point of our pull-up, how high will we be?" The commanding officer replied, "No more than 900 feet above the terrain." I explained to him that on the two previous runs I had required nearly 15,000 feet to come out of the pull-up and that if I flew like that the next day, I'd dig a hole 14,100 feet into the desert floor!

I asked for permission to make a few more high-altitude simulation runs. The CO gave me permission to run the simulations again even as he admonished me, "You may not always have the extra day or second chance in the real world. That's why it's so important to practice correctly in the simulation drills. Your life and the lives of your buddies may depend on it."

The next day, I managed to stay well within the 900-foot limit, and later, I flew the real exercise with confidence. I never forgot that lesson. Simulation is invaluable in preparing you for all kinds of situations—some of them may well involve life and death, or at minimum, the life and death of your business, your career, your job, your marriage, or your important relationships. When given the opportunity to practice for success, give it your best effort.

Another name for experience is practice. Rehearse at every opportunity. Repeat and repeat and repeat your performance until you are completely satisfied that you've done all you can do.

Practice under the most realistic conditions possible. I recall the days prior to my launching out into seminars and public speaking events. I attended numerous lectures and observed closely the delivery manner of the speakers and the content covered. I listened to cassettes of speakers who were similar to me in age, background, and beliefs. I then wrote a twenty-minute speech and rehearsed it in the privacy of my study until I had it memorized. Rehearsal in my study, however, wasn't a simulation.

To create a simulation, I rounded up my family members and gave my speech to them. They listened patiently and offered suggestions, including one that I consider a different avocation! I branched out. I invited a group of friends over for dinner and gave them my after-dinner speech for dessert. If you'll pardon the pun, it was a piece of cake!

After giving the speech several times to friends, I contacted service clubs in my city that met periodically for lunch or dinner. I volunteered to give my presentation. The groups—Kiwanis, Rotarians, Optimists, Lions, various women's groups—offered no fees or honorariums to their meeting speakers and were accustomed to a variety of guest speakers.

Today I deliver about two hundred keynote addresses each year to major corporations, institutions, and public audiences. When I'm asked how long it took me to move up the public speaking ladder to earn the fees that I receive today, I answer politely that I delivered more than eight hundred unpaid simulation speeches before I ever received one dime.

I suspect the same is true for every concert soloist, every author, every race car driver, every actor, every athlete, every frame maker, every mechanic, every surgeon, every preacher, every attorney, every nurse, every teacher, and virtually every other professional at the top of his or her field. The simulations of childhood and classroom laboratories and volunteer performances are background upon which success is built.

Practice before a supportive audience. Your first simulations should be before or with groups of supportive family members and friends. The emphasis here is on *supportive*. You'll have more courage and you'll receive more encouragement at the outset if you "perform" in front of those who truly want you to succeed and who will listen to you or watch you intently with an eye toward helping you achieve success.

The value of simulation is that it allows you to perform and to get it right without the fear of failure creating stifling or choking pressure. With a successful string of simulated performances under your belt, you'll have a strong level of confidence and greater self-esteem by the time you face the real thing. In fact, you may feel as if the real thing is just another simulated drill.

What types of activities lend themselves to simulation? Virtually anything that you consider worth the extra effort of doing right!

- · Interviewing for a new job or new position
- · Hostessing a major event
- · Preparing a dinner for an important party
- · Dancing in exhibition
- · Giving a presentation to stockholders
- · Writing a summary report for your boss
- · Teaching a lesson

Closely related to simulation is the ability to visualize your performance. Valeri Borzov, the great Russian sprinter who won two gold medals in the 1972 Olympic Games at Munich, said in an interview after one race:

As I placed my feet against the starting blocks, I began to run the race in my mind. The spectators, naturally, could not know this. They only saw Borzov walk slowly to the starting line, carefully place his feet against the starting blocks, and freeze in that pose until the command "Ready!" Mentally, though, I was somewhat ahead of that. I was already running. By learning to draw a mental picture of the race while I was still at the starting line, I was able to react to the starting shot with split-second speed. And when the shot was fired, my inner robot—programmed to get me out of the motionless state—switched on and took over.

In enhancing your preparation through simulation, close your eyes and imagine yourself giving your speech . . . performing the surgery . . . making the presentation . . . singing the song . . . in the environment in which you will be giving your real performance. Focus on how the room looks, what you can hear, how you feel, and what you do. Create the episode in your imagination as vividly as possible. And then hear the applause, the compliments of colleagues, the praise of your superiors, the kudos of your mentor.

In summary, then, the six keys to a successful simulation are these:

1. Learn techniques from a successful, highly skilled role model. Find the best example you can to emulate.
2. Memorize the material in exact sequence, or copy a master's performance precisely.
3. Rehearse the performance until it is mastered.
4. Drill in realistic but nonthreatening environments until the successful performance becomes second nature.
5. Ask for, and receive, the constructive criticism from your role model, teacher, coach, or supportive family or friends. Get their feedback and adapt your presentation in ways that may be necessary before you attempt to move into the world-class arena.
6. As you engage in simulation, visualize your successful completion of the activity.

Plan for Rewards

As you make plans for reaching your goals, include plans for a reward once a goal is reached. It may be a dinner out on the town, a trip, or a gift to yourself. Don't expect others to reward you. They may not fully see, or appreciate, the changes or growth you are experiencing. They may not know how to reward you in a way meaningful to you. Don't expect that of them! Reward yourself.

In rewarding yourself, make certain that you avoid the tendency to make the reward something indicative of your old life or the old patterns you are hoping to leave behind. For example, a hot fudge sundae is not a suitable reward for losing ten pounds.

Rewards allow you to celebrate your way to the goal.

Behavioral psychologists use the phrase "reinforced for successive approximations" related to intermediate goal setting. Generally, this technique is used to train animals to perform a certain trick or stunt. Let's anticipate, for a moment, that you want a dog to jump up on a fire truck and pull a chain that sounds the siren. Here's a procedure to reinforce for successive approximations:

1. Reward the dog for going near the truck.
2. As the animal spends more and more time near the truck, reward it only if it climbs onto the truck.
3. Once the dog remains on the truck, reinforce it only if it

places a paw near the chain that—when pulled—will turn
on the siren.

4. Once the dog's paw remains near the chain consistently,
reinforce the behavior only when the dog paws at the chain
and forces it to start the siren.

Granted, we aren't animals to be trained, and yet, to a certain
degree, we can use this same technique in rewarding ourselves
for achieving successively closer approximations of the goal-
oriented behavior we are seeking to adopt.

For example, if your resting pulse rate is presently in the
mideighties, you may aspire to bring it to a more excellent condition of sixty to seventy beats per minute. You know that to bring
your pulse rate down, you'll need to combine aerobic exercise
and a more healthful nutrition program. Set for yourself the intermediate goal of bringing your resting pulse rate under eighty. On
the day that you awaken to find a pulse of seventy-nine, celebrate!
Go to a play or concert. Treat yourself to a new hairdo or a mani-
cure. Rejoice in the achievement of an intermediate goal. And
then set your sights on a resting pulse of seventy-five. In other
words . . . celebrate your way to your goal!

Developing New Goal-Oriented Habits

Much of the activity of our lives is rooted in habit. We do
countless things every day without thinking about them—from
the way we brush our teeth to the way we tie our neckties to the
order in which we put on our socks and shoes.

Planning for success also means planning for new habits and
beginning to establish them in our lives.

Begin each day with this question: What am I going to do today
that will make the best use of my time and energy and thus lead
me a step closer to reaching my goals?

Keep your goals firmly in mind as you plan your day's agenda.
At first, you should question each appointment and stop to think
about each activity that you add to your day's schedule. Over
time, this way of thinking will become a habit. You'll no doubt find
that you'll have

· greater ease in saying no to projects or activities that are a
genuine waste of your time.

- greater ease in shortening the length of appointments or in choosing not to schedule appointments with people that you recognize are inhibitors or discouragers in your quest for greater success.
- shorter time periods scheduled for items that are low in priority in order to allow longer time periods for items that are high in priority.
- less patience with slow-moving agendas or meetings that drag on without reaching consensus. Rather than become frustrated, voice your concern and see what you can do to push the meetings forward toward consensus, decisions, or conclusions.

During the day, each time you are faced with a decision, ask yourself, Does this action substantially help me toward achieving my goals?

You will no doubt be amazed at how many things seem to come against your desire to reach your goals once you have them in place. Those interruptions, those waylaid plans, and those sidetracks were always there before . . . you just weren't aware of them. Now that you are headed for goals, you see them for the slow-down or aversion tactics that they represent.

Before you leave your workplace or before you go to sleep at night, make a list of your most urgent priorities for the following day in order of their importance. I divide my activities into A, B, and C lists.

- A is for *action immediately.*
- B is *before the end of the day.*
- C is *can wait until the next day.*

Become aware of interruptions and distractions that block your success. Constant telephone calls are among the most common. Coworkers who stop by to chat are another. Messy files that slow down your ability to find important items . . . disorganized scheduling (such as keeping two or more appointment books running at the same time) . . . cluttered desks. Take an objective look at your life. And then take action.

You may want to ask your secretary to hold your calls for a period of time so that you can concentrate on creative projects. Then return your calls and make calls in one period, which will tend to give you a break from work that requires intense concentration or creative flow.

You may need to close your door for an hour or two, even though you normally have an open-door policy.

You may need to spend a day or two getting organized, cleaning out your office, or combining all of your appointment books into one master schedule.

Block the Prime Time of Your Life

My friend Bob Smullin, who founded the Day Focus System—which is similar to the Day-Timer System—believes that all time management problems generally are harbingers of a more deeply rooted problem: a lack of clear focus in one's career or personal life. He said he has never met a man or woman with a clear focus who also has a time management problem. On the other hand, he knows scores of individuals who have time management problems because they lack a clear focus.

The study of time, as a decision-making resource, is fascinating. We all take time for granted, living as if we're immortal. Without a good grasp of time and its power, we are likely to lose our focus in time's unrelenting passing.

Time has a dual structure. On the one hand, we live our daily routines meeting present contingencies as they arise. On the other hand, our most ambitious goals and desires need time to be assembled and cemented. A long-term goal connects pieces of time into one block. These blocks can be imagined and projected into the future as we do when we set goals for ourselves. Or these blocks of time can be created in retrospect as we do when we look back at what we have accomplished.

It is not in the image of our big dreams that we run the risk of losing our focus and motivation. It is the drudgery and routine of our daily lives that present the greatest danger to our hopes for achievement.

Good time management means that you maximize the daily return on the energy and mental effort you expend.

I call this LIVING IN PRIME TIME!

On the East Coast, prime-time television is from 8:00 to 11:00 P.M. For the rest of the nation, prime time is from 7:00 to 10:00 P.M. Surveys have shown that the most viewers are available during those hours, and accordingly, commercials are much more expensive during prime-time hours. If a program generates an extremely high Nielsen rating, such as the Super Bowl or "60 Minutes," the cost of commercials might be increased a hundredfold.

Start thinking of your days and weeks in terms of prime-time blocks. When is the very best time of day or night for you? When do you rate yourself as sharpest, most cost-effective, in terms of performance? Are you a morning person or a night person? Your peak hours will vary with your age, physical condition, and biological clock.

One of the most effective time management consultants in the nation, in my opinion, is my colleague Lyle Sussman, professor of management at the University of Louisville. He and I have toured major cities addressing business leaders and employee groups in seminars sponsored by universities. His action steps on how to maximize productivity have helped thousands of executives, myself included. I have improvised a sample check-off list drawn from his outstanding guidebook *Smart Moves,* cowritten by Sam Deep and published by Addison-Wesley.

I call this list . . .

Twenty Ways to Live in Prime Time

1. Commit yourself to yearly goals for personal development and professional accomplishment. Translate yearly goals into quarterly goals and into "to do" lists that are revised weekly and daily.
2. Buy or construct your own comprehensive calendar planning system. Record in this planner all the people and projects you manage, and all pertinent addresses and phone numbers. Write down in the action section every commitment you make *at the time you make it.*
3. Create a time analysis chart of your activities. Break your day into fifteen-minute blocks. Note your chief activity or activities for each block. After logging your activities for a week or so, you'll have a representative sample of how your time is spent. Study the results. Decide what you can do to make better use of your time.
4. Stop wasting the first hour of your workday. Having that first cup of coffee, reading the newspaper, and socializing are the three costliest opening exercises that lower productivity.

5. Get enough rest, nutrients, and exercise. If you don't feel good, you can't do good. Maintain your health, and build your stamina. Treat your body the way you would if it were a space shuttle you were about to be launched in. Treat yourself as if you are worth the effort and expense it takes to nurture yourself!

6. Recognize when your peak energy or prime time occurs during the day. Allocate the most difficult projects to that period. Work on easy projects at low-energy times.

7. When you recognize that your energy level is dropping, take a break. For many people, this occurs around 3:00 or 4:00 P.M. For you, it may be in the early morning or evening or right after lunch.

8. Do one thing, well, at a time. It takes time to start and stop work on each activity. Stay with a task until it is completed.

9. Don't open unimportant mail. At least 25 percent of the mail you receive can be thrown away without taking the time to open it.

10. Handle each piece of paper only once—and never more than twice. Don't set aside anything without taking some action.

11. Carry work, reading material, audiotapes, and your laptop computer (if you have one) with you everywhere you go. Convert downtime into uplink time.

12. Spend twenty minutes at the beginning of each week and ten minutes at the beginning of each day planning your "to do" list. Ask yourself, What will I accomplish this week and this day?

13. Set aside personal relaxation time during the day. Don't work during lunch. It's neither noble nor nutritional to skip important energy-input and stress-relieving times.

14. Periodically, each day, focus on your long-term dreams. You will keep your motivation vivid and strong.

15. Establish time limits for meetings and conversations in advance. Consult your watch when a deadline approaches. End the conversation when it arrives.

16. Write answers in the margins of letters you receive, and mail the original back to the sender.

17. Take vacations and leave your work at home. The harder you work, the more you need to balance your exercise and leisure time.

18. When possible, plan your work so that your tasks end

when your day does. Take work home only as an exception, not the rule. Your professional life needs a whole human being, one with a satisfying personal life.

19. Throughout the day, ask yourself, What's the best use of my time right now? As the day grows short, focus on projects you can least afford to leave undone.

20. End the day by listing all of tomorrow's important tasks. In the morning, incorporate these projects into your daily "to do" list.

Schedule longer, uninterrupted blocks of time for special projects.

Contrary to popular notions, most books, works of art, inventions, and musical compositions are created during uninterrupted time frames—not by adding a few lines, strokes, or notes every so often. Each book or program I have written has been done by working twelve to seventeen hours a day for a specific number of days. True enough, I might have sacrificed a ski trip or a week or two at the beach. But because I focused on prime projects in prime time, the return on invested resources has been richly rewarding.

Plan for interruptions.

Mark out time on your calendar to accommodate them.

Prepare for delays.

Anticipate the delays that may be caused by others in terms of time. Have a Plan B for when your Plan A hits a snag—a traffic delay, a person who shows up late, a waiting room stay that is longer than anticipated, a plane that is late in taking off. Ask, How can I make the most of ten minutes here and five minutes there toward reaching my goals?

Make the most of your "spare moments."

My wife, Susan, carries a small piece of needlework with her at all times. She uses the "spare moments" of her life to make Christmas and birthday gifts. Virtually all of the projects are completed in five-minute spurts of time—a few stitches now, a few stitches later.

Keep a CURRENT calendar of your commitments with you always.

I cannot overestimate the value of keeping a current calendar with you always. I carry a thirty-day calendar with me at all times, and a twelve-month calendar is never more than a briefcase away from my touch. My twelve-month calendar is a set of twelve legal size monthly calendar sheets stapled together. I purchase them at a local stationery store and write on them goals, priorities, appointments, anticipated completion dates for projects, and so forth. Then as one month is ended, I make a photocopy of any sheets that I have corrected, and add a new sheet to the back (so that I always have twelve months).

Balance the Short View and the Long View

Make certain that you have PRIMARY, INTERMEDIATE, and LIFE goals on your plan—that you have accommodated means of achieving them in terms of present-day time.

Planning inevitably involves balancing short-range goals and long-range goals. Recognize at the outset that every goal has a certain length of time for its achievement. (I like to think of that as its unique growing season.)

It's also important to recognize that a long-term growing season is actually made up of many short-term seasons. Take, for example, the oak tree that we used as an analogy at the beginning of this discussion about the winter season. An oak tree produces an increasing number of acorns as it grows to maturity. A fully grown oak tree has already been through numerous seasons of growth.

Consider a grapevine. The vine is planted as a seedling and spends the next seven years in a cycle of dormancy, pruning, growing, and fruit-setting seasons before it reaches full maturity and yields its maximum harvest.

So, too, the long-range goals of your life will no doubt undergo many short-term-goal cycles.

Ask yourself, If I knew I had twenty years left to live, what would I do differently in terms of goal setting and establishing priorities?

Then ask yourself, If I knew I had only one year left to live, what would I do differently in terms of goal setting and establishing priorities?

How can you mesh those two answers into a plan?

In chapter 16 we'll discuss a 90-day cycle of success that includes very specific elements of planning. For the present, I encourage you to ask yourself,

- · What is my most important personal goal this month?
- · What can I do to move myself ever closer to reaching that goal? Where are the activities that will bring me closer to the goal MARKED IN TIME on my calendar?
- · What is my most important professional goal for this month?
- · Have I shared this goal with anyone who can help me reach it? Where ON MY CALENDAR is an appointment with the person who can best help me?
- · What is my foremost goal this month for improving my level of health and physical fitness? Have I blocked out times for regular exercise?
- · What is my goal this month regarding income, savings, and investments? Do I have an appointment with someone who can help me make the most of my assets?

Remember always . . .

**A plan is not truly a plan until ALL of
the subtasks related to your goals
are mapped out in time.**

If you do not have your plan translated into hours, days, and deadlines, there's little likelihood you will enact it. You will spin your wheels in frustration, procrastinate, or hurl headlong into activity without direction. I once overheard a flight instructor say to a cadet, "Where are we at?" The cadet responded, "I'm not sure, but we're making great speed, sir!"

Forward motion without direction leads to failure.

Forward motion WITH direction, and sequenced in time, leads to success.

If Your First Plan Fails . . . Try Again!

Plans are not set in concrete. They are put on paper . . . generally best written with pencils that have erasers. Why? Plans must be flexible. You need to be able to revise them as you encounter the factors that are still unknown to you.

Do you know why the majority of people never achieve their goals? First, they fail to plan. Second, if they fail, they fail to plan *again*.

Don't give up after the first round. Many a war has been won, even if the first battle was lost.

If your first plan flops, pick yourself up, dust yourself off, and start over. Temporary defeat is not permanent failure.

There's not a champion alive who has not experienced temporary defeat. There's not a joyful person on the earth today who has not also experienced deep disappointment and pain. Life has both winning and losing moments. Learn from the losing experiences to enhance your opportunity to have more and better winning experiences!

Expect to learn from your mistakes and any obstacles you encounter and overcome along the way. Each failure should be just one more set of facts taken into consideration as you continually engineer better and better plans.

Have freedom from the urgent, freedom for the important.

Effective time management creates freedom. Freedom provides opportunities to make decisions. We make our decisions, and our decisions, over time, make us.

Freedom from the urgent will allow us to succeed through the seasons and live fulfilling lives.

Most of us have allowed the urgent to crowd out the *important*.

Each day we will continue to encounter deadlines we must meet and fires we must put out that are not necessarily of our own making. Endless urgent details will always beg for our attention. We seldom realize that the truly important things in our lives don't make such demands on us, and therefore, we usually assign them low priority.

Our loved ones understand when we are preoccupied with urgent business, but it's hard for us to understand many years later why they appear preoccupied when we finally have time for them.

All the important arenas of our lives are there awaiting our decisions. But they don't beg us to give them our time. The local university doesn't call us to advance our education and improve our life skills. I've never received a letter from a medical or health facility demanding me to get my annual physical exam and enroll in a fitness program. My bathroom scale has never insisted that I lose thirty pounds. (Although I did buy an electronic talking scale, and when I stepped on it, after my shower, it groaned, "Ugh, will one of you please get off!") I have never been subpoenaed by an ocean, a park, or a church for failing to appear for spiritual enrichment. The easiest thing in the world to do is to neglect the important and give that time to the urgent.

Set your sails for success.

Through the ages, people have frequently been compared to ships. About 95 percent of all people you or I will ever meet can be considered to be ships without rudders. They are subject to every shift of wind. They move through life adrift.

Those 95 percent hope that their individual ships will drift into a rich, successful tropical port. That rarely happens.

The more likely outcome is for the ship to end up on the rocks, run aground, wallow around in the backwash of mediocrity, or become lodged on a sandbar of indifference.

Research has concluded repeatedly that the single common denominator of all top performers is this: a clear written focus and PLAN.

If, in the course of reading this chapter, you have completed a plan based on your goals . . .

Congratulations! You have just joined the fewer than 2 percent of all business and professional people who have a written plan of action for their careers and personal lives!

Final Words as the Winter Season of Your Success Draws to a Close . . .

Dream dynamic dreams.
Let them give rise to great goals.
Forge those goals into realistic
                    workable
                    time-bound
                    plans.

And you are ready for SPRING!

Gearing Up for Spring

🌷 *Have you started to take action toward your goals as prescribed in your plan?*

🌷 *Are you procrastinating in starting a task you want to do?*

🌷 *Do you have a strong, vibrant vision of yourself as the successful farmer of a bumper crop?*

Unless your answer is yes to each of these questions, you need to begin your quest for success in SPRING.

Spring

THE SEASON FORECAST

To the unsuccessful person: Spring is a time for daydreams and renewed but unfocused energy. It's a time for spring-fever rebellion—for desiring to escape reality and romp at play. The ground has come alive, and a desire is born within also to come alive. Yet rarely is that desire rooted deeply. Wildflowers spring up, bloom, and wither in a matter of days.

To the successful person: Spring is the time for definitive action—for saying, "If a harvest is to be, it's up to me!" The winter's plans give impetus to self-reliance, self-motivation, and enthusiastic activity. Spring is the time for gathering the best seeds, preparing the best soil, and planting ideas, energy, and enthusiasm into a new crop of success.

To the successful person,
spring is the second
superb season of success.

8

The Season for Breaking Ground

Spring is where the action is.
Hibernation ends.
Animals stretch and yawn.
Flowers bud.
Leaves appear as if by magic.
The ice melts.
Rivers flow again.
Birds take wing and build nests.
The sun changes direction and intensity.
The soil thaws.
Seeds take root.
Spring is the time for clearing the plot and planting seeds.
Spring is the season for taking action . . . personally.

Self-Reliance

Self-reliance at the beginning of the action season of success is the number one personal quality that can turn a salesclerk into an entrepreneur, a waiter into a restaurateur, an accountant into a financial director, a secretary into a manager, a teller into a banker, and an unrecognized employee into a corporate leader.

Tomorrow's leaders not only have dreams, goals, and plans. They are willing to work hard and to take responsibility for turning their plans into energy, perspiration, and effort. They don't sit back and wait for someone else to turn their plan into action. They take charge of executing their own plan.

In the 1940s, the leading physicists and aeronautical engineers believed that the sound barrier could not be broken and that anyone or anything that attempted to break the barrier would be shattered into countless pieces just before approaching the speed of sound.

Chuck Yeager didn't think there was such a thing as a sound "barrier" . . . so he flew right through it. He didn't just plan to fly faster than the speed of sound. He accelerated his airplane to that point and beyond.

Roger Bannister didn't just dream about running a four-minute mile. He didn't stop with planning for it—conditioning his body into peak performance ability. He pushed his body through the four-minute-mile barrier.

Jackie Robinson didn't just dream of playing in the big leagues. He didn't stop with improving his game skills to the point of excellence, making plans all the while for the day he might don a major league uniform. Jackie Robinson played through the color barrier.

Golda Meir and Indira Gandhi broke through the barrier that said women could not be elected leaders of democratic nations.

The dream of freedom among Eastern Europeans and former Soviets is a harsh, long-fought, emotion-packed reality!

Most human limitations are self-imposed. They arise from lack of two essential human qualities working together: self-esteem and self-reliance.

Some people have good self-esteem. They see themselves as having value, importance, worth. They regard their work as valuable. Still, they don't take the extra step of assuming that the success they achieve in life will be largely through their own efforts. They anticipate recognition from others—which frequently does not come. The truly successful person takes responsibility for his own success.

God has given each of us the equal right to become as successful as we can become. We must, however . . .

Put up the dream—as a banner before our eyes, stated in clear terms and objective goals.

Put in the knowledge—and skills and experience to build up ourselves.

And then . . .

Put out the effort. In other words, *stop stewing and start doing.*

Self-reliance is taking the position: "It's up to me to plant."

Don't expect anyone to do your planting for you.

Some time ago *Time* magazine had a cover story that portrayed America as a land of sore losers, spoiled brats, blame fixers, and crybabies. Those are indicting words compared with what we use to describe the pioneers who founded this nation not that many generations ago.

The common cry we hear today is, "Why me, Lord?" when we should be saying, "Try me, Lord! I can handle anything with Your help!"

The juvenile mind blames others—his parents, his boss, his company, the government, the immigrants, fate, luck, the weather, his horoscope—anything but himself. The mature mind asks, What is there within me that caused this to happen? What did I fail to consider? What can I do next time to succeed?

Instead of working on what is going on inside him, the blame fixer turns his attention to what is going on around him. It's always easier and more convenient to assume the answer or the blame lies elsewhere or with others.

Self-reliance has set me free to be all I can be.

I consider life a do-it-with-God, do-it-for-others, do-it-to-myself program. God allows each of us to lead a good or bad life, depending on how we choose our role models, our thoughts, our actions and responses. It takes just as much effort to lead a bad life as it does to lead a good one.

My grandfather, William Ostrander, owned a bookstore and bindery in San Diego during the 1930s and 1940s, and I used to love to spend Saturdays there sampling and browsing through the shelves of books. It was like a candy store of wisdom to me. He had a poster on the wall that I copied in my notebook because my grandfather said it was an important lesson for me to learn when I was young. My grandpa never put anything off. The poster read,

He was going to be all that he wanted to be—tomorrow;
None would be kinder and braver than he—tomorrow;

A friend who was troubled and weary he knew
Who'd be glad for a lift, and who needed it, too,
On him he would call and see what he could do—tomorrow.
Each morning he stacked up the letters he'd write—tomorrow,
And thought of the clients he'd fill with delight—tomorrow,
But he hadn't a minute to stop on his way,
"More time I will give to others," he'd say—"tomorrow."
The greatest of leaders this man would have been—tomorrow;
The world would have hailed him, had he ever seen—
        tomorrow,
But, in fact, he passed on, and he faded from view
And all that he left here when his life was through
Was a mountain of things he intended to do—TOMORROW.

The point is . . . it's *your* job to start planting *your* field TO-DAY.

The time comes when you must turn motivation into motiv*action*. Nobody else will do it.

Start Planting with a Simulation

When you have decided to make positive changes in your life, have set reachable goals, and have put those goals into the form of a plan, your first step will generally be to implement a simulation of your idea or goal.

Television producers call it a pilot.

Race car drivers call it a time trial.

Actors call it a dress rehearsal.

Scientists call it a field test.

Tennis players call it a warm-up serve.

A simulation is an enactment of your goal in an environment as close to true performance as possible. It is a time for testing your abilities, ideas, and level of skill.

Suppose that you've always wanted to speak in public and you desire to give seminars on the importance of having a positive attitude. You've made the decision to enter this field. You've researched the library for examples of successful individuals who have overcome enormous obstacles to achieve their goals. You've attended lectures and observed both the content and the delivery of excellent speakers with proven track records of success. You've listened to cassettes of speakers whose messages mirror your beliefs. You've formed your ideas about the importance of a positive attitude and how to have one. And finally, you've written a thirty-minute inspirational speech and rehearsed it in the privacy of your bedroom until you have it memorized. The time has come for a simulation—for you to field-test your performance in a realistic but nonthreatening environment.

I shared with you in an earlier chapter how I began my present career of public speaking. There's no substitute for a simulation. With each speech, I polished my delivery and content. I saved the anecdotal humor that regularly received positive response. I quickly discarded the material that evoked no visible positive response or was received with lukewarm nonchalance by an audience.

If you do it right in drill, chances are, you'll do it right in the coliseum.

If you say it right in rehearsal, chances are, you'll say it right on opening night.

If you develop the right instinctual responses during practice workouts, chances are, you'll make the right move during the game.

What I did not tell you is that I conduct a minisimulation before every speaking engagement I have today. I'm still mentally rehearsing before I begin a speech.

Use the Seconds Before Your Performance to Visualize Your Success

Are you up next?

Is it almost your turn?

Are the next lines yours?

Use those few moments to visualize the successful completion of your task.

Have you planned a major dinner party? Sit down in your favorite chair for a few minutes an hour before your guests arrive; close your eyes and visualize yourself going to the door to greet your guests. Visualize the meal being served, the conversation around the table being lively and thought-provoking, the ambience one of generous hospitality, the mood warm. Visualize what you will be doing. Think through the evening all the way through dessert to coffee and conversation in the living room. Bid your guests good night as they leave your home, smiling and feeling as if they have been treated as the most important people in the world.

Are you waiting for a sales appointment—sitting in the lobby outside the door of the person whom you desire to place an order? Use those moments to visualize your meeting. See yourself greeting the person with confidence. Imagine walking into the room, your hand outstretched for a hearty handshake and a genuine smile on your face. Imagine yourself being more concerned about his or her problems, life, and needs than you are about your sale. Imagine expressing yourself fluidly and succinctly. Visualize closing the deal.

Self-Esteem Plus Self-Reliance Equals Motivation

The best and most long-lasting brand of motivation is that labeled positive desire. It grows when you really believe it's possible to change your life for the better—that you are both worthy of that change and capable of achieving it. Motivation is an inner drive that keeps moving you forward despite discouragement, mistakes, and setbacks.

Fear is a powerful negative motivator. Bullies and tyrants can cause us to run fast! Sometimes the bullies and tyrants in our lives are disguised as parents, employers, coaches, world leaders, and even spouses. They "motivate" in the form of threats, power plays, and punishments. I recently saw a sign that read, "Please cut off my legs so that I can run faster." That's the motivation tactic that some people use and some people have come to expect.

When I was a boy, I saw another sign above a farmer's pasture. In the pasture was the biggest, ugliest, meanest-looking bull you'd ever hope to see. The sign was a cryptic lesson in fear motivation for us would-be trespassers. It read, "Don't attempt to cross this field unless you can do it in 9.9 seconds. The bull can do it in 10 flat!"

In reality, fear restricts, inhibits, tightens, panics, and forces. It creates distress, anxiety, and hostility. Although it may cause a person to make temporary changes or to exert temporary effort, it ultimately scuttles plans and defeats goals. The person who is running in fear tires easily and quickly becomes embittered and even enraged.

Positive desire, conversely, is an inner force that propels motivation into positive action. It excites and energizes. It encourages enthusiasm and excellence. Desire is the emotion that builds, plans, attracts, achieves goals, and leads to a happy present and a bright future.

Spring Is the Season for Tapping in to Your Motivation

Motivation that is not tied to a specific goal is scattered by the winds of change or buffeted away the minute problems arise. Motivation without a goal is unfocused, is diffused, and evaporates easily. However, when motivation becomes focused on a well-defined goal and game plan, it becomes a powerful force for success and achievement.

I think of motivation as steam. If released into the open air, it disappears without accomplishing anything. On the other hand, if the steam is harnessed into the catapult engine on an aircraft carrier, it becomes powerful enough to hurtle a sixty-ton steel jet aircraft from a dead stop to 130 mph in five seconds. I know. I left some of my gold fillings aboard a navy carrier when I was a pilot.

When you let your enthusiasm for a dream dissipate rather than trap it with a goal and allow it to energize that goal, you are left feeling unenthusiastic and lethargic about working your plans. A what-will-be-will-be attitude can set in.

It is critical that you channel the motivation you felt for a dream into motivation for reaching a goal and working a plan.

If you don't focus on a plan, you may find your engines revving without achieving forward motion. That can lead to inner agitation and frustration. Motivation properly harnessed to a plan causes you to move forward to accomplish virtually anything you set your thoughts on.

How do you do this?

See yourself enjoying a fresh beginning.

Visualize yourself being enthusiastic as you work toward reaching your goals. Visualize yourself being enthusiastic as you start to work your plan.

Concentrate and focus your enthusiasm on the FIRST STEP you are taking in your plan.

Imagine a mist of steam going through a narrow valve. As the steam is forced into a narrow opening, it builds pressure. That's what happens as you focus your motivation and enthusiasm on a single goal and an immediate step of your plan.

Many of us can generate enthusiasm for living our dream lives. Everything inside us seems to leap in response to the idea of living the way we've always intuitively longed to live—experiencing success in every area of our lives, with all parts of our lives working in harmony.

Generate that same enthusiasm for each subtask of your plan. See your plan as an extension of your goals, and your goals as an extension of your dream; become excited about reaching a new level, accomplishing a short-term step that leads to long-range results. Again, focus on the immediate "next step" in your plan. Narrow down all of your motivation, and aim it toward the next item on your agenda, the next stage of your plan.

For example, do you have a goal of doubling your income through innovation and hard work as you produce a product you know is worthy? Set yourself a short-range goal of increasing your income by 20 percent. Channel your enthusiasm for your long-term goal into reaching that interim step. Don't think about anything else. Focus on the immediate challenge.

A marathoner may dream of winning Olympic gold. Still, three years out of four are not Olympic years. The marathoner will set his sights on Boston, New York, the Pan American Games, and so forth. Each race becomes an important win. Each race becomes an opportunity to beat her best time to date. Each race becomes the event toward which all training is aimed. Each race is its own goal.

Do you have a dream of being thin and fit? Do you awaken every Monday morning with your dream clearly in focus, ready to take on the entire fifteen pounds that you need to lose and to tackle the hundred daily sit-ups that are your eventual goal? If so, the chances are great that you'll be off your diet and too sore to do sit-ups by Tuesday morning. Instead, channel your motivation toward losing three pounds . . . this week! Channel your motivation toward the goal of doing twenty sit-ups every morning, Monday through Friday.

In setting your goals, you established both long-term and

short-term ones. By putting those goals into a plan, you charted out a sequence of steps. You should have a sense of security as you begin the spring season of your success that if you execute your plan, you will arrive at your goal, which represents the implementation of one more facet of your life-dream. In other words, you should be able to see the big picture of your dream—clarified as goals and lockstepped into position as a plan.

The spring season is the time to zero in on one goal at a time and to put all of your energy and motivation behind it.

Consider the farmer who goes out to plant a field. He knows that a successful corn harvest is part of the overall dream for his life. In fact, he may have set a very specific goal of bushels per acre before him. He has a plan for achieving that goal—of planting the best seeds in optimally prepared soil. He has confidence that if he works his plan and achieves his goal, he will implement part of the dream he holds for his life.

Now . . . as the spring season dictates, he faces the challenge of planting. Of beginning. Of putting those first seeds into the ground. He climbs on his tractor, the planter behind him loaded with good seeds, the ground in front of him barren, level, and moistened ready for planting. And he begins to move forward. He does not see the entire field in front of him. On the contrary, he focuses on just one pass of his tractor through the field. He puts all of his energy into pulling one set of straight rows, making sure that the seeds are going into the ground precisely as planned.

Should the farmer take his eyes off the immediate swath of ground in front of him and let his mind wander over the entire field, he'll lose focus. No telling where he'll end up at the other end of the field!

Crooked planting leads to difficult cultivation. Any farmer can tell you that. The same is true for planting your energy into achieving your goals. Stay focused. See only the immediate goal. Don't let your mind wander to next-step goals until after the immediate goal is reached.

Put all of your attention on *today's* agenda—not next month's.

Put all of your energy into *this* workout—not the workout you hope to have six months from now.

Put all of your focus on the *immediate* project before you—without letting your mind wander to the other ten things you have planned to do this year.

Put all of your effort into acing *this* serve and winning *this* point —not on playing the remaining games of the set.

Stay concentrated.

Stay directed.

Stay on track.

Procrastinators: Those Who Never Break Ground

In my studies of human behavior I have come across three basic personality types who are very poor planters indeed. They are three types of procrastinators—people who never seem to switch on the gadget to get started.

Victims are preoccupied with the past and concerned about things they cannot control. Over time, they develop a loser's mind-set and their conversations are peppered with phrases such as "should have," "could have," "might have," and "if only." They suffer from "Ida" disease—"if only I'd a dime," "if only I'd done this," "if only I'd said that."

Victims fix the blame for failure in their lives on others. They see themselves being controlled by external circumstances rather than having control over their destiny.

Victims believe they are always at the wrong place at the wrong time. They trust their horoscopes more than their inner dreams. They are experts in excuses. They love to put the onus on the government, their failed childhoods, the teacher who gave them an *F* (without any regard to whether they earned it), and the police officer who caught them (without any responsibility on their part for doing something for which to get caught!).

Victims believe they will never win a fight against City Hall. They believe they are the bearers of rotten luck. The most optimistic thought they can muster is, *Well, it could have been worse, I suppose.*

Victims don't plant because they don't believe that the seeds they put into the soil have a potential for growth. And if they do grow, they'll be wiped out by weather, pestilence, or infestation. If the seeds should perchance—as a quirk of fate—grow and produce a harvest, Victims are certain that the plants won't yield enough to pay the growing costs. Therefore, they conclude, it's better not to plant. *Nothing risked, nothing lost.*

Alas, for Victims, nothing is usually the only thing gained!

Failure Avoiders rarely seek out a new field to plant. They are happy with the present. They like to keep things going smoothly, just the way they've always been. They are rut walkers. They tend to focus their energy on making sure that things stay safe and predictable. Since seed planting requires a new risk, they avoid the possibility at all costs.

They are happy to make it through the week and frequently post signs where they can remind themselves, "Thank God, it's Friday," or "Only two more days till Friday."

Failure Avoiders have a weekday job so they can make a living, which they intend to enjoy on weekends. Failure Avoiders survive, but they very rarely soar.

Field-of-Dreamers imagine that the field is already planted. They draw great inspiration from the fantasy tale *Field of Dreams*. They figure if they build it, success will come. In their mind's eye, they've planted—when in reality, they haven't. In their mind's eye, crops are growing—when in reality, there are no seeds in the ground. In their mind's eye, they see themselves as successful planters—when in reality, they have yet to get behind a plow.

Field-of-Dreamers may think of a market-shattering concept or an engineering breakthrough in the shower, but somehow they never get out of the shower to do anything about it. Field-of-Dreamers are forever looking for their potential to ride up in a carriage or their success to walk out of the nearby cornfields to play ball on their lot.

Field-of-Dreamers never bother to plant because they don't think they need to, or because they think they already have.

Ask yourself today,

- Who is my scapegoat? Who am I blaming for my lack of success?
- What keeps me from getting started? Why am I procrastinating?
- Am I a Victim?
- Am I a Failure Avoider?
- Am I wandering around in a field of dreams rather than planting in my dream field?
- Am I hoping to hide so that success can't find me?

Are you a procrastinator?

If so, you need to face up to that today, or you will never move from winter to spring in your cycle of seasons toward success.

Face yourself honestly as you answer these specific questions about procrastination behavior:

1. Do I put off the tough jobs or avoid difficult assignments in the hope that things may change and I can get out of responsibility?
2. Do I put off important tasks by stalling with reorganizing my desk, cleaning my files, or sharpening my pencils?
3. Am I afraid of new situations, change, or risk?
4. When I am faced with a difficult or unpleasant situation, do I have a tendency to get sick or even have accidents?
5. Have I ever delayed something or done something so badly that someone else finally had to do it—which is exactly what I had in mind in the first place?
6. Do I avoid confronting others, even though I may have a valid complaint, a just cause, or some information that could really help the other person?
7. Do I tend to blame "them" or "it" for my failures or delay in reaching my goals?
8. Do I resort to criticism or sarcasm to get out of doing something difficult or tedious?
9. Do I put off physicals and dental checkups because I think I'm too busy?
10. Am I working at three-quarters or half speed in my job and using the excuse that it's too boring?
11. Is my planning book full of goals that have not been met?
12. Do my daily to-do lists stay filled with the same things day after day after day?

If the answer to even one question is yes, take action!
Face your fears.

Recognize that planting is risk taking.

To a great extent, planting is a risk. Once a seed is entrusted to the ground, you have no more control over it. It no longer is in hand or visible. It has been turned over to a process of growth over which human beings have little to no influence.

Planting for your own success means taking risks, too. It means being willing to make commitments, even before you are sure of your ability to keep them. (It also means, of course, giving your best effort to fulfilling those commitments and not taking them lightly.)

Planting means telling employers what you are going to offer them in the way of service, even before you ask about the pay scale or benefit package. (It also means researching the products and/or services of the organization in advance of the interview so you can volunteer relevant ideas.)

Planting means giving what you have to others who are in need, even though you may be dipping into your own luxury. (It also means, of course, providing for the basic needs of your family as a first priority.)

Planting means taking that bold step toward progress, even though all the details may not be in place. (It also means, of course, having enough details in place so that you aren't making illogical choices or haphazard guesses.)

Ask yourself, What keeps me from planting?

Because planting in the spring season of success requires risk, few people in our society are inclined to take this step. They dream dreams, set goals, and make plans—and then never follow through.

If that is your case, ask yourself, Why?

Are you like many in our society who have been so dependent on parental support for so long that you've never cut the cord to live on your own?

Have you become so addicted to a standard of living that you are unwilling to take one step back in order to move five steps forward?

Are you comparing yourself to storybook characters—for example, those of prime-time television—who play a great deal and have access to incredible luxuries but never seem to spend an overtime day at work? Are you expecting something for nothing?

Do you feel that all problems should be solvable within the time it takes to watch a prime-time sitcom or murder mystery? Do you expect the products advertised on television to cure your ills within sixty seconds? Are you expecting a fast-food delivery of success into your life?

Have you come to a false-dreamworld conclusion that loving relationships "just happen," as if by magic, and that a good relationship involves no quarreling, no negotiating, and no difficulties? Do you face the fact that a satisfying love-saturated relationship requires a degree of independence and a great deal of self-esteem on the part of both persons involved?

Do you avoid commitments of any kind—moving from one instant-gratification source to another, going with the flow wherever that may lead, even if the result might be pregnancy, venereal disease, drug or alcohol dependency, or shattered loyalty?

After years of study in this area and some painful experiences of my own, I'm thoroughly convinced that people often procrastinate and resist change because they are afraid of the perceived costs of success. The costs are there, to be sure. One must face old habits and seek to change them. One must have courage to distance himself from a peer group that isn't helping him toward greater success. One must take responsibility for leading others—for example, family members or business associates—down an uncharted, unfamiliar path. The successful person also must be a positive example and role model for others.

Very often, change means delaying personal gratification as you push hard to reach goals that will eventually bring great personal fulfillment. Perhaps the toughest challenge of all is facing criticism and jealousy voiced by family, friends, and colleagues. Yes, success has a cost. The fear of paying it keeps many people from pursuing the success that they could enjoy.

Ask yourself today, What is it about greater success that I fear?

Seven Techniques for Overcoming the Tendency to Procrastinate

Many a person lives on Someday Isle. They're convinced that "someday I'll do that" or "someday I'll go there."

The science of physics recognizes two kinds of inertia—both of which can be related to procrastination. The first law states, "Standing objects tend to remain stationary." The second law is the inverse: "Moving objects tend to stay in motion." We experience these laws nearly every time we are passengers in a car. When the car accelerates again after coming to a complete stop at a stop sign, we are in a state of stationary inertia, and unless the driver puts his foot on the gas pedal, we remain stationary. We feel our mass as we are forced back into the seat when the car takes off from the light. A few miles down the highway, however, a light may turn red very suddenly, and the driver slams on the brakes. Our tendency as passengers is to keep right on going, right out of our seats. Only our seat belts prevent us from moving forward. We brace ourselves to stop—putting on our own internal "brakes."

Procrastination is stationary inertia. We aren't moving, and we therefore don't move!

Procrastination overcome, however, moves us into the arena where the law of motion takes over. We frequently find that once we've started a project or process, we stay with it until completion. One of my favorite sayings from my friend Dr. Robert Schuller is posted on my word processor: "BEGINNING IS HALF DONE!" (I've modified it to say, "BEGINNING IS HALF WON.") The first step toward success will be the biggest one that most people take.

How can you overcome the tendency to procrastinate in breaking ground so that you may plant in the spring season of your success? Here are seven techniques I've found very helpful in my life and in the lives of others who have achieved success.

1. Take five minutes to identify what you are putting off.

On a blank sheet of paper, note several important activities that you realize you are delaying or have put on hold.

2. Look at your list of tasks and do one of them right now.

Put the energy you've been directing toward excuses into the activity you've been avoiding. You'll no doubt discover that action eliminates anxiety. Enjoy the satisfaction of a job completed, a chore done, a discussion held, a decision reached, a letter written, a project started.

3. If getting started is the hard part for you, set a designated time slot in the day to work on the task.

For example, you may choose to mark your calendar for Tuesday at noon. Set aside thirty minutes of your lunch hour for work specifically on that one job, project, or personal goal (such as a physical workout) that you've been avoiding or find difficult to start. You'll be surprised at how much you can accomplish in one focused half-hour period each week.

4. Don't worry about perfection.

What counts is quality of effort, not perfect results. Don't let yourself get bogged down with a preoccupation for perfectionism. Recognize that nothing in life is ever going to be perfect and that your concern for perfection may significantly slow you down in reaching goals you have set for yourself. Too many people are waiting for "just the perfect setting," "just the right situation," or "just the right opportunity." That perfect context may never come along!

Virtually any project, job, or situation can be edited in progress. Midcourse corrections are nearly always possible. As a man once said to me, "It's easier to steer a car that's in motion." Get started, and decide to manage changes in direction as the need for them may arise along the way.

5. If what you are putting off involves other people, consult with them.

Your reasons for delaying action may be imaginary. Lack of communication often turns molehills into mountains, making procrastination seem more justified and starting a project more of a chore than it really is.

6. If you fear the consequences associated with the action you've been avoiding, ask yourself, What's the worst thing that could happen if I did this today?

The worst-case scenario most likely would be a minor inconvenience or a temporary setback, not a collapse of an entire relationship, project, or career.

7. Vividly picture how you'll feel once the task is done.

You'll have a sense of relief. Freedom from anxiety. Freedom from nagging pressures. Freedom from self-doubt. Accomplishing put-off tasks usually gives a person a great boost of confidence and energy. Use that energy to pursue yet another chore or decision about which you have been procrastinating!

TNT for
Ground Breaking

Ground breaking requires TNT. It means blasting your way out of failure or apathy. It means blasting a hole in your future. It means overcoming procrastination and breaking the ground necessary for you to move forward to seed planting!

My definition of TNT is this:

Today
Not
Tomorrow

That's constructive TNT. Put some of it to work for you today.

9

The Season for Planting Seeds

Are you aware that most seeds are ideally planted in the spring? Even plants that are planted in autumn—such as bulbs, trees, and large bushes—are usually first grown from seeds or cuttings propagated in the spring season.

Seeds and spring are inextricably linked.

For that reason, we need to turn our attention to a number of factors of success that may be likened to seeds—factors that are critical for success.

Make Certain You Have
Seeds in the Planter

Many people equate motion with progress. That isn't necessarily so. A person can create a great deal of motion by riding a stationary bicycle or walking on a treadmill. Unfortunately, she won't arrive anywhere. She is exerting, not progressing.

Make certain that you have seeds in the planter before you go out to plow your field. Running a tractor at high gear over barren ground won't result in a field unless the seeds are in the planter and are being properly thrust into the soil at the correct depth and distances from one another.

Three principles are at work here. Each is critical to your success during the spring planting season.

First, plant seeds one at a time.

Don't plant all of your seeds in one hole at one time. Any farmer knows this. Digging a giant hole in the center of an acre and planting several bushels of seeds there won't result in a harvest. In fact, it won't result in *anything!*

In terms of your success, you need to make a concerted effort to plant seed after seed after seed.

Day after day after day.

Into the life of person after person after person.

And into project after project after project.

Don't assume that because you write one stirring memo, you will be promoted. String that good memo with a good phone call and a good presentation and a good habit of arriving at work on time and putting in a full day's work to a good idea to a new innovation to a good suggestion . . . to yet another good memo and phone call and presentation and so forth.

One day's successful dieting must be connected to another day's successful dieting to another day's successful dieting . . . and so forth for several weeks or months before your goal is reached.

One compliment or one good deed doesn't make a relationship. Friendships and marriages are built by linking one loving, generous, and kind act to another . . . after another after another after another.

One visit to church a year (or decade) isn't going to build up your faith to withstand life's crises. Feed your spirit week after week after week after week.

Can you imagine feeding a tiny baby just once a day? Hardly. The baby would fail to thrive. Babies require multiple feedings at fairly set intervals.

So do fledgling enterprises.

New careers.

Budding businesses.

Count on investing long hours during the planting season. Count on planting as many seeds as possible. Count on planting one at a time.

Concentration is necessary for seed-after-seed planting.
Do you have well-developed concentration skills? Work to develop them. You'll need them to stay focused for accurate planting.

Perhaps the greatest lesson we can learn about concentrated action is that it actually requires two skills. The first is the ability to focus tightly on the task. The second—and often overlooked—skill is the ability to dismiss the background noise and the potential penalties of failure.

"Just concentrate and you'll sink that free throw." We've all heard or overheard a coach say that. But what if the score is tied, the clock has run out, the crowd is going insane, and you missed your last two free throws? The goal is to concentrate so tightly on the shot that you fail to hear the crowd or see any of the activity around you. It's as if you enter a time warp where only you, the basket, and the ball exist. *That's* concentration!

Suppose your supervisor comes in with a demand, "Type this letter for me and try not to make any mistakes. I need it in five minutes for the board meeting." You face the task of not only typing rapidly and error free but of blocking out all of the sights, sounds, and hustle-and-bustle motion of the office around you. *That's* concentration!

"Your grades are terrible. Blow this final exam and no car for a month!" Can you imagine a parent saying that to a teen? Can you imagine being a teen who hears that from a parent? I can, on both accounts. It takes more than keeping your nose in the book to prepare for the test. It means blocking out all the other noise of the house, all the invitations from friends, all thoughts of things you'd rather be doing. *That's* concentration.

Second, plant carefully and precisely to avoid mistakes.

A farmer checks his planter repeatedly to make certain that it is working properly—that the seeds are going through the machine as they should, entering the ground at the correct depth, being spaced in the row at proper distance. Planting is a precise process.

A farmer doesn't scatter seeds to the wind in willy-nilly fashion. To do so means that crops grow in clusters that are difficult to cultivate and nearly impossible to harvest.

Furthermore, mistakes mean extra work. Planting is a time for all of your energy to count, not for you to spend your time mending mistakes.

Frequently mistakes happen because we fail to take sufficient time for planting. Therefore . . .

Third, plant joyfully, without stress.

Don't force your planting. Don't hurry through it, eager to get to the next phase of your success. Planting takes time. Give it the time it requires.

Planting in a hurry yields only an internal feeling of stress and frequently an outward result that's disastrous.

Pare down your to-do list to focus on planting. Don't try to do anything else during this season.

Plan your time carefully so that you don't become swallowed up by people to see, detoured by extraneous (to your goal) activities, or overwhelmed by a mountain of phone messages to return.

Working hard to solve a problem is not to your credit if you created the problem in the first place.

Hurrying to plant seeds can result in hasty decisions, which can lead to problems, which can lead to devastation, frustration, and pain, which eventually can lead to failure.

When you enter the planting season of your success, do so with calm, focused attention, highly intentional behavior, persistence and endurance, care, and joy.

Plant the Best Seeds Possible

Buzzwords in American industry for the last fifteen years have been *quality* and *quality control*. Ford became famous for its TV commercials trumpeting, "Quality is Job One!" The resulting upward trend in Ford sales in the face of tough competition attests to both the drawing power and the selling power of quality.

Phil Crosby's book, *Quality Is Free: The Art of Making Quality Certain,* helped set the pace for American industry's pursuit of excellence by introducing tools such as the Quality Management Maturity Grid, the zero-defects concept, and the fourteen-step Quality Improvement Program.

Crosby's interest in quality control began when he was a junior technician testing fire control systems for B-47's. After several years of battling mistakes, errors, and apathy, he hit upon the basic principle that has dictated his success—and that of major corporations: "Why spend all this time finding and fixing and fighting when you could prevent the incident in the first place?"

The principle behind quality is actually a very simple one: I do things right the first time.

Quality not only pays off in the business world. It pays off in every area of life. I believe strongly in quality.

Do quality work.

Give quality service.

Purchase quality products and services.

In the spring season of your success, quality is critical. Plant the *best* seeds you have in the *best* soil possible, the *best* you know how.

Quality is like a two-sided gold coin. One side of quality advocates that you do things right and do them right the first time.

The other side of the coin is that quality involves a willingness to invest money in what lasts longer and serves better. The correlation between quality and cost is often very strong.

Of course, not all things with expensive price tags are quality-made items, built to serve well and last long. Many items in our world are priced according to their "style" or their "name," not according to their ability to function long and well. On the other hand, items built to function long and well nearly always take longer to make with more quality controls built into the process; therefore, they are more expensive. Make certain that you are getting your money's worth. At the same time, make certain that you are buying the best quality.

Value transcends price tag.

Buy things according to their worth—not their ability to impress. A tailor-made suit is one example of an item made for quality. It is made for better fit (which results in less wear and tear), is generally made of top-grade materials, and is usually made in classic long-lasting styles. A tailor-made suit may cost more; it usually lasts far longer and provides a great deal more wearer satisfaction.

If you were buying a parachute, where would you shop? At a discount store? At a flea market? I doubt it. My guess would be that you would shop at a store specializing in parachutes—a store willing to guarantee the product you purchase. You'd be highly interested in the failure rate of the chutes manufactured by various firms. You'd want to talk to a salesperson who was an expert.

If you needed a heart operation, where would you go? Why, to the best hospital you know! You'd seek out the most highly respected surgeon in that particular specialty of medicine. And you'd want to know that he had successfully performed hundreds of operations similar to yours.

Dare to seek that level of quality in every area of your life! In every relationship. In every purchase. In every activity. In every conversation.

When you need expert advice on a matter . . . go to an experienced, highly trained person in that particular field. Ask for recommendations from those with whom the expert has consulted.

When you are purchasing equipment for a manufacturing enterprise, purchase the best you can find. Buy the highest-grade components. Seek out the best raw materials.

When you are developing a relationship, invest quality time and creativity in the relationship. Make your time with the person special. Make him or her feel honored by you and honored to be with you.

When you are making choices in your personal life—furniture, appliances, gemstones, you name it—choose the best you can afford. And if you can't afford what you want, save for it. Make quality your goal. Delay a purchase until you can have an item of proven quality.

Don't deal in junk. Deal in quality merchandise.

Don't give half-baked suggestions. Become an expert.

Don't dabble in experiments. Find out what works.

Don't guess. Have a sound basis for what you say, do, and propose.

In the central valley of California, about three hundred miles north of where I live, thousands of acres have been planted with fruit trees and vines—from apples to kiwifruit, exotic pears to oranges. The yield from these trees is measured in three ways: (1) the size of the fruit, (2) the quality of the fruit, and (3) the total tonnage of each grade (size/quality) of fruit in the harvest.

The highest price goes to the fruit of optimal size and highest grade.

Seek the optimal.

The optimal size of fruit isn't always the largest fruit. Oversized fruit can often be misshapen, sunburned, or bruised. Optimal refers to what is perceived as the "ideal size" by the consumer. The grade of the fruit refers to what is ripe, of maximum flavor.

Much goes into developing an orchard or vineyard that produces large quantities of optimally sized fruit with maximum grade, but one prime factor behind highly valued acreage is this: good root stock.

There's no substitute for a good beginning. Good fruit comes from healthy trees well tended. Healthy trees rise from healthy cuttings or healthy seeds.

Again, I encourage you to plant the best seeds you can plant.

Where do good seeds come from?

Why, from the fruit of the previous harvest! If that harvest wasn't one of your own growing, seeds still must come from somebody's harvest. Seeds don't spring forth from air. They come from the fruit produced by someone, somewhere.

Your success will be built from the success of another person or persons. You will base your success on what you have learned from others . . . what you have watched others do . . . what you have learned through emulating . . . what you have read or heard from others.

Your success isn't created in a vacuum. You are getting your seeds from somewhere!

Make sure they are from a person who has lived an optimal life —a life regarded as worthy, valid, solid, important, credible, valuable. Glean seeds from the fruit of that person's life.

Watch what successful people do. Copy them. (You'll copy somebody, whether you intend to or not. You may as well copy the best.)

Listen closely to what they say and how they say it.

Study their lives. To what do they belong? To what do they subscribe? What do they attend? Where have they traveled? How have they acquired their skills and experience?

Observe their habits. Are they ones that lead to health and wholeness—not physical health alone, but total health in personality, spirit, emotions, relationships, finances, community involvement?

The person to emulate is not someone who is larger than life or lives at a scale grander than grand. Such a person may not be well balanced or in a giving, generous relationship with those who are poor or in need. Choose a person who is optimal in his relationship with others and the community as a whole.

Choose also to emulate people who produce fruit rich in flavor. Every person's life has a texture—a certain amount of warmth, verve, joy, enthusiasm, and delight to it. Don't glean from a person with stale ideas, sour opinions, or syrupy-sweet insincere comments. Instead, glean from a person with a fresh perspective, a genuinely distinctive personality, and a pleasing sweetness.

Good fruit is invariably rich in nutrients. Choose the seeds you will plant from those who bear fruit in life that is valuable for growth and balance. Choose to study the ideas of others—whether portrayed in spoken or written words, or through art forms—that are rich in "mental vitamins." Associate yourself with people who cause you to think, to feel, to create, to explore, to ponder, to evaluate life in exciting, original, and beneficial ways.

Yes, good seeds come from optimally sized, high-grade fruit.

Find them.

Invest in them.

And then plant them in your life and the lives of others so they can grow.

Give Your Seeds the Test of Integrity

Seeds are bought and sold on the commodity markets of the world. Good seeds are always those with high rates of germination.

How can you test the seeds that you are gleaning from others? Put them to the Integrity Test. Ask three questions.

First, ask, Is it true?

Is the information you have received accurate? Can you trust the advice you've received because it's rooted in actual experience, not theory? Is the information or advice based on research with high validity?

On what is the information based? Research? Opinion? Historical fact? Projected trends? A good guess? A nice idea? A whim?

Who is the source of the information or advice? Does this source have a good reputation for reliability and truth telling?

Is the arrangement based on mutual commitment and integrity? Can both parties be trusted? Have they proven themselves to be truthful and trustworthy in the past?

Don't plant seeds of doubt, innuendo, or good guessing in your field. Don't spread gossip. Don't base your relationships on "I hope" or "maybe" statements. Don't align yourself with those who have a track record of dishonesty or unfulfilled commitments.

Second, once you have tested the veracity of the situation, project, or person, ask, Is this what I believe I should do?

In other words, ask, Is this right for *me?* You have a natural intuitive sense about what is right or wrong for you. The situation may be a good one. The time may be right. The opportunity may be a good one. You may still feel uneasy about it. You may have qualms about whether you want to spend your time and energy in a particular enterprise. Trust your intuition.

A friend is an excellent swimmer. At the age of ten, she was approached by a coach who had trained several swimmers who went on to compete in the Olympics. She was asked to weigh seriously a decision to pursue a rigorous training program that included a multiyear schedule of swim meets in anticipation of the possibility of being in the Olympic Games someday. She opted not to pursue the opportunity.

I asked her, "Why not? On what did you base your decision?"

She replied, "Swimming wasn't the only thing I wanted to do in my life. To become an Olympic swimmer meant to turn down many other opportunities and activities that were equally important, or more important, to me than swimming. To train as an Olympic athlete literally meant that I would have no time to pursue my music studies. Or my art classes. Or to be active in Camp Fire Girls or to go on youth group retreats with members of my church. My life would have been spent mainly in school and at the pool. My schedule would have revolved around swim meets. Pursuing this goal also meant asking my family members to make a commitment of time and money that would pull them away from some of their goals in life. Being an Olympic athlete is a wonderful achievement. It's a fabulous goal. I'm grateful that I was considered to have 'raw talent.' But . . . the opportunity just wasn't right for me."

Not all of the opportunities you encounter will be worth *your* pursuit. It won't be that they aren't worth pursuing. Just not by you.

You can plant seeds of many types. You can even cultivate and nurture them into a harvest. But not all seeds—or all crops—will bring you joy and a deep sense of fulfillment. You must choose the seeds that are right for your life. Your success is uniquely of your choosing.

Another friend, a writer, was asked nearly two decades ago to help out with the political campaign of a person running for a local office. She accepted the position at 6:00 P.M., but after thinking about it overnight, she phoned the next day at 8:00 A.M. to resign.

I asked her, "What prompted your decision?"

She said, "I thought long and hard about what it would mean to be a political writer—concerned with slogans and speeches and press releases. On the one hand, it was a new challenge. On the other, I couldn't think of anything I'd enjoy writing less."

The candidate won the election in which my friend was asked to help and eventually went on to become the governor of the state in which my friend lives. I pointed out to her one day that she might well have been the press spokesperson for the governor's office had she pursued that initial campaign position. She replied, "Yes, perhaps. I think I could have done the quality of work that would have made me an invaluable asset and someone worth taking into the statehouse for just that type of position. I also think I would have been miserable had I done that. I would have missed numerous other opportunities that have brought me great joy and satisfaction. Accomplishment and success in the eyes of others . . . yes. A feeling of personal success . . . no."

Ultimately, you must decide to pursue what brings *you* the feelings and achievement of the success you want. Don't play to any audience other than the one you see in your mirror. Do what is consistent with your values, your beliefs, your understanding of your personality and what brings you fulfillment.

You can do many things. You can do a number of them well. Choose to pursue only the ones that cause delight and enthusiasm to ignite in your soul.

Third, ask yourself, Is what I say consistent with what I do, or is what I want consistent with what I already like?

In other words, do you enjoy the process of planting certain seeds, or do you just enjoy the idea of their harvest?

I recently met a young man who told me that he was taking premedicine courses in hopes of becoming a doctor one day. I asked him why he had chosen that course of study, and he responded, "I want to help people. I like solving problems—such as diagnosing what is wrong. And I like the life that I see doctors living—their houses, their afternoons on golf courses, their cars."

I asked him, "Have you ever worked at a hospital?"

He answered, "No."

"A clinic?"

"No."

I asked, "Have you talked over your plans with a practicing physician?"

"No."

"In other words," I pressed him, "you don't really know what it's like to work day after day as a physician or surgeon?"

"No, not really. I just think I'd like the profession."

I suggested to this young man that he start talking to doctors, start hanging around hospitals (and getting a part-time job at one, even in a menial area), and start reading medical journals. There are many careers in which a person can help others, solve problems, and make a good living.

As you begin planting seeds in your field, you will sense immediately whether you enjoy the process in which you are involved. If you don't, you may want to consider going back to the planning stage. *Don't* give up your dreams. *Do* realign your goals and plans for reaching them.

The joy of success must be evident along the way—as part of the process of planting and cultivating—not simply lie at the end of the road as the by-product of your success. If you can't experience fulfillment, feel satisfaction, or enjoy a deep sense of purpose and joy as you work, you are probably in the wrong line of work. You're planting the wrong kinds of seeds. You're growing the wrong crop—for *you*.

William Shakespeare interpreted our individual differences and our responsibility for recognizing those differences when, in *Hamlet,* he had Polonius say,

> This above all: to thine own self be true,
> And it must follow, as the night the day,
> Thou canst not then be false to any man.

Shakespeare wasn't saying, "If it feels good to you, do it." He was saying, "You should walk the road for which your feet were created. You don't need to copy others or live up to the expectations of anyone but yourself."

Plant Shade Trees for Others

Even as we become self-reliant and take responsibility for planting the seeds that will grow into the trees of our own success, we face an equal responsibility of planting shade trees for the benefit of others. One of God's great rules for the harvest of success is that the crops we sow and reap must be for the benefit of others, too—not crops grown and reaped at their expense. The harvest of seeds of selfishness always results in personal and group famine, pestilence, and drought.

People who live the seasons of success principle display the quality of earning the love and respect of other people. Success does not mean standing victoriously over a fallen enemy. It is standing side by side with persons you have helped. Success is a matter of raising not only your own water level but the water level of all around you so that all the ships in the harbor can embark on prosperous voyages.

You are truly successful when you can extend a strong hand to someone who is reaching, searching, or just trying to hang on. There is divine purpose in bringing out the best in one another. Selfish people live narrow lives. Real leaders expand their dreams, goals, plans . . . and efforts . . . beyond themselves to say, "I live every moment, enjoying as much as I can, relating as much as I can, doing as much as I can—and giving as much as I can."

As you swing into the action and planting season in your quest for success, consider these words of Albert Einstein:

Strange is our situation here upon Earth. Each of us comes for a short visit, not knowing why—yet, sometimes sensing a divine calling. From the standpoint of daily life, however, there is one thing we do know: that we are here for the sake of other humans—above all, for those upon whose smile and well-being our own happiness depends, and also for the countless, unknown souls with whose fate we are connected by a bond of sympathy. Many times a day I realize how much my own outer and inner life is built upon the labors of my fellow humans, both living and dead—and how earnestly I must exert myself in order to give and return as much as I have received.

I like Einstein's philosophy. There is more to his theory of relativity than math and physics. He was equally concerned about our "relativity" one to another.

We live in a "me" world—facing the challenge of turning a "me" generation into a "we" generation. The elusive preoccupation we have in self-gratification and self-indulgence has too often been defined as personal success. Personal success, in my opinion, is only success if it also results in success for those with whom your life is intertwined.

Narcissism—that "me first" philosophy of life—is manifested in too many gold chains and designer fashions, too many presents around the Christmas tree, and an overt emphasis on youth, physical beauty, sexuality, and things. It results in a preoccupation with things to own, things to adorn, and things to show others—including the slides of places visited. Don't confuse narcissism with success. Narcissism results in a patch of weeds that gives us interesting flowers and foliage for the day, but nothing that produces lasting fruit. Eventually, narcissism creates a cancer in the society as a whole—like thorns infesting a field of good grain. It kills the efforts of others to improve the whole and, within our own souls, wipes out our ability to see beyond ourselves and our gratification.

Why do we stand in awe at the power and immensity of the roaring sea, the vast unknown reaches of outer space, the beauty of an unfolding flower, the splendor of a sunset? In part, it is because these things represent a magnificent creation available for the pleasure of all who will view it. The sun does not blaze its way into the horizon for its own glory. We view the beauty.

So, too, is the visage of the successful life. We truly achieve success only when others can look at us and say, "There is a splendid example of what humanity should be like. There is a person worth emulating. There is someone who is giving without self-preoccupation."

To reach that point, of course, we first must believe that we are called and challenged as human beings to exhibit this kind of success to others. We must see ourselves as "worthy" of success. Feelings of self-acceptance and self-worth—or self-esteem—must go hand in hand with self-reliance.

> **We must believe we are both worthy and capable of**
> **achieving success that will benefit others**
> **as well as ourselves.**

I recently took my wife and our six children on a tour of China. We went during Easter season. I wanted my family to witness the largest congregation of human beings on the earth as they struggled in their rebirth of springtime—a time of great growth and dreams rekindled for their future. We read the Chinese version of one of my favorite New Testament verses posted in Sun Yat-sen High School. The verse is from Galatians 6:7: "Whatsoever a man soweth, that shall he also reap" (KJV). The Chinese version read this way:

> If the past has taught us anything it is that every cause brings its effect, every action has a consequence. We Chinese have a saying, "If a man plants melon seeds, he will reap melons. If he sows the seed from beans, he will reap beans." And this is true of everyone's life—good begets good and evil leads to evil. True enough, the sun shines on the saint and the sinner alike, and too often it seems that the wicked prosper. But we can say with certainty that with the individual as with the nation, the flourishing of the wicked is an illusion. For unceasingly, life keeps books on us all. In the end, we are all the sum total of our actions. Character cannot be counterfeited, nor can it be put on and cast off as if it were a garment to meet the whim of the moment. Like the markings on wood, which are ingrained in the very heart of the tree, character requires time and nurturing for growth and development. Thus also, day by day, we write our own

destiny for, inexorably like the rings on a tree, we become what we do.*

Sow what you intend to reap. That way you will always enjoy a good harvest, regardless of the quantity your field yields.

* William Nichols, *A New Treasury of Words to Live By* (New York: Simon & Schuster, 1947), p. 14.

10

The Season for Taking on the Identity of a Successful Farmer

We all know the exuberance of spring. The exhilaration of feeling alive and getting outdoors after a winter of being cooped up inside.

The world seems to turn lush green before our eyes.

Flowers burst into bloom.

Birds sing.

The very air seems alive again.

It's difficult on a beautiful spring morning to walk without a spring in your step, a smile on your face.

Take that exuberance with you as you plant. Let the feeling of springtime energize you. Make enthusiasm the hallmark emotion of your planting season.

What Is Enthusiasm *Really?*

Enthusiasm may sound like a phony concept to you—too reminiscent of high-school cheerleaders and pep talks at sales meetings. Recognize that, for the most part, we live in cynical times.

Even our top national news media personalities and national role models sometimes seem to believe that it is their solemn duty to focus on the weeds in society while stepping on the flowers. Choose to hear a different drummer.

Don't worry about whether people will call you naive, unsophisticated, out of touch with reality, or a Pollyanna. Being naive can be a good quality if it means that you have never experienced the impact of evil, crime, or the ravages of human-afflicted abuse in your life. Being unsophisticated is a great quality if it means that you are genuine, curious about your world, eager to learn, and unjaded by those who would seek to steal your dreams or rob you of joy. Being out of touch with reality isn't necessarily bad; it depends on what you define as reality. And Pollyanna was a wonderful girl.

Consider the alternatives to genuine enthusiasm for life. Coldness. Hardness. Minds closed to new ideas. Lives that shun new opportunities. Failure to grow. Decay.

The word *enthusiasm* actually has very little to do with an outward display of exuberance or showmanship. It has much to do with an inner fire. The word stems from the Greek word *entheos,* which means "inspired." The word *entheos* is actually derived from two older Greek words: *en* meaning "within," and *theos* meaning "of God." *Entheos* literally means having a God-given spirit inside you—one eager to create and to enter into relationships that bring blessing!

To be enthused means to be infused with life!

Enthusiasm is a choice.

It's a choice easily made when your actions yield results, the sun is shining, and everything seems to be going your way. But what about the days when it's raining on your parade? When life seems to be a boring routine? Where is *entheos* then? It's where it always was—inside you.

Enthusiasm is like the pilot light in a gas turbine that is always burning on low, ready for you to turn the control knob to ignite it into a flame. When it gets cold outside, that's when the knob needs to be turned up to its highest point. The same is true for the times in your life when things seem the bleakest or most miserable. That's the time to be most enthusiastic!

When faced with a routine chore—such as typing a letter, filing papers, filling out forms, prospecting, cleaning up, doing yard work—approach each task as if it was the first time you faced it. Look for the best way to do the job. Be eager to see how quickly you can get the job done with the best long-term results. Each time I speak to an audience, I pretend that it's my first time. I have been speaking five days a week in a different city each day for more than ten years now. Still, I remind myself before each speech that although this may be my two thousandth time behind the podium, it's the first time I've addressed this particular audience with this particular presentation.

We've all watched children—or been children—who visit a place for the first time. The excitement of discovery is contagious. How eager children are to explore everything about a new environment! They go into a new situation generally with the attitude, "What can I see that's new? What will surprise me? What can I explore?" These are good attitudes to take with us as we enter an unfamiliar city, embark on a new job, start a new venture, attend a lesson, listen to a lecture, begin a project, meet a new person.

Go into the field where you will be planting seeds in the spring season of your success with this attitude: What is here for me to learn . . . experience . . . explore . . . discover . . . as if for the first time? Be on the alert. There *is* something new and exciting about each appointment you have, each person you meet, and each piece of information you receive. Dig it out. Find it. Discover it. Unearth it.

It may be the thousandth appointment you've had in your sales career. Approach it as if it's your first. What new thing can you learn in the minutes ahead of you?

It may be the fiftieth hour of lecture you've had in the course. Go into it expecting to hear something you've never heard before and to see the lecturer in a new light.

It may be your five thousandth piano lesson. Expect it to be different from every one that has preceded it.

It may be the forty thousandth time you've kissed your spouse. Imagine that it's the first.

Enthusiasm is not just a nice idea.

Enthusiasm actually pays off in real dividends that can be measured and evaluated.

In his book *Optimism, the Biology of Hope,* Dr. Lionel Tiger makes a strong case for the possibility of a brain function that is responsible for creating good feelings about the present and future. Dr. Tiger suggests that we have developed this capability in our "internal pharmacy" ever since prehistoric times when as hunters we optimistically entertained the idea of a successful hunt and sufficient food to last through cold winter months. He suggests that people who are pessimistic, depressed, or dependent tend to look to external means in an attempt to cure their frustrations—eating megadoses of sweets, consuming too much alcohol, taking too many vacations, smoking marijuana, taking Valium, snorting cocaine, going on shopping sprees, making too many appointments with psychiatrists and interior decorators, or choosing to just party, party, party—rather than rely on their built-in capability to anticipate a bright future.

I tend to agree with Dr. Tiger that optimism is the natural biology of hope. I'm equally excited about the discovery of natural internal opiates that appear to be even stronger than any morphine-based or man-made substances in guarding us against pain. Evidence is increasing that optimistic, self-expectant people enjoy a *natural* high that helps them withstand discomfort, overcome depression, and turn stress into energy and the strength to persist.

Medical researchers have discovered that the body produces natural internal opiates called endorphins. Secreted and used by the brain, endorphins reduce the experience of pain and screen out unpleasant stimuli. In fact, the presence of endorphins actually causes the feeling of well-being. Studies on clinically depressed patients show a severe lack of the natural endorphin chemical. This may be the beginning of a breakthrough in understanding the origins of depression and joy. More important, behavioral scientists are learning that we can actually stimulate the production of endorphins through optimistic thoughts and a positive attitude.

In one related study, actors were wired to electrodes and connected to blood catheters. They were then asked to perform various scenes. When they played roles in which the characters were angry, depressed, or without hope, the endorphin levels in the brain dropped. But when the scene called for emoting confidence, love, optimism, and enthusiasm, the endorphin levels shot up.

Do you sing because you're happy, or are you happy because you sing? The answer is yes to both questions. The action is inseparable from the results. Positive self-expectancy evokes the result of the natural high.

The advice to whistle while you work is more than fairy-tale talk from a Disney character. It's sound psychological counsel.

Therefore, sing while you plant.

Choose to smile more.

Choose to wake up to music instead of the jolt of an alarm that sends you into fire-drill behavior at the start of your day. Try an alarm that plays upbeat inspirational music.

Greet yourself positively in the mirror: *What a day for opportunities! What a great day for planting seeds! What a good day to be in the springtime of my seasons of success!*

Shift to Planter Talk

As you enter the spring season of your success, it's time to engage in positive "planting" talk.

Change your "I will" statements to "I am" statements.

- I am learning a new skill.
- I am losing weight.
- I am adopting a new habit.
- I am working toward a promotion.
- I am starting my own company.

Don't infuse your statements with the word *try* or *maybe* or *hoping*. State the affirmative purely.

Don't say, "I'm hoping to go into business for myself." *Do* say, "I'm self-employed."

Don't say, "I'm on a diet." *Do* say, "I'm reaching my best weight and gaining health."

Don't say, "I'm trying for a different job." *Do* say, "I'm in pursuit of a new and better job."

Help Your Neighbor Plant

Farmers have a long-standing tradition of helping one another in times of planting and harvesting. They know that the optimal time for planting lasts only a few days—perhaps before the next rain or immediately after the last one. The same is true for persons seeking to use the seasons of success to grow their own rich harvest of achievement. The windows of opportunity for planting come frequently, but they rarely stay open for great lengths of time.

There's a time to strike the iron if you want to forge a piece of iron into a horseshoe—or if you want to bring about a forward-moving positive change in your life. That time is when the iron is red-hot and malleable.

Plant when the season is right for planting. Assist others in planting, too.

Be on the Alert for Allies

Many people see a bogeyman in every shadow, a threat in every face, an enemy around every corner. They are on enemy reconnaissance in life.

Instead, choose to be on the alert for allies.

Look for those who can help you. Look for those who offer assistance, positive ideas, or encouragement. Align yourself with people who believe in what you are doing and want to see you succeed.

Goodwill is amazingly contagious. Encourage another person to reach his goals. Cheerlead him forward as he makes his plans and exerts energy toward reaching the goal. Chances are, you'll receive that much encouragement and inspiration back and more.

Help others implement their plans. They'll help you, too.

Give helpful advice when you have advice to give and others are willing to receive it. Others will feel more free to give you advice that can help you toward your goal.

Offer practical assistance. You'll find that you receive more offers of practical assistance.

Look Carefully at the First Signs of Growth

You will experience both mistakes and successes as you begin to plant and to take action during the spring season of your success. How you regard them and handle them will determine to a great extent your long-term achievement. Don't assume that all things green will result in plants that bear good fruit in abundant quantities.

Weeds and wheat come up at the same time.

Look for the first signs of success in your action. Capitalize on them. Expand them. Build on them. Encourage them. Nurture them. Work harder at them. And be encouraged by them.

Rejoice that you seem to be on the right track, and make a renewed effort to set your face toward the completion of the tasks ahead.

Don't be lulled into a false sense of security. The initial response may be a good one; it is rarely the final one. There's much more to be done before success is firmly in hand.

At the same time, watch for weeds. Take careful stock of what isn't working. Be realistic about it. Cut your losses before they multiply. Don't throw good money after bad. Eliminate waste. Streamline the flow of your energy and ideas.

Weeds are much easier to pull out when they are two inches high than when they are two feet high. The same is true for problems that arise at the beginning of a project or new venture.

Have a talk with the troublesome employee or discouraging colleague before the morale of the entire team is infected and affected.

Hold a conference with your salespeople at the first sign of a downturn on the trend chart.

Keep tabs on debits and credits. Don't let a trickle of red ink turn into a deluge.

Be continually on the alert for opportunities.

The road to failure is littered with missed opportunities. In waiting for luck to come in the front door, we often miss opportunity entering through the back window. Look around. Wipe the sleep from your eyes. Pay attention. See details. Listen intently to what you hear.

Opportunity may be knocking. Too many of us are listening for a knock at the door rather than a knock inside our hearts and minds.

Opportunity is waiting to burst out of our lives, not seeking to invade us.

Opportunity is resident within you. It's in the way you face today. It's in the way you think about who you are and what you will do with the next twenty-four hours of your life. It's in the way you perceive the ultimate destiny of your life.

Opportunity isn't something that is advertised through the

want ads, purchased in the form of a lottery ticket, overheard in the passing comments of a stranger on the street, or realized through a change of scenery. Opportunity is a mind-set.

Opportunities are literally everywhere. But you won't see any of them unless you first choose within yourself to see them, embrace them, and pursue them. Once you begin to look for opportunities, you'll see them with increasing frequency. The more you look for them, the more you'll find them all around you.

It's a little like looking at the black-and-white drawing used frequently by psychologists. If you focus on the white image at the center of the drawing, you'll see an urn. If you focus on the black images at either side of the drawing, you'll see the profiles of two people facing each other.

In virtually every situation, you can choose to see an opportunity or a problem. You can choose to envision the field fully planted, sprouting, and growing toward a harvest. Or you can see the barren field before you.

You can choose to see the problem resolved and a stronger you emerging from it, or you can see it capsizing your life.

You can choose to see the need met and you and your family entering a new realm of strength, health, possibilities, wealth, and charitable outreach, or you can choose to see the need remaining unmet and poverty overtaking your spirit, mind, and body as well as those of your family and community.

Pessimists see a problem behind every opportunity.

Optimists see an opportunity behind every problem.

There's a difference, of course, in being optimistic and being opportunistic.

Opportunistic people frequently seek to capitalize on opportunities at the expense of others. A true opportunity benefits everyone associated with it. A true opportunity is a double-win, everybody-comes-out-ahead situation.

You can be alert for opportunities without being opportunistic to the detriment of others. Simply ask yourself, What's the best thing that can happen for everyone involved? Your answer represents an opportunity waiting to be realized!

Each encounter you have every day of your life is an opportunity.

Each person you meet holds an opportunity for you.

Each experience you have is rooted in opportunity.

From each encounter, person, or experience, you have the opportunity to grow, to learn, to change, to add to your level of awareness, to become more than you presently are.

Consider the case of Edwin C. Barnes. Barnes had a burning desire to become a business associate of the great inventor Thomas A. Edison. He didn't want to work *for* Edison; he wanted to work *with* him.

Barnes was presented with an opportunity to become an office worker, earning a minimum salary, in Edison's laboratory in Orange, New Jersey. He didn't dismiss the idea, saying, "This isn't what I want. I'll wait until a partnership comes along." No. He saw it for the opportunity it was to get his foot in the door.

Months passed without any change in Barnes's status or his relationship with Edison. Many in his shoes might have felt as if the job was leading them nowhere. Barnes took a different approach. He saw the position as an ideal opportunity to do three things: (1) to become thoroughly familiar with the office environment, learning what each person did and imagining ways in which to make the workplace more pleasant and efficient, (2) to become acquainted with other people and to learn how they did their jobs and what their jobs entailed—thus building a network of colleagues and a thorough understanding of all the job descriptions in the laboratory, and (3) to be on the lookout daily for an opportunity to reach his ultimate goal. He wisely assumed that he could see that opportunity from *within* the laboratory much more readily than from outside its walls.

The time came when Edison invented a new office device called the Edison Dictating Machine. Edison's sales staff, however, didn't believe that the invention would sell. They couldn't see any potential for it in the workplace. Barnes, however, knew that the difficult-to-sell, awkward-looking, new-to-the-market machine was his opportunity.

He approached Edison, stating that he'd like to sell the dictating device. Since no one else showed any enthusiasm, Edison agreed to give Barnes the chance. And Barnes ran with it. He sold that dictating machine with such success that Edison gave him an exclusive contract to distribute and market the machine throughout the United States. Barnes succeeded in his goal: He was working *with* the great Edison.

Don't Assume the Harvest Is in Hand Just Because the Seeds Are in the Ground

Most people have a tendency to count their chickens before they're hatched. It's a tendency we must work hard to overcome as we move through the seasons of success.

Planting sets us up for success. It isn't, however, the same thing as success.

Neither should we assume that just because we are given a rock-free field with good soil, we will experience a great harvest from it.

Success isn't handed to anyone on a silver platter. No one has a sure lock on happiness, a good job, or lots of money. Inherited fortunes can be lost in a day. The same is true for lottery winnings, health, marriage, or happiness. Success is something at which we must continually work.

Time and talents are given to us. So is energy. So is the ability to imagine and to envision the future. So are dreams and ideas.

Those are the givens of life. Each of us has been given a field in which to plant. Some with better soil. Some with fewer rocks. Some in areas with better climate for growing. But each field has the potential for growing success. Fertilizer may need to be added; rocks may need to be hauled away; plants need to be chosen in harmony with the climate and location. A harvest is possible. The one constant is this: All fields must be tilled.

Do you deserve success? Absolutely! You owe it to yourself to achieve it.

Do other people have the obligation to make you successful? Absolutely not!

Are you looking to someone else today to enable you to live the dream life you want to live? Are you expecting someone else to pave your road to success? Face the facts. Your success is your responsibility, not that of anyone else.

Be cautious if the victory seems too easy. Napoleon once said, "The most dangerous moment comes with easy victory." It isn't that you shouldn't rejoice in your win. It's that success is not a constant. It is always in transition. It is always in an ebb-and-flow pattern.

I have lived most of my life near the Pacific Ocean. I enjoy watching the tides rise and fall. A tide moves in a little higher with each successive series of waves. The tide comes in not with one wave but with hundreds of waves. The overall trend is upward, even though a few waves in each tide-rising cycle may appear to be low tide in nature. In other words, they don't make it as far up the beach as the preceding few waves.

See the overall trend in your life. Don't judge your ultimate success—or failure—by the first wave.

Ultimately, you will never arrive at the absolute of success. Success is a concept akin to growth. You never fully grow up, no matter how old you become in years. There's always more maturity, more growth, more development, more refinement, more achievement possible.

When you reach the point where you say to yourself, "I have it made; I've got all of the success I can possibly have," be wary. You are on the verge of overconfidence. Overconfidence can lead to pride and carelessness. That can lead to a disastrous fall.

> Humpty Dumpty sat on a wall.
> Humpty Dumpty had a great fall.
> *It's not the way the nursery rhyme ends, but the fact*
> *remains—*
> Humpty Dumpty FIRST thought he had it all.

Humpty would never have sat on the wall if he hadn't first thought he was invincible.

When you feel that you have fully arrived, you're in for disappointment.

Irritability erupts when new problems arise.

Anxiety attacks occur when fear of failure rears its ugly head.

Careless and reckless moves are made when new plans aren't.

Success isn't permanent. Don't expect it to be. You'll be planting many times in your life. The seasons roll around. Make the most of each one, and you'll feel constantly renewed and invigorated in life.

Avoid the Temptation to Take a Spring Break

The planting season is not the time to go on vacation. It's the time for effort.

Concentrate your energies and put them to the task.

Avoid the temptation to interrupt your task for group-griping sessions, pity parties, or grudge-collecting activities. When tension or anxiety enters the room you're in, take a deep, slow breath, lower the tone and pitch of your voice, sit back and relax your muscles, and respond calmly to problems with solutions. Above all, return immediately to the task before you as soon as the person has left, you have hung up the phone, or the crisis has passed.

Avoid, too, the temptation to goof off with friends. There are times and places for everything. Keep those times and places from intermingling. Work when it is your planned time for work. Play when it is your planned time for play. Don't allow those who play to tempt you into relaxing from the tasks you have set before yourself.

By choosing to stay focused on your immediate project, endeavor, or task, you will encourage others to stay focused on their work priorities.

Don't Compare Yourself
to Other Farmers

Avoid the tendency to look over the fence into the other person's pasture. During the planting season, it's easy to look over at others who planted a little earlier than you did and to become discouraged because their crops are already up and thriving when your seeds are barely in the ground.

Comparison rarely benefits anyone. You'll always be able to find someone who is smarter . . . younger . . . older . . . wiser . . . richer . . . more clever . . . better looking . . . or working harder and longer and more effectively than you are.

When you make comparisons in which you place yourself on the short end of the stick, you're in for discouragement that will keep you from pursuing your goals.

You can also find others who don't measure up to what you have become, are, or are aspiring to be. Avoid the tendency to compare yourself to them. You'll lower your goals and settle for average when you could have excellent. You may come to think that you deserve more success than others or that success lies ahead for you, no matter what you do. Both are false assumptions.

In truth, success isn't a pie with a limited number of pieces. The success of others has very little bearing on your success. You and everyone you know can become successful without anyone suffering any setbacks, harm, or downturns. Neither is your success measured by what others say or accomplish. Only you can truly define your success, and only you can measure it.

The late Henry Fonda once said that a thoroughbred horse never looks at the other racehorses. It simply concentrates on running the best and fastest race it can run. That's true for us human beings, too. On our track to success, we must resist the tendency to see how others are running or how rapidly they are coming up behind us, passing us, or pulling away from us. The only thing that truly counts is how fast we run our own race—and whether we have the endurance to reach the finish line.

Run to the best of your ability. Encourage others to do the same. You and the others will benefit and succeed.

Nurture Yourself for Strength

Planting takes effort. This is not the time to cut back on good nutrients in your life.

Nutrition involves far more than physical nutrients taken into your physical body for health. It means providing appropriate and helpful nutrients for every aspect of your being.

In the fantasy movie *Short Circuit,* a robot comes to life after being jolted by lightning, and upon being befriended by a human being, he immediately begins to demand "input, input"—just as a baby cries for food and water. Be a person who craves more input into *your* life. Make certain, however, that what you feed yourself is top quality. What goes in becomes what you think, and what you think determines to a great extent who you are and who you will become!

Select television programs and movies for their quality of performance and enriching story value. Ask yourself, What will this add to my life? If the answer is "very little" or "nothing," skip the program or show.

Subscribe to magazines and newspapers that provide information helpful or useful to you.

Read books that trigger new ideas and inspire you to climb higher mountains mentally and spiritually.

Take advantage of your opportunity to hear the best music,

attend the most uplifting concerts and plays, and to hear the best inspirational speakers on the circuit. Check your local community college calendar for seminars, short courses, and guest lecturers.

Feed yourself spiritually, too. Don't neglect to nurture your value system and faith. Attend church regularly, set aside time for prayer and reflection, and, in addition to contributing money to your church's service programs, volunteer time for you and family members to get personally involved with a service project.

Expect to Be a Good Farmer

Have confidence in yourself as you plant that you are going to learn how to be a good tiller of the field you've been given.

In the movie *Jean de Florette,* a French language film that won many European film awards a few years back but is little known in America, the leading character has a dream of turning a family inheritance into a successful farm. No matter what adversity strikes, he keeps believing in the possibility of his success. Despite experiencing extreme drought, having used all of his resources, and facing the possibility of bankruptcy, he envisions the "mathematics" of his success.

My studies of great achievers have shown me that no matter how different their personalities, their work habits, or their occupations, those who have accomplished much in life have expected to succeed at their endeavors. They have had the ability to picture vividly their success and to reassure themselves in the face of long odds and difficult obstacles that they will come through them. It is in part because successful people expect to succeed that they keep their eyes open to new opportunities. Also-rans and other unhappy individuals who don't expect to succeed don't seem to see opportunities or advantages.

The motto of a low achiever is, "If you don't expect too much, you won't be disappointed."

The motto of a high achiever is the opposite: "I expect the best of others and of myself. I've come to understand that I may not always get what I want in life, but in the long run, I'll get what I expect."

Visualize your success.

When a child of ten to twelve months of age first considers the possibility of walking, she sees before her adults and older children who are walking. She begins to picture the possibility of walking as being a profitable, desirable experience. As her parents give her encouragement by holding out their arms or placing something of interest on top of a table just out of reach, the child is reinforced in her desire to walk. By experimenting, the child begins to take unsure, wobbly steps forward.

Invariably, the young child's first attempts at walking result in a substantial number of falls, a bump on the head, a near miss in pulling herself up, a few hard landings on her rear end, and no doubt a couple of frightening close calls (to the parents, at least, if not to the child).

But the child does not have an association between falling and failing. The baby's next thought is always one of "I'll try to get up again." The young child is intent on getting that object on the tabletop, being lifted up into her parent's beckoning arms, or experiencing the new "high" of taking two successive steps without a tumble.

Strive to be like that child.

Don't see a "fall" as a final failure. See it in the total perspective of learning how to walk or, in our terms, of how to succeed in growing through the seasons of success. Regard it as a learning experience, a trial-and-error real-life incident, and get up again.

Falling on a ski slope is inevitable for the beginning skier. However, the response to the fall is important. If you say, "No problem—I'll get up and make it down the hill successfully the next time," you're far more likely to become an accomplished skier. If you shoulder your skis after the first fall, you never will make it past the bunny slope.

Most of our childhood experiences were filled with trial and error. We had numerous experiences in which we needed to get up after a fall, dust ourselves off, and start over.

Remember the first time you rode a bicycle?

Attempted to skate down the driveway or across the pond?

Played football with the neighborhood guys?

Belly flopped into a pool?

Your "success coordination" as an adult must also be developed. You may fall. In fact, you're likely to fall a few times. Furthermore, you're likely to fall the more you try new things.

But you needn't fail as long as you keep getting up and trying again.

You aren't a failure until you quit trying.

Don't lock on to images of failure.

Once the brain is locked in on what you don't want, it's almost impossible to get away from the idea. I once had the opportunity to play in a foursome with Lee Trevino during the Andy Williams San Diego Open, which I originated as a charity benefit for the Salk Institute. Just before our group teed off in the Pro-Am, Lee did a little psych job on us: "Do you fellas breathe in or out during your backswing?"

I tried not to think about it and ended up so successfully thinking about it that I whipped my drive back in front of three thousand Trevino groupies! We never did find my ball.

Even as you acknowledge the *possibility* of setbacks, don't concentrate on them. Don't anticipate them. If you do, you'll be overwhelmed by them. Keep your mind focused on the goal.

Are you aware of how the FBI trains its agents to spot counterfeit bills? The FBI schools agents by training them to see all of the characteristics of bona fide bills—they deal *only* with genuine money. An FBI agent learns to recognize authentic $1, $5, $10, $20, $50, and $100 bills until his or her appraisal of them becomes second nature and virtually instinctual. An agent studies a bill—both sides of it!—until he or she learns every feature that makes it a genuine issue of legal tender.

That way, when FBI agents encounter counterfeit bills, they immediately recognize them as such. Their minds aren't cluttered with what "might be wrong" or "what usually is left off" or "mistakes that are commonly made." They know what they're looking for. They are specialists in the real thing. False bills seem glaringly obvious to them.

If you allow yourself to think about the penalties of failure or all the things that could go wrong, you're far more likely to infuse your performance with those penalties and mistakes!

Continually tell yourself what *to* do. Don't concentrate on what *not* to do.

The mind has a fascinating capability. What you think about most is generally what you do most readily. Program your mind with a negative idea, and when given the opportunity, you'll more than likely act on that idea. Program your mind with a positive image or idea, and when given the opportunity, you'll more than likely choose that image or pursue that idea.

A mistake most people make is to set goals in negative terms. A tennis player may set a goal of not double-faulting a certain number of times during a match. An employee may set a goal of not being late so often. Goals to *lose* weight, *not* talk so loud and fast, and *not* get upset so often are goals phrased in negative terms. We need to stay away from negative goal setting.

Understand this about the mind: A fear is a goal in reverse. The mind can't focus on the reverse of a concept. The word *double fault* reminds the tennis player of the condition he wants to avoid. Being late reminds the employee of the problem, not the solution. When we think we need to lose weight, our minds store the self-image of being overweight. It is extremely difficult, if not impossible, to concentrate on *not* being upset. It's the same thing as saying, "Don't make mistakes." The mind always moves you toward your current dominant thought.

We should say, "First serve in," for the tennis player. "I'm a punctual, on-time person" . . . "I'm reaching my desired weight" . . . "I speak slowly, clearly, and confidently" . . . "I remain calm and relaxed under pressure"—all are positive goal statements that pull us in the direction of the desired behavior rather than away from the undesired habit.

If I say to you, "Don't think about a big dish of ice cream sitting on a table next to you," or "Don't think about Saddam Hussein," what are you most likely to think about? Images of both ice cream and Hussein are likely to pop into your mind, regardless of whether you want them to appear on your mental screen. If I say, "Don't think about getting thirsty for a tall glass of freshly squeezed orange juice," you're likely not to think about anything else!

I told my children one Sunday morning as we were laughing at our imitation of "The Cosby Show," "Don't giggle like this when we get to church." You can guess what happened as the offering was being collected.

Once the brain is locked in on what you don't want—or what you don't want to happen—it's almost impossible to get your mind away from that idea.

Don't anticipate specific setbacks.

Don't anticipate specific problems.

Don't identify specific failures.

Keep your mind firmly fixed on the successful completion of your plan. Go into each stage of your goal with that mind-set.

Play it for the first time, Sam.

In their book *My Voice Will Go with You*, Dr. Sydney Rose and Milton Erikson advise golfers to play every hole as if it were the first hole. In other words, don't remember what went wrong last time. Simply swing again, looking to hit the ball correctly this time. A duffer thinks about the sand trap. He recalls how he hit into it during last Saturday's round. He thinks, *Better play it safe and stay as far away from the sand as possible.* Sure enough, he plops the ball right into the middle of the trap. Or he overcompensates so much that he goes out of bounds on the opposite side of the fairway.

The true pro, on the other hand, keeps his eyes fixed on the flag. He sees only the green and thinks only about where he wants to position the ball on the green—or in the fairway approaching the green. He says to himself, "I can make this." He swings aiming for the hole in one, even on a par five.

Refuse to let negative suggestions or negative images take root in your mind. They're weeds!

Specialize in making positive assumptions.

Assume that you will succeed at accomplishing the task, and that you will be healthy and well from the beginning of the task to its completion. Don't have an "I'll do this even if it kills me" attitude. Such an attitude will actually cause your entire system to clench, adding to the possibility of stress, injury, and frustration.

Speak well of your health. Encourage your family members and those with whom you work to focus on good health and wellness. Too much attention paid to minor health irritations places an undue value on being sick. Like a personal version of workmen's compensation, a negative health focus—if habitual—can lead to a host of allergies, aches, and ailments that frequently become exaggerated. How you think about your health to a great extent influences how much time you devote to thinking of your health, how much you talk about it, and how much you allow it to keep you from executing the plans you have made for your success.

Assume that you are of a strong constitution, not a weak one.

Assume that you have sufficient energy to get the job done, not that you have a limited amount of energy that must be conserved.

Assume that you have the strength to endure until you've finished the task ahead of you, not that you will have to take yet another break to rest.

Keep your mind focused on the goal ahead of you, not on the internal workings of your body.

Of course, you should not ignore your body or bypass warning signs of serious illness. One of your foremost personal goals should be that of achieving and maintaining the best health possible. Have that annual checkup. See the doctor when something goes awry. Don't exert yourself to the point of physical injury. Avail yourself of the opportunity for positive recreation and education about your body and fitness. At the same time, take the attitude that you will do everything you can to achieve the best possible health, and then give your concern for your health a rest. Move on. Concentrate on other things.

Recognize that Farming Is a Way of Life —Not Just a Way to Make a Living

One of the toughest challenges in growing success is delaying the gratification of harvest while at the same time anticipating the joy of it.

We sometimes try to force the growing process in our keen desire to partake of fruit that isn't yet ripe or to reap a harvest from plants that are only in the germination stage.

The successful businessperson generally plows most of the first profits back into the business.

The successful entrepreneur delays personal investments until the business is solidly established.

The person who seeks political office is usually someone who has been successful in community affairs for a number of years— helping other candidates; building a network of supporters, colleagues, and sound advisers; and giving of himself at every turn possible.

The person who is successful in reaching personal goals frequently avoids purchasing items until she can pay cash for them, builds a retirement fund even though it means stalling on luxury purchases, or waits to purchase "rewards" until goals are reached.

The Proof Is in the Starting . . .
and the *Finishing*

A decision is only a promise. Proof comes at two points: the starting and the finishing of the race. What a wisher lacks and a doer has is motivation in ACTION. None of your dreams will be actualized . . . none of your goals will be reached . . . none of your plans will be implemented . . . unless you put hand to plow and move forward.

A failure to start is the number one reason that the majority of people who set goals never reach them.

The number two reason is close behind. Many people who make plans and start them fail to finish the race.

Be aware at the outset of any project, plan, or process that you will encounter setbacks and unexpected experiences that have the potential for thwarting you or stopping your forward momentum. Don't concentrate on them. Don't allow the unforeseen circumstances to worry you or cause you to become so discouraged that you never take a first step. Rather, see them as challenges that you will face, and make a decision at the outset of your effort that you will overcome them, whenever and wherever they arise.

Too many people expect life to be a rose garden without thorns. They want the glory without paying a price for it. They want the fame without the work. They want the gain without the pain. They want the wealth without the risk. They want the beauty without the possibility of blemish. Life isn't like that. You're living in a false dreamworld if you think it is. A true dreamworld says, "Life may have unforeseen thorns, but I'm going to pursue my dream of growing roses nonetheless. Life may have pain, but I'm going to work through the pain. Life may pose problems, but I'm going to walk through them and face them until I solve them."

True success in the planting season comes only to the farmer who stays with the project until the entire field is planted.

It doesn't matter if he hits a sharp-edged rock and blows a tire. He changes the tire and moves forward.

It doesn't matter if he runs out of seeds. He knows in advance that he will, and he simply stops to reload the planter.

It doesn't matter if he hits a spot in the field that is too moist or too dry. He may leave that swath and come back the next day.

It doesn't matter if he finishes the entire acreage in one planting session. He picks up the next day where he left off.

Planting is a process.

What if you see revisions that you need to make in your plan?

Make them! Don't scrap your plan at the first hint that one part of it may be awry. Instead, revise it.

Many people give up after failing in the first round of their plan. They don't have the ability to revise their game plan and keep going. Make a midcourse correction. Use the information you've acquired to reset your sights, refocus your energies, redirect your efforts.

What should you do if you realize that your plan needs a *major* overhaul?

Back up and redo your plan. Don't give up on your goal. Simply backtrack and replan.

The key is to keep replanting.

Many a farmer has had seeds washed out of his field by torrential rains. Many a farmer has lost an entire crop in the first few weeks after planting.

The farmer aimed at a successful harvest doesn't waste time bemoaning the loss. He puts all of his energy into replanting and doing so as quickly as possible!

Men and women of true accomplishment will tell you that they usually had to come up with several plans and give each one their best effort until they hit upon the one that finally worked for them. Few people score a major victory their first time out. Few batters hit a grand-slam their first time at bat in the majors. Few runners win their first marathon. Few writers score their biggest hit on the first short story out of the typewriter. Few businesspeople turn their first idea into the enterprise for which they are most famous by the time they retire.

Are you aware that Margaret Mitchell, who wrote *Gone with the Wind,* submitted her manuscript to eighty publishers and was rejected by all eighty . . . before the eighty-first publisher accepted it and published it?

Did you know that Tennessee Williams's first play was booed so loudly that the producers came forward and apologized to the audience?

The great baseball professional Ted Williams grew up very near my old house in San Diego, California. My dad and I kept a diary on his batting average as we listened to radio broadcasts of the games he played for the Boston Red Sox. Dad would always remind me not to worry about Ted's striking out. In his finest year as the greatest hitter the game has ever known, Ted Williams came away from home plate nearly 60 percent of the time having failed to get as far as first base.

I have never forgotten that as I have stepped up to take my swings and compile my own batting average of life.

The trouble with most people is that they stop trying in troubling times. The person who does never makes it to the wonderful season of . . .

SUMMER!

Final Words as the Spring Season of Your Success Draws to a Close . . .

Face the inertia of your own spring-fever laziness.

Motivate yourself to action.

Break ground.

Plant good seeds in good soil.

And get ready . . .

SUMMER is coming!

Anticipating Summer

☼ *Are you putting out maximum effort as you work your plan, moving ever closer to your goal?*

☼ *Are you continually monitoring your progress, making adjustments in your goals and adapting your efforts to continue your cultivation of success?*

☼ *Are you establishing relationships that will enable you to reach your goals quickly and with maximum results?*

☼ *Have you set your face to overcome obstacles, persevere through trials, and endure to the end?*

☼ *Is your optimism high for the harvest?*

Unless your answer is yes to each of these questions, you need to begin your quest for success in SUMMER.

Summer

THE SEASON FORECAST

 To the unsuccessful person: Summer is marked by long, hot, tedious days. One endures but without joy. The unsuccessful person marks time, walking through one long day to the next, seeking relief, respite, and relaxing vacations as momentary salves for the season's anxiety and tension.

 To the successful person: Summer is the time for continual, regular cultivation, watering, and fertilization. It is the time of great growth. Summer is the season for feedback, progress reports, and midcourse corrections. It is the time for renewal of commitment, perseverance, and cultivation of new skills and knowledge that appear needed through the actual doing. It is the time for negotiating and forging strong alliances with others. Summer is the season for intense, concentrated, focused effort.

To the successful person,
summer is the third
purposeful season of success.

11

The Season for Effort

Summer is the season of growth.
Sunshine and exciting activity.
Vacations and times of reflection.
Breaks between work cycles.
In the rhythmic cycle of success, summer is the most intense
season. It is your time for

- receiving progress reports and analyzing feedback.
- making midcourse corrections.
- cultivating additional knowledge and skills that become necessary.
- continuing to till your field with vigor and regular applica-
  tions of positive energy.

Summer is the time for persevering, maintaining habits
through self-discipline, negotiating, cooperating, and "watering"
the plants that have sprung from your seed planting with positive
self-talk.
For many people, the summer of their careers is one long, hot,
stifling, irritating period. They can hardly wait to retire from it all.
In many ways, summer is the flip side of the cold, bleak despair

and lack of dreams they experienced in the winter season. Since they did not set dreams, identify goals, or make plans for reaching their goals, they are left with little but drudgery—walking through the days with nothing but tension-relieving activities to break the monotony of work, work, and more work.

For others, summer is the season when they give up. They no longer care about their jobs, careers, businesses, or family relationships. Although they may not bail out of the job, they have shelved it mentally. They show up for work but without enthusiasm. They dread the clang of their alarms on Monday morning. They are already looking forward to Friday afternoon by noon on Monday, and they are the first out the door when the whistle blows Monday afternoon.

Summer doesn't bear these characteristics for the person who has made good use of the winter and spring seasons in the success cycle. After you have converted your dreams into goals and your goals into plans, and your plans are starting to be implemented, summer becomes a time marked by momentum. Everything that you have begun intensifies, enlarges, progresses, develops and, in the process, becomes more of a reality in your life.

By now . . .

· New routines of the spring should be habits.
· New projects started in the spring should be taking direction.
· New relationships should have moved to a point of decision making, commitment, and comfort.
· Short-term goals should be within reach.
· Skills you began acquiring should be developing to maturity.
· Your enthusiasm for the future harvest should be growing, even as you see real evidence before your eyes of success in the making.

Summer Is for WORK

Summer is the season for the toughest work.
It is the time to . . .

· make more calls.
· travel more miles.
· exert more energy.
· generate more ideas.

· establish more contacts.
· get up earlier.

Summer is the time always to be on the lookout for a better way, an improved method, or a higher quality product or service.

Summer is the season for increase . . . growth . . . development . . . forward motion . . . and upward trends.

Work has no substitute. It is a prime ingredient for success, and nothing else can replace it.

Do you expect to be luckier or to work harder?

One of the greatest myths for years in American schools was that Oriental children are naturally more intelligent than American children. Studies have revealed, however, that they're not smarter . . . they just work harder.

Researchers at the University of Michigan tested one thousand randomly selected children for the study from each of these three cities: Taipei, Taiwan; Sendai, Japan; Minneapolis, Minnesota. They found that Chinese and Japanese children in kindergarten and first and fifth grades did, indeed, score higher on standard math tests than the American children. However, in tests of general cognitive ability, children in the three locations showed no differences in their perceptual, verbal, or general abilities.

What made the difference in the math scores? The researchers discovered that the Chinese children spent forty hours a week in school working at academic tasks—compared to twenty hours for the American children. The Japanese children spent about thirty-three hours in school.

Oriental teachers spent more time giving information to their students: Chinese teachers gave twenty-six hours a week, Japanese teachers twelve hours, and American teachers six hours.

The Chinese and Japanese children attended school 240 days a year, American children only 178 days.

(Originally, American children were given two and a half months away from school so they could help their parents harvest crops. One can only guess what crops they are helping to harvest today!)

A second major area of difference in these studies related to values. While fifth graders in Minneapolis spend about 46 minutes a day doing homework, Chinese children spend about 114 minutes—more than twice as long! They don't call the exercises homework. They call them home education. Oriental children enjoy doing homework and aren't ashamed to admit it. Most American children don't like it and seem proud to say so.

American mothers and fathers tended to believe that their children succeeded in school according to their ability. Japanese and Chinese parents were more likely to say that their children succeeded according to their effort.

Ask yourself,

· How much time am I willing to put into my success?
· Do I believe it will come because of my innate ability and glowing natural personality . . . or because of the concentrated effort I apply to my goals?
· Am I willing to do what it takes to become a success?

Go full speed ahead with 100 percent effort.

I once read an article about Tom Cruise in the *Washington Post*. What got Tom Cruise where he is today? Hard work. Don Simpson, producer of *Top Gun,* learned about Cruise's dedication to work at a school for race car driving. "We were supposed to study a racing manual," recalled Simpson for the reporter. "But I preferred watching TV. Tom Cruise would come in the room and say, 'Hey, turn that thing off, we've gotta study.' Then he'd make me quiz him until midnight."

Simpson said to Cruise, "You go 100 percent at everything, don't you?"

Tom replied, "That's the only way I know how to do it. Full speed ahead at 100 percent!"

Summer Is the Season for Making the Most of Long Days

Summer is marked by work. The days are long. The weather is usually conducive to working. Summer is for perspiring and for exerting maximum effort.

Are you aware that you can program your mind to make the most of time?

One of the most fascinating features of the mind is that you can set it to alert you to important moments. When you really want to —or need to—awaken in the morning by a certain hour, you can set the alarm in your mind, and usually, you will awaken within ten minutes of the appointed time you designate. Most people have an intuitive sense of what time of day it is, even if they work indoors and don't have access to a clock. Many people have conditioned themselves over the months and years to do certain things at certain times—such as take pills, check on small children, and so forth.

You can also program yourself to become aware of your optimum time of day for maximum output. Listen to your body. Discover within yourself what works best for you. For many people, the early morning hours are times for maximum productivity. If that is the case for you, set aside that time of day for doing your most creative, mind-taxing work. Don't clutter those hours with meetings, routine activity, or phone calls (unless, of course, those phone calls involve creative, thought-involving work).

For other people, the afternoon hours are a time when they really begin to come alive mentally. They drag through the morning hours, and finally, a burst of energy seems to kick them into high gear. If that is the case for you, choose those hours as being exclusive for you to engage in your most important tasks.

This same ability of the mind to deal with time enables a person to filter out distractions. You can learn to set your mind to filter out noise and to ignore incidents that would otherwise interrupt you.

To get the most out of life, you need to learn how to put the most into your hours.

Monitor your use of time to turn long hours into smart hours.

The average American adult spends nearly thirty hours per week in a semistupor, attempting to escape from the priorities and goals he or she never sets. Children spend even more time this way. Where can you find them? Plunked down in front of a television set, the primary purpose of which is to sell them products that they don't even know they need!

According to the President's Council on Physical Fitness, youngsters in America are in much worse shape physically than they were only ten years ago. More and more people claim spectator sports as their favorite athletic activities! If the trend continues, most of us will rust out rather than wear out.

When you kill time, you kill your opportunities for success. Imagine what you could really do in thirty hours a week!

- How many books, magazines, or journals could you read?
- How many miles could you walk or jog, and how much of God's creation could you enjoy while doing so?
- How many people could you converse with at length—letting your minds wander together to explore new ideas?
- How much handwork or housework or yard work or carpentry work could you get accomplished?
- How might you improve your relationship with your spouse or your children by spending that time together?

Thirty hours. Every week. Think about it.

That's nearly sixteen hundred hours a year.

How do you invest that time?

What do *you* get out of those hours—or put into them—while most Americans are watching television programs that portray lives and life-styles they really wouldn't want to lead for very long if given the opportunity? (How many of us really want lives in which we encounter murders, violence, infidelity, and family difficulties at every turn?)

At least one-twelfth of that time—well over a hundred hours—is devoted to exposing you to products. Again and again and again. How many times *have* you seen the commercial that keeps playing over and over in your head? Do you really need the product being promoted? Would your life be any worse off if you had never heard about that particular product or brand name?

Does *your* activity during those sixteen hundred hours a year bring you closer to the success you dream about or keep you from pursuing your goals?

Time is the most precious element of human existence. It's worth far more than money. I know many multimillionaires who would gladly give $1 million just to live another year or two.

The successful person knows how to put energy into time and draw success from time.

Shining sun is for making hay.

Farmers have a saying: "Make hay while the sun shines." The analogy is true for all walks of life. Summer is the time for working, not watching. It's the time for doing, not dozing. It's the time for making the most of your health, resources, and energy, not the time for kicking back or taking a break.

Here are some tips for making the most of your time:

1. Seize the moment. Learn what to do in life's "spare minutes." Ask, What can I do in just a five- or ten-minute waiting time?

· Work on a piece of handwork.
· Bring your calendar up to date.
· Write a note to a friend.
· File your nails.
· Make a list.
· Outline a presentation or upcoming project.
· Review your goal cards.
· Call a colleague.
· Read a brochure or magazine article.
· Memorize a memorable quote, verse of Scripture, or short poem.

Dozens more ideas are not only possible but plausible for things that can be started and completed in a ten-minute time span. Furthermore, life is filled with numerous ten-minute waiting periods. You probably encounter several during a day: waiting for planes (either to arrive or to take off) . . . waiting for an appointment (one you initiated, or one someone requested of you) . . . waiting for your family (to get ready) . . . waiting for the server to bring the food you ordered . . . waiting for an open barber chair . . .

In addition, you have the normal coffee breaks within your work environment.

Use these times—scheduled and unscheduled—for accomplishing something other than drinking coffee. Run up and down a couple of flights of stairs. Order flowers for your spouse. Write a greeting card to a homebound person who is a part of your church or synagogue.

Time wasted is time lost. Time lost means opportunities and growth lost. Opportunities lost mean less success down the road.

2. Turn off the tube. Listen to audiotape classes instead. Or take a walk with your child. Or help with household chores so both you and your spouse can relax together.

There's more benefit from turning off television than refusing to fill your mind with mental junk food. When you turn off television, you must create something else to do. Overcoming boredom is one of the greatest impetuses you can ever experience for your creativity. Your mind engages once again in the world around you. You become a participant, not a spectator. Try it tonight! After momentary pangs of withdrawal, you'll probably like the feeling you have after spending an evening doing something other than sitting passively in front of a big box with moving colors and disruptive sound effects.

3. Get up an hour earlier in the morning. You may need to inch up on that hour, getting up ten minutes earlier each week for six weeks. That extra hour, however, may well become your most productive or personally rewarding hour of the day. If you have small children, that hour can be your "alone time"—time to read, think, catch up on the news, have a good breakfast. Use that hour to prepare yourself for the day—checking your lists and agendas. Energize yourself spiritually with a few moments of meditation, prayer, or inspirational material.

4. Enjoy the process, not just the result. Finally . . .
Don't fight the passing of time. Don't fear it, chase after it, squander it, or try to hide from it under a superficial cosmetic veil of fads and indulgences. Life and time go together. *Do* enjoy each phase of life.

Don't frantically run through your life as if it is a race to see who comes in first. *Do* learn to savor each period of life and to get the most out of each rich encounter.

Don't think of old age as a frightful plight. *Do* see it as something of a postseason garden you will be able to plant and from which you will be able to reap.

Do make the most of each day, and draw maximum joy from each moment.

Summertime Requires Consistency of a Quality Application

Many people today are concerned with "quality" time—time generally defined in part as that spent with children, spouses, and friends. While I certainly believe that "quality" time is important, I believe two other aspects of time are equally important, especially during the summer season of success.

First, one must spend "quantity" time. Are you aware that the average father spends less than one minute a day in direct one-on-one communication with each of his children? How can we possibly expect good family relationships with so little communication?

Second, one must spend "regular" time. Many supervisors and company presidents go for weeks, even months, without seeing many of their employees. There's no substitute for regular meetings and open-air forums in which supervisors and workers can share ideas.

Both of my parents worked. They had their share of personal and financial problems, not the least of which was supporting their three children. Somehow, though, they always found time to spend with each one of us before we went to bed at night. That was quality time, to be sure! It was also, however, quantity time. Day after day, month after month, the hours spent together added up to a significant quantity of time. Equally important to me as a child, those bedtime chats were times that I knew I could count on. No matter what the problem I was facing or the questions I was pondering or the big idea I was weighing, I knew a time would come within the day when I could ask my questions or discuss my problems with Mom or Dad.

Quality is the nature of the task performed.

Quality refers more to the nature of the task performed than to the time allotted for doing it. For example, you can spend time with your child in play, but unless you devote all of your quality effort to throwing that football around or give your undivided attention to the game your child wants to play, the play itself is *not* quality play.

Quality has no substitute for the work you do in the summer season of your success. The manufacturing of a quality product or the rendering of a quality service should be one of your foremost concerns.

Adopt Japan's *kaizen* philosophy.

The term *kaizen* (kȳ'-zĕn) is the key to Japan's competitive success. *Kaizen* means continuing improvement in personal life, home life, social life, and work life. In Japan, the saying goes, "If it isn't broken, it's obsolete." Quality must be sought every day. It is never static.

In the United States, on the other hand, the old saying goes, "If it isn't broken, don't fool with it." If things are going along successfully, leave them alone.

The belief that there should be unending improvement is deeply ingrained in the Japanese culture.

Back in the 1950s, Toshiro Yamada, now professor emeritus of the faculty of engineering at Kyoto University, was a member of a Japanese study team visiting American companies to learn about the secret of American industrial productivity.

At a recent banquet, Professor Yamada said he had been back to the United States not too long ago on a "sentimental journey" to one of the plants he had visited in the 1950s. Shaking his head in disbelief, he said, "You know, the plant was exactly the same as it had been nearly forty years ago."

Another popular Japanese saying is, "If a man has not been seen for three days, his friends should take a good look at him to see what changes have befallen him." The idea is that he must have changed in three days—that change is ever ongoing.

Kaizen means never-ending efforts for improvement in quality. Unless each of us embraces this philosophy, our standard of living will never improve again.

Summer Is a Time to Become Efficient

Practice and more practice.

Work and more work.

The result should be greater efficiency.

Have you ever watched a runner run? I'm not talking about a beginning jogger. I'm talking about someone who has been running for years. A true runner displays such efficiency of motion it hardly looks as if the person is working.

Even though success takes time, effort, and a concern for quality, above all it takes a meshing of the three together so that you . . .

**Strive to produce a maximally quality
product without wasted effort and
with a minimum of time invested.**

Another way to state that is this: Work smarter!

ADIA Personnel Services conducted a survey of executives about what it takes for a person to become a top-notch manager. Of the 1,102 executives polled, 58 percent said that good management skills were crucial to getting ahead. Being results oriented came in a close second (54 percent), as did being ambitious (47 percent)—in other words, those who set a goal and are eagerly pursuing it are already well on their way! The ability to seize opportunity was considered an important trait by 24 percent of those polled. Only 9 percent of the executives felt that taking on extra work was a significant ingredient.

The point is not to put in *more* time but

- to give all of your attention to any given task at any given time.
- to work with time rather than against it—giving your best efforts to prime-time opportunities, focusing your energy on tasks during the hours of a day in which you are biologically "up," and making the most of each hour.
- to eliminate time-wasting activities from your schedule.

Is it real work or fake work?

Some time-wasting activities disguise themselves as work. A survey conducted by Robert Half International concluded that top executives spend 22 percent of their time—as much as eleven work weeks a year!—writing or reading memos. The one hundred executives polled also said that 39 percent of those memos are a waste of time. If they are correct, many executives are spending one month a year writing memos that don't need to be written!

Ask yourself about any task, and especially about any memo,

- What happens if I don't do this? Will anything be different for better or worse? What will be the consequences if I don't put this into writing?
- What will be the likely outcome of this memo? Will it change behavior? Will it establish a new policy? Will it shed light?
- Will a two-minute conversation be just as effective?

Consider the fact that a single memo may take up several man-hours. It requires time from you in dictating, writing, editing, re-typing, sending; your secretary if you have one; the delivery persons who carry your memo from one place to the next; and possibly a mail room person or two en route. And that doesn't include the time of the recipient of your memo and perhaps even a secretary, much less the perceived need on the part of many to respond to every memo received.

In addition to memos, question the use of reports. Are you getting the information you need and only the information you need? Can your reporting mechanism be streamlined? What information do you rarely consult? Do the reports you receive affect the way you make decisions? If so, what part of the reports holds most sway?

Being busy isn't the same as being productive.

I'm continually amazed at the number of people who fill their weekly and monthly calendars with activities—scheduling all of their time to go places and do things—and they call this activity goal setting. They seem to think that by being busy, they're achieving a goal. As far as I can tell, the only goal they are reaching is one of being overly tired, overly extended, or overly obligated.

Don't fall into the trap of thinking that the more you schedule, the more you succeed. You can go to a group meeting or seminar every night for the next year and arrive nowhere close to your goals. In fact, you probably won't even get out of the starting blocks on the race toward the goals you want to reach.

Make certain that you choose truly helpful activities. Activity just for the sake of activity is wheel spinning. It's revving the engine without ever engaging the clutch.

A part of every living process—including the dynamic growth of your successful life—is rest. The heart rests after every beat. Sleep at night follows activity at day. Creative pauses punctuate projects completed.

The farmer doesn't water his crop every day. Plants must have time to absorb and use the moisture given them. In fact, too much water can drown the plants or cause them to continue to put out foliage without putting on fruit!

Neither does the farmer cultivate his field every day or apply fertilizer every week. He cultivates his field as weeds arise. He applies fertilizer as signs of nutrient depletion are manifest.

Give yourself what you need to stay fueled.

Be attuned to what you need to achieve success and how periodic your need for that element arises. One thing you will need personally—I guarantee it—is a continual renewal of your confidence and your physical body.

Goals, to be genuine and worthy goals, must be demanding. They require something of us—more brain power, real effort, quality performance. They take something out of us. They tax our talents, skills, and abilities.

By midsummer, we often feel exhausted and ready to give up. Many a garden has been abandoned and the seedlings left to die because the gardener no longer felt like gardening.

Take time during the summer months of your season of success to replenish yourself.

Revisit the dreams and goals of your winter season. Take time to reflect on them and to reassert to yourself that your dreams are valid, your goals are worthy to be reached. Renew your vision for your life. The Old Testament wisdom still holds true: "Where there is no vision, the people perish" (Prov. 29:18).

Replenish yourself physically. Take time out to reassess your health. Go away to a spa. Give yourself a longer-than-usual vacation. See your life from a faraway perspective. I am always amazed at how much more clearly I am able to view my work when I am miles away from it. In recent years, my family and I have enjoyed getaways to the seashore. There's nothing like relaxing on a beach away from my work obligations to renew my body—and at the same time to renew relationships with my family members, gain a new perspective, reposition myself, and reflect on life's truly important priorities.

Renew yourself mentally. Professors have a time-honored practice of taking sabbatical leave. Every seven years, fully tenured professors are traditionally granted a semester, or an entire year, to renew themselves professionally and intellectually. Most devote this time to a special research project, a trip abroad to conduct on-site research or to peruse original source material, or a series of guest lectures in another location. The experiences are stimulating. The timing is concentrated.

You can do the same for yourself. Take a break to learn something new. In our farming analogy, take time to read something other than farm journals for a while. Explore a new interest. Acquire a new skill. Don't allow it to derail you from your goals or purposes; rather, seek what will complement your goals and enrich you personally.

Renewing Yourself Keeps Confidence High

Taking time out periodically to renew yourself helps you maintain the self-confidence you need for this season of intense effort. You will come away from these experiences with a deep-down-in-your-roots feeling of having worth and being valuable, apart from your current progress or status.

Self-confidence isn't something you were born with. It's something you must develop. Many of us were cultivated like weeds as children. We played inferior roles to the adults around us, who frequently reminded us of our faults and shortcomings more than our successes and abilities. If you had that type of childhood, you face a special challenge in building up your self-confidence as an adult. Here are some basic points to remember about yourself:

1. Realize that the most important opinion about you is the one that you hold.

Ultimately, nobody else is responsible for your life but you. Nobody else is accountable for your actions but you. Therefore, nobody's opinion about you is as important as yours.

2. Recognize that the most important conversations are the ones you have with yourself.

Whether or not you are aware of it, you have a running conversation with yourself from the time you get up to the time you go to sleep. Your thoughts and ideas are "you talking to you." Have daily conversations with yourself that are supportive and reinforcing. We know the value of talking to people who praise us, reward us, recognize us, are happy to see us, and let us know that they genuinely enjoy talking with us. Talk to yourself with those same qualities—silently as well as audibly.

3. Develop a strong system of internal values.

Weigh what you hold to be true, good, and lasting. Write down some of your values for periodic review. Read material that reinforces what you hold to be significant in life. Know what you believe and why you believe it. At times, have discussions—even debates—with yourself. Draw conclusions about life. Think about deeper issues. Your values will greatly affect how you relate to others. The stronger your values are, the greater the impact. If you are lacking in internal values, you will tend to draw from and even use other people—almost as a leech fastening itself to their value systems. Instead, seek to become a server, one who can help others and give strength to others.

4. Don't stop in your failures.

Don't wallow in your mistakes. Keep moving.

5. Don't demand perfection of yourself.

An *A* is usually awarded to the person who scores 90 percent or better, and sometimes the score doesn't even need to be that high. A passing grade can be as low as 60 percent. Elections are frequently won with 51 percent, as is majority stock holding!

Give your best effort, and continue to move forward. Perfection is not only unrealistic to expect and virtually impossible to achieve, but it greatly deters your ability to move forward. The person who is constantly looking over his or her shoulder at what might have been done better can't possibly be focused on the future. Drive with your eyes ahead; don't drive by concentrating on the rearview mirror.

6. Give each job or task your best effort.

Countless individuals say when confronted with a chore, "I'm too good to be doing this." They have contempt for their current means of subsistence, their current colleagues, their current situation in life. Don't despise your environment, your associates, or the tasks ahead of you. Instead, encourage them and throw yourself into giving them your best.

People who look down on their current situation will rarely do what it takes to overcome the present and achieve a better tomorrow. They are likely to be forever stuck in the present they despise. They are dissatisfied, restless, and unhappy. Frequently, they lose the present they have and sink even lower. They haven't failed at their jobs; they've failed at themselves. No job is too unworthy to do well. There are no small parts—only small actors.

7. View the big picture of life.

Step back from the landscape of your life today and take a long walk, ride a bike, or jog into the countryside. Observe the wonder and abundance of nature, and remember that everything in your world is interconnected. You are a part of a much bigger whole. Listen to the subtle rhythms of your environment. Recognize that you have rhythms and cycles of change in your life. Relax and open up to the vast creative and interrelated world around you.

To develop confidence, you must see yourself ultimately as a unique creation. You must recognize, with pleasure, that nobody else is just like you. No one else has exactly your temperament, history, associations. No one else has your footprints, your fingerprints, your voiceprint, your genetic code. No one else has precisely your set of capabilities, talents, and skills. You are one of a kind.

Marvel at your uniqueness. You have a unique contribution to render to your family, your community, your world. You have something to give. This world will be different because of your involvement, your actions, your responses.

Most of us sell ourselves short when it comes to potential. Researchers confirm again and again that we use only a fraction of our brain power; we accomplish only a portion of what we could accomplish. Bask in the fact that you have virtually unlimited potential.

The confident person ultimately realizes that the impossible is possible. It just takes a little longer.

Value is there. It just needs to be dusted off.

Purpose is there. It just needs to be polished.

Make this summer season a time for growing in self-confidence, a critical trait as you continue to work hard and give of yourself to the tasks before you.

Work hard.

Work smart.

Above all, work to *your* best. You'll enjoy the feeling you have at the end of the day and the season.

12

The Season for Evaluation

A farmer constantly monitors his field, asking such questions as,

- "What does it need?"
- "How is the fruit setting on?"
- "Are predators or harmful insects invading?"
- "Are the plants as healthy as they can be?"
- "When should I next water?"
- "Would an application of fertilizer help?"

Begin your evaluative process as a life-farmer by concentrating on what is going right. Ask yourself, What are the areas in which I can sense growth? What gives me the most joy? In what am I being most productive?

The turning point in my personal career came in the middle 1960s when I became associated with the Salk Institute for Biological Studies near my hometown of La Jolla, California. Although my position was not a scientific one, I had a unique opportunity to observe scientists at work. I noticed that as an investigator approached a particular disease and a series of experiments related to it, he studied first how a healthy organism functions. He looked first at the studies that showed positive results. Instead of focusing only on the diseased tissue, he looked first at life, health, and progress.

Start out with your successes. And then hold that same positive frame of mind throughout the evaluative process.

Summer Is the Season for Feedback

Summer is the time to take stock of where you are. More than ever, you need to put into place certain criteria by which you will monitor your progress and make adjustments to arrive on target as your success draws closer.

Ask yourself,

- Do I feel good about my progress to date? Why? Why not?
- Am I going where I carefully decided I want to go?
  If not, ask, Have my feelings changed about my destination? Have I veered off course? If so, isolate what caused you to take a detour.
- Am I on my way toward becoming the person that I hope to be?
  How are others responding to you? Are they respecting you more? Or do they fear you? Are you attracting the right kind of attention? Are you a good role model for your business associates, friends, family members, children? If not, what can you do to change?
- Is my body signaling distress?
  Are you burning out because you're not getting the proper balance of physical exercise, rest, and good nutrients?
- Have I already reached my goals?
  If so, how can your goals be expanded to stretch yourself further? Or are your goals still so far out of sight that you are frustrated? If so, analyze them. Can you create more subtasks?
- Are my goals still clearly in focus?
  Have you become so caught up in the doing of your plan that you've lost sight of the reason for your efforts?
- Am I feeling irritable and frustrated?
  How are you communicating this to others? Are you having trouble sleeping? Do you eat too much or too little lately? Are you puttering around aimlessly? Are you sleeping too much? Do you feel listless?

These are all telltale symptoms of unmet needs, so ask yourself further,

- · What do I need personally to stay on track to achieve the goals I've set for myself?
  What specifically do you require to meet certain needs in your body, mind, and soul?
- · How does what I'm doing now compare with my last best effort?

Answers to these questions will give you a progress report that you can trust.

Don't be discouraged by your answers. Consider them to be midterm grades. You are your own greatest critic. Unfortunately, many of us are also our harshest critics. We have a tendency to be impatient and want to see more progress toward our goals than is reasonable to expect for the amount of time we've been pursuing them.

Recognize as you appraise your progress that you aren't qualified to be all-knowing, all-seeing, or all-feeling. Only God is omniscient, omnipotent, and omnipresent.

Prayer, in whatever form or custom your particular religious affiliation calls for, can be extremely helpful to you in getting to the heart of your answers. Are you uneasy about something in your life? Are you bearing a burden of guilt, remorse, or regret? Pause to listen to the heartbeat of your soul.

Extend to yourself the same patience you would extend to a stranger . . . or a young child . . . or a patient recovering from a serious injury. Don't expect more from yourself than you expect from others you love.

In addition to inner feedback, seek constructive external feedback. Ask others to evaluate objectively how they see your progress. They will have a perspective you don't have. Do they see growth? Do they see progress? Ask them to be concrete in expressing to you what types of changes or growth they see in your life.

Remember, however, to seek feedback only from people who are truly interested in seeing you reach your goals. Don't seek feedback from a competitor, an enemy, a person who abuses you, or any person who doesn't have your best interests at heart. Neutral doesn't count. Get feedback from someone who is on your side but will still be objective and honest with you.

I've observed time and again, misery truly does love company. Jealousy makes for some of the most miserable people I know. Surpass the achievements of your particular social crowd or your business colleagues, and look out for the slings and arrows of the many who will wish you were back where they are. Dodge the snide remarks and catty comments. Let them roll right off you. Don't internalize them.

Only pay attention to feedback from those who have similar goals or who are working actively alongside you to achieve goals of their own.

Motives and fears run deep. Study them in others. The authoritarian boss who supports you and comforts you when you're down may like you best when you are in just that state—down and dependent. When you start succeeding (beyond his expectations and comfort level), he may be among the first to suggest that you cut back, back off, or set your goals a little lower. Recognize that for the insecurity that it is. Respect him as a person, but don't accept his feedback as genuine and helpful. It will rarely be either objective or well-intentioned.

Even parents aren't immune to emotional conflicts that can pollute the feedback they give their children. Many parents have had difficulty accepting the success of a child or encouraging further success. Even without a conscious or evil thought, they have said to their children,

· "You shouldn't . . ."
· "You couldn't . . ."
· "I wouldn't . . ."
· "You really can't . . ."

If you hear remarks like that—from parents or from anyone— let them be a red flag in your mind. Evaluate closely what people are saying. Ask yourself, What is the motive here?

What causes a person to give negative feedback or to fail to receive feedback? Here are several Feedback Glitches I've observed through the years:

1. A person may feel she has "outgrown" another person. Therefore, she refuses to accept what a seemingly "inferior" person suggests.
2. Anger virtually always clouds feedback. If an unresolved issue or problem stands between you and another person, you will never be able to communicate genuinely toward the growth and betterment of the other person.
3. Jealousy taints feedback. Ask, Why would this person give me negative comments? What's in it for him? Is he attempting to tear me down to build up himself?

Be willing to say to yourself, "I'm on the right road. I'm doing OK. I'm succeeding." We too frequently become adept at pointing out our flaws and identifying our failures. Become equally adept at citing your achievements.

Identify . . .

- things you are doing now that you weren't doing one month ago . . . six months ago . . . a year ago . . . five years ago. What habits have changed? What progress has been made?
- areas where improvement has been made. Chart your progress. Use the same type of charts that businesses make in forecasting or reporting trends over multiyear periods. Note areas of growth.
- goals you have reached. List them. Take note of them. Reflect on them.

Doing well once or twice is relatively easy. Continuing to move upward is tough, in part because we so easily revert to old habits and former life-styles. Over the long run, you need to give yourself regular feedback to monitor your performance and reinforce yourself positively. If you note that you are starting to experience a downward trend, feedback sessions can help you recognize it and take steps to reverse its course.

If you can learn to give yourself the right feedback, you will find it much easier to turn goal achievement into habit.

Ask yourself several questions as you analyze the feedback you are taking in . . .

Question 1: Is this a brick wall?

Recognize brick walls for what they are.

Some people assume that they must keep running toward a

brick wall to succeed. They seem to feel that if they keep running at it full speed, crashing their skulls into it, they will eventually cause the wall to crack, crumble, or disappear, or at least, a hole will be formed that they can sail through. Repeatedly running into a brick wall will wear you out.

Back up and think smart. There's more than one way to get to the other side of that wall. You may not be able to crash through it. But you may be able to climb over it, especially with the boost of a friend or two. You may be able to tunnel under it. You may be able to go around it by following it in one direction or the other to its end. In fact, you may be able to catapult over it and enjoy the ride even as you sail through the air to a successful landing on the other side.

Consider the difference between a bee and a fly.

Trap a bee in a bottle and then turn the base of the bottle toward a light source. Even though you leave the bottle un-capped, the bee will not escape. It will fly repeatedly toward the bottom of the bottle until it wears itself out trying to get to the light. Bees are perfectly equipped for life in a hive, not for life alone in a bottle. They are unable to adapt to that environment and eventually perish because they are unable to overcome their genetically programmed instincts.

Trap a fly in the bottle and turn its bottom toward the light, and you'd better cap the bottle or the fly will escape. The fly will not simply bounce off the bottom of the bottle to reach the light. It will fly in every direction—up, down, toward the light, away from the light—and sooner or later, the fly will find its way out the open neck.

Adaptability is the key. Don't get stuck by refusing to check out alternatives. Don't get bogged down in just one way of doing something.

Change is just as predictable as taxes and death. It's something you can count on. Don't buck it. Adapt!

The great prayer of Reinhold Neibuhr is one I've not only mem-orized but recommended to just about everyone I know:

> God, give us grace to accept with serenity the things that cannot be changed, courage to change the things which should be changed, and the wisdom to distinguish the one from the other.

Question 2: Is this the best time to tackle this slope?

Sometimes you may need to back off a project or task to gain more information or skill so that you may accomplish it with greater success at a future date.

I once had an interesting day on a ski slope in Aspen, Colorado. I was just learning how to ski, and I took the wrong chair lift to the top of a ski run marked with a black diamond symbol—the mark for an EXPERT skier. Even though I was a beginner, I smiled and began to fantasize that I was just an older version of Phil Mahre about to be reborn on the slopes. The name of the ski run was *Adios,* which in cases such as mine is loosely interpreted "good-bye, pronto."

My original imagination of the desired result—my whipping across the snow at lightning speed, deftly maneuvering my way over moguls and down steep inclines—quickly gave way to fear. I could equally imagine a fractured fibula, a possible broken neck, or perhaps a "tree implant" in some part of my body that didn't need one.

Someplace between the thoughts of sheer exhilaration and stark terror is a point of reason. Back off. Take the ski lift back down the mountain and enjoy the view along the way. It may be slightly embarrassing but far less painful in the long run.

Admitting that you have encountered something you aren't ready to tackle isn't a sin, a crime, or a serious threat to your success—unless you let it be one. Having surveyed *Adios* trail, make a commitment to yourself that you will one day ski that run! Don't assume that you will never make it to that point. Assume that you will—and that the next time you make your way up the slope, you'll be able to ski down it.

Question 3: Is the problem I'm perceiving a REAL problem?

A farmer knows the difference between a predator in his field and just another insect. A predator causes damage whereas non-predator insects may be helpful.

As a life-farmer, you need to know how to determine when your field is infested with a problem. Real problems must be dealt with quickly, quietly, and efficiently, or they will affect the quality or quantity of your success. In some cases, a problem can keep you from doing what you must do to cultivate or reap a harvest. Take action.

Many nuisances, however, disguise themselves as problems. They aren't real problems—just gnats buzzing across the field of your success. Your major challenge is determining which problems are real ones.

Was the Malibu rock a real problem? Have you ever heard or read about the $1 million Malibu rock?

The rains had been pounding southern California for most of two weeks one February. Rocks were falling down the slopes, most of them unnoticed and unpublicized. Some of the homeowners who lived in the 19700 block of Pacific Coast Highway in Malibu looked up and paid new attention to a rock that had been located directly above them since the day they had built their costly homes. They saw the 116-ton rock, perched a little more than 180 feet above Pacific Coast Highway between Topanga Canyon Boulevard and Malibu Canyon Road, and they began to perceive it as a problem—a major problem. They envisioned it sliding down onto their homes, causing great property damage and possibly injuries or death.

One homeowner sent a telegram to the California Department of Transportation, holding it responsible for anything that happened should that rock dislodge and come crashing down the mountainside. That, of course, put the department in action. The state ordered the owners of the property on which the rock balanced to have the rock removed immediately. The Iranian Import Company, which owned the land, declined to take action and so the state hired a construction company to remove the rock. Bids were put out, and the lowest one was for $92,000!

The job was only supposed to take a few hours at the most. A net was going to be raised by helicopter and then fastened to the rock by a crew in bulldozers. Then the helicopter would gently lower the rock onto the highway, where a cushion of mud had been spread to break its fall and prevent it from rolling onto the houses. It all sounded simple enough.

Shortly after dawn, three Caterpillar D-9 tractors started up the hill. It was past noon before they were in place. Then workers had trouble getting the thirty-by-thirty-foot 2,500-pound net laced together. A twin-turbine jet helicopter picked up the net and draped it over the rock. The tractors, pulling in tandem, attempted to budge the rock from its perch. It did not move.

Crowds of people and reporters arrived to watch as the day turned to night. One news photographer got stuck on a ledge near the rock and had to be rescued by helicopter. The crowd cheered. The rock didn't move.

The next day, the rock was bombarded with 32,000 gallons of water from a 400-foot fire hose. The rock still didn't move. Someone said in exasperation, "The darn thing must be welded to a steel beam down the middle of it!"

Superman arrived at the party to promote one of his films. The crowds were enjoying the rock-moving party atmosphere. The rock became the most watched rock in the Los Angeles basin!

Just before sundown, three days after the assault had started, a herculean effort involving a one-inch steel cable and a skiploader caused the Malibu rock to come tumbling down, crashing through the net holding it, breaking chains, and shooting sparks as it fell 180 feet onto the mud cushion on Pacific Coast Highway. It took another three days for the road to be cleared of the rock and mud. All things considered—including loss of business revenue and salaries and per diem school funds because the road was closed—the removal of that rock cost nearly $1 million!

In retrospect, many questioned whether that rock was really a problem at all. The fear had been that it would dislodge in the rains. Yet 32,000 gallons of water under pressure had failed to move it an inch. The rock was probably there to stay. Indeed, the only thing that might have dislodged it might have been a major earthquake, at which many of the homes below it might very well have been heavily damaged or destroyed anyway.

Was the rock a problem?

Was it a problem worth spending $1 million to resolve?

Make certain your problems are real ones. Put in the effort it takes

- to ascertain the problem—to define it, measure it, size it up.
- to determine the impact of the problem should a worst-case scenario ensue.
- to determine which course of action you should take to resolve the issue.

In the case of the Malibu rock, the better choice probably would have been to notice the rock before one built a house in its pathway to the sea!

Question 4: Is an opportunity lurking in my problem?

One of the best places to find opportunities is within problems.

In the 1930s a German immigrant in Philadelphia was selling knockwurst and sauerkraut in his small restaurant. Unable to afford plates and silverware as other establishments, he gave his patrons inexpensive cotton gloves to hold the knockwurst, draped in sauerkraut, while they ate it. You can imagine his problem—dozens upon dozens of dirty gloves to take home to wash each day—not to mention the gloves that his customers inadvertently or purposefully took home to use while gardening or doing odd jobs.

To solve his glove problem, he split a German roll down the center one day and placed the knockwurst and sauerkraut in it. He explained to his clientele the first day that the bun—which cost just a few cents to produce—was taking the place of his serving gloves, which were now being discontinued. One of the customers noticed the owner's dachshund snoozing in a corner of the restaurant, and he said, "What happened to the other dog you used to have around here? Is that missing dog the reason you're trying to cover up your knockwurst in a fancy roll?" Everyone laughed, but on that day, the hot dog was born.

The opportunity was within the problem!

Question 5: Am I spending resources wisely and effectively?

Summer is a time for being keenly aware of your resources—spending them wisely, replenishing them as they are depleted, and looking for new ways of enhancing them.

Ask yourself several key questions regarding your resources, keeping in mind that your resources include your creativity, motivational level, and energy as well as financial resources and important goal-related alliances . . .

1. What are my spending habits? Can I account for my outflow of money, time, energy, skills?
2. What are my savings habits? Do I put away at least 10 percent of each paycheck into a savings or long-term invest-

ment account? Am I acquiring and saving precious memories? Am I maintaining my friendships and family relationships—"saving" them as opposed to losing them?
3. What are my assets? What am I doing to increase my fixed assets?

Assets and resources, of course, also refer to far more than money. Wealth is far more than what you have; it's what you are. Wealth is counted not only in dollars and cents but also in decency and sense.

The Summer Season Is a Time to Clarify Long-Range Goals

As you begin to pursue the activities that bring you immediate short-term successes and accomplishments—in other words, as you begin to achieve some of the items that appeared in your plan during the winter season of your success cycle—you should review your *long-range* goals. Sometimes the doing of a goal helps us refine, redefine, or reset our goals, generally to a higher mark.

Long-range goals are worth both the work and the wait entailed in their achievement. They rarely, however, provide sustained reinforcement and feedback along the way. To stay on track toward long-term goals, you need to do two things:

First, review your long-range goals and the small subtask action steps you derived from them.

Are these still the subtasks that will lead you to your long-range goal? Has anything happened along the way to cause you to want to change a part of your long-range goal or its implementation plan?

Look closely at the beginning and ending of these long-range tasks. Corporations do this regularly. The long-term goal may be to show increased profit year after year. The short-term goals are expressed in terms of percentages and volume sales and decreased problems or returned goods. The action steps that help reach the goals, however, are such activities as contests, quotas, and campaigns.

Second, intersperse long-range campaigns within your summer season.

In developing your rhythm of short-term action steps in the summer months of your success, identify very specific campaigns. Enter into a contest with yourself.

Lose Ten Pounds Campaign may be part of a much longer-range goal of becoming thin and fit. You may want to run this particular campaign during the months of June and July. Give yourself a start date and a stop date. Identify a reward that you will give yourself if you achieve your goal by July 31. It may be a new swimsuit or an evening out on the town.

See How Much I Can Gather Together for Goodwill Campaign may be your action step for your intermediate-range goal of cleaning out the house and garage (which relates to your long-range goal of reevaluating all of your possessions, which relates to your life-dream of living in an efficient, streamlined, uncluttered environment with only high-quality possessions).

In this campaign, give yourself a start date and a stop date—perhaps the next four Saturday afternoons. Schedule the campaign on your personal schedule. Identify levels of reward—perhaps one level of reward for one pickup load of goods, another level of reward for two pickup loads, and so forth. Get the entire family involved. You may want to give a specific reward to each person based on the contribution to the project.

Get the Book Written Campaign is a long-range task I engage in periodically. As I begin to write a book, I break the subject down to a working outline. Once I have the outline, I take the main subject areas and work them into chapters. For each chapter heading, I establish a file folder into which I put research material as I gather it throughout the year. Copies of magazine and newspaper articles, bibliographies of other books on the subject, and clippings and scribbled notes of all kinds make their way into the file folders. Once I have assembled all of the research material into folders, I get out my tape recorder and take an entire Saturday—a twelve-hour period—to dictate all of my thoughts and ideas about the book on audiocassettes. Then I have the tapes transcribed into double-spaced, typewritten pages, which I refer to as general inspirational source data. Now comes the crucial phase.

I go to my year-at-a-glance calendar and block out forty days. I make a commitment to devote twelve hours a day on each of these days to sitting at my word processor and writing.

Through trial and error, I've learned that I can compose 10 double-spaced pages of rough-draft book manuscript in a twelve-hour sitting. In forty days, I can generate approximately 400 pages. During the editing process, I expect my editor to cut, reshape, and consolidate the rough draft down to about 320 to 350 pages of typed text. Those pages will result in about 220 to 230 pages of typeset book.

The entire project takes on a "campaign" aspect to me. I don't write a book per se. I complete a set of incremental tasks, setting time parameters around each stage, and rewarding myself in small ways as I complete each segment, each stage, each step in the process.

For me, the task of sitting down and writing an entire book would be overwhelming. In fact, I probably wouldn't bother to begin such a Matterhorn of a project. But tell me that I need to write ten pages during twelve Saturday hours, and I will tell you that I can do it. Tell me that I need to block out forty days a year for writing, and I can do that.

In addition, it's easier for me to monitor my progress toward the long-range goal of completing the book if I have incremental steps that I can check off—both literally and figuratively, in my case. When I get behind, I know what it takes to catch up. If I get ahead of my pace, I know that I can take one of those Saturdays for a day at the beach with my family.

I like to set several award ceremonies during my book-writing campaign. The first comes at the midpoint of the project after I have completed about two hundred pages of rough text. I like to go out and have a midseason dinner celebration with my family. The next celebration comes when I submit the rough draft to the publisher. I have an end-of-the-regular-season celebration dinner. I now consider that I'm moving into postseason play-offs. When the final draft is accepted by the publisher, my wife and I go away together for the weekend. On publication day, when the book comes off the press and enters the market, my entire family and I go away for a three-day cruise, a deep-sea fishing excursion, or some other adventure that we have visualized together and anticipated during those hours when I am stuck in front of the word processor and am not readily accessible for one-on-one nurturing.

Writing a book is not my project alone. It's a family activity. My family members participate in the rewards; they, in turn, recognize my need for their patience, encouragement, and quiet-foot-steps-around-the-house on "writing days."

By the page, writing a book is a cinch. By the volume, writing a book would be impossible for me. Interim celebrations at the end of specific action steps not only make the process easier but truly enjoyable.

No matter what your particular goal, you can find a way to break it down into action steps that take on the nature of a contest or campaign.

Get your family members, friends, or colleagues involved. Take on the challenge together. By setting step-by-step goals that can be reached and rewarded, you'll find that your forward progress is faster and more fun.

Become Your Own Best Expert About Yourself and Your Goals

In taking note of your progress continually, you'll be in a much better position to spot problems as they arise and to deal with them before they loom large, become messy, or create havoc.

You'll also be more likely to see your growth and successes along the way.

Survey your field.

How *is* your crop growing?

A farmer enjoys watching the stages of growth throughout the summer months. You can, too, as a life-farmer!

13

The Season for Endurance

Summer storms can be violent.

Thunder and lightning, with great gully-washing downpours of water, can drown a field in the "flash" of a flash flood. Hail can pound young plants back into earth. Winds can whip fruit and grain from stems and stalks prematurely. Long dry spells can result in parched ground and plants that crumble like paper.

We frequently do not have control over the storms that hit us. Personally, storms may come in the form of disease, accidents, the death of loved ones. We struggle against seemingly overwhelming urges, desires, irritations, and temptations as well as seizures of laziness and complacency. In our external world . . . neighbors may move; loved ones may be transferred; children may leave. A leading manufacturer may choose to close a plant or leave a community entirely. A major business in town may fold. New laws may be passed, adding the need for additional safeguards or reporting—both of which cost money. Policies, practices, and politics may change.

Opportunity rides the dangerous wind.

In 1980 my plane made an emergency landing in Portland, Oregon, as the Pacific Northwest shuddered under the devastating force of Mount Saint Helens's eruption, the worst volcanic fire storm in the continental United States in a century.

Television and newspaper reports dominated the national news. "Forest annihilated . . . rivers choked . . . fish and wildlife destroyed . . . tourist areas buried . . . acid rain cloud moving south and west . . . farmers finished . . . weather cycles permanently changed . . . California next . . . only the beginning" . . . so the headlines read.

Less than a year after the havoc, I visited the area. No one would deny that the damage had been tremendous. But most of the salmon and steelhead trout managed to survive. Finding the rivers clogged with hot mud and debris, the fish followed alternate tributaries home, some of them less than six inches deep.

The wildlife on and near Mount Saint Helens returned quickly. Lakes and rivers soon were teeming with life, their waters full of rich, life-supporting nutrients generously supplied by the exploding volcano. Wildflowers bloomed as did tourist business in the area. Farmers who were wiped out by the thick layer of ash at least could be heartened by the fact that they had rich mineral deposits in their soil on layaway for future crops.

Most important, the citizens of Washington State joined together to rebuild the area out of the storm's ashes and devastation. In Chinese, the symbols for *crisis* are identical to those for the word *opportunity*. To the courageous, crisis is an opportunity riding on the dangerous wind.

When you have your life, your health, your family, time ahead of you, faith, and optimism . . . you've got valuable resources and great wealth! You've got what you need for seizing opportunities.

Storms. Volcanoes. Devastating losses. Each and every one a threat to your achieving a maximum harvest of success. It's easy during the summer months to feel at times as if you are fighting a losing battle.

You CAN control . . .

During a summertime storm—when I feel as if life is whirling out of my control—I find it helpful to reflect on the many resources over which I do have control. Let me share with you at least twelve things over which you have vast or sole control:

1. You CAN control what you do with most of your time in a day.
2. You CAN control the amount of energy you exert or the amount of effort you give to a task.
3. You CAN control what you think about—your thoughts and imaginations.
4. You CAN control your attitude.
5. You CAN control your tongue. You can choose to remain silent or choose to speak. If you choose to speak, you can choose the words you will say. As you speak the words, you can choose the tone of voice you will use.
6. You CAN control with whom you will develop friendships . . . whom you will choose as role models . . . and whom you will seek out for mentoring counsel and inspiration. You CAN control to a great extent with whom you will communicate.
7. You CAN control your commitments.
8. You CAN control the causes to which you give your time and ideas.
9. You CAN control your memberships.
10. You CAN control what you do with your faith.
11. You CAN control your concerns—and whether you will choose action or worry in response to them.
12. You CAN control your response to difficult times and people.

What about failure?

Failure is often a result of a mistake we made—of judgment, decision, or performance—in an arena over which we do have control. How do we accommodate errors for which we feel we have some degree of fault? Facing mistakes successfully and positively is one of the most important lessons you will learn during your summer season.

One of my friends and mentors these past twenty years has been the inexhaustible positive thinker, Norman Vincent Peale. I have traveled with him on the international speaker circuit on a regular basis, and I always marvel at his vitality and enthusiasm for life. One thing I have noticed about Dr. Peale is that I rarely see him without his wife, Ruth, by his side. Ruth is not only present for moral support. She is an active part of his professional life.

I believe in including my wife, Susan, in all of my professional projects as well. She travels with me as often as her responsibilities allow. We believe firmly that the family that travels together grows together and stays together.

I heartily recommend that you include your family in your plans and projects. They will be of invaluable help to you when it comes to feedback and also will be allies when you confront errors, mistakes, and problems.

One of my favorite parts of Dr. Peale's marvelous presentation is his statement to the audience that a man or woman without problems is one who is planted safely in the cemetery. He relates that if he personally goes too long without a problem, he knows that he is either asleep or hiding. Then Dr. Peale raises his head and hands skyward and asks a question of God, "Lord, don't You love me anymore? You haven't given me a challenge or setback for days. How about a nice, big, healthy, jumbo-sized problem just to let me know You really care about me?" Next, Dr. Peale chuckles with a twinkle in his eye, "God always hears my call and grants my request."

I firmly believe his approach to daily challenges has kept Dr. Peale perennially young and active. Did you know, though, that even Norman Vincent Peale has struggled with discouragement? When he was in his fifties, he gave up before he reached one of his major goals. He had written a manuscript and had sent it to a host of publishers without success. He looked at the stack of rejection notices piled high, and in frustration, he threw the manuscript in the wastebasket. His wife reached in to salvage it. He said to her sternly, "We've wasted enough time on it. I forbid you to take it from the wastebasket."

The following day, she decided to take the manuscript personally to yet another publisher. When she arrived at his office, the publisher noticed that her parcel looked odd, unlike any other book he had ever seen. It was too big and bulky and the wrong shape to be a book manuscript. When he unwrapped the odd-shaped package, wrapped in brown paper, the publisher discovered to his amazement a wastebasket containing the manuscript that we have come to know as *The Power of Positive Thinking*.

Ruth Peale followed her husband's command—not taking the manuscript from the wastebasket—but she refused to let him give up on his goal. Had she given up, Dr. Peale's classic book, which has sold scores of millions of copies, would not have been published, much less any of the many other best-sellers he has written since then.

Have you ever suffered a severe setback? Have you been handicapped by illness or injury? Have you taken a risk and failed?

You are in the company of some of the most famous and successful men and women of all time.

Failure is as much a part of life as risk taking and winning.

The greatest successes frequently come after numerous painful failures. The key is to learn from your mistakes, not repeat them, and move forward.

One of the best role models I've found for illustrating how to handle failure and disappointment is Thomas S. Monaghan, founder, president, and chairman of Domino's Pizza, Inc. Domino's has 3,300 pizzerias spread across America, but not one of them has tables. Domino's is the king of home-delivered pizza—virtually anywhere you want it.

The success Domino's enjoys today grew out of failure. First, a bad partnership nearly dragged the business under in 1965. In 1968, the business suffered a devastating $150,000 loss as the result of a fire, and insurance covered only one-tenth of the loss. By 1970, the management of the debt-ridden pizza chain was assumed to be a principal creditor—a bank. Ten months later, Domino's owner, Thomas S. Monaghan, resumed control and faced more than one hundred lawsuits, fifteen hundred creditors, and an overall debt of $1.5 million.

No one would have blamed Monaghan for labeling his business a failure, folding his pizza tent, and fading into the sunset. Monaghan, however, had only begun to fight back.

You see, Monaghan knew about adversity. He was only four years old when his father died. He had grown up in foster homes, worked as a farmhand, a pinsetter in a bowling alley, and a newsboy.

The pizza business started in 1960 when Monaghan was only twenty-three years old. He and his brother bought a nondescript pizza parlor next to the campus of Eastern Michigan University in Ypsilanti, Michigan, a tiny community between Detroit and Ann Arbor. Tom viewed the pizza parlor as a way to supplement his income from a corner newsstand he operated.

In a year, he became the sole owner of the shop, called Domi-Nick's. He dropped out of college to give the pizza parlor his concentrated effort. A year later he added another shop near the campus of Central Michigan University, and on the first delivery run he ever made there, he met his future wife, Margie, in a girls' dorm on the Central Michigan campus.

As the business grew, Tom encountered numerous failures. His business literally grew by trial and error. He learned fast preparation techniques in that first little pizza shop, elbow deep in flour and tomato sauce, as he hustled to make deliveries to the college campuses before the dorms closed for the night.

In the beginning, he offered five pizza sizes, from a six-inch pie to a sixteen-inch pie. He eventually learned that he couldn't make money by selling the six-inch pies, and he settled only on twelve- and sixteen-inch sizes.

As he charted his progress, he learned that residential customers who ordered for home delivery were by far his most loyal and profitable customers. He zeroed in on them as his market.

In 1970 when faced with financial ruin, Monaghan did what he had always done in his life. He dug in his heels, viewed his mistakes as a learning experience, and prepared to climb out of the hole he was in to heights he had never before experienced.

And he did it. He instituted a new policy. In his own words, he stated it this way: "Domino's has a single goal. Its mission: to delivery a high-quality pizza, hot, within thirty minutes at a fair price." Everything Monaghan did was aimed at that goal. He trained crews to turn out a pizza in six minutes flat. He outlined delivery routes in premapped zones. He put his pizzas in crush-resistant, thermally insulated boxes.

By 1990, Domino's sales were heading upward to $2 billion, and store openings had established new records for the food service industry.

Thomas S. Monaghan is more than an astute businessman. He is a successful person. He cites these as the five principles that have guided his life since he was a nineteen-year-old marine, preparing to ship overseas:

1. *Spiritual.* "What good would it do to gain the world and lose my soul?" he asks himself. Monaghan once aspired to study for the priesthood.
2. *Family and social.* As important as his company is to him, it comes second in his life to his family, which includes his wife and four daughters.
3. *Mental development.* Monaghan squeezes in time to be a director of Cleary College in Ypsilanti, Henry Ford Hospital,

"Detroit Renaissance," and National Bank of Detroit. He spends fifteen minutes of quiet contemplation before starting work each morning.

4. *Physical development.* His routine includes morning workouts on his Nautilus equipment and jogging.

5. Monaghan believes that if he takes care of the other four principles of his life, he will make all the money he wants and also have the ability to enjoy it.

These five principles Monaghan links to the simple golden rule that governs his life: "Just figure out how you want to be treated yourself, and then treat others that way—your customers, your employees, your franchises, your suppliers."

All that sounds idealistic in today's harsh business climate, but it's working for Monaghan. He's now in the international market with pizzerias delivering piping hot pizzas to customers in Australia, Canada, Japan, the United Kingdom, and Germany, among others.

Too often we let our failures result in a message we give ourselves about our lives:

- "You always foul up."
- "You never get it right."
- "It's always your fault."
- "You're a failure."

Failure thinking is a mind-set that traps us in failure. It creates a downward spiral of failure thinking and failure acting.

Do you have a pessimistic explanatory style?

Dr. Martin Seligman has spent more than twenty years and conducted more than one hundred experiments with almost fifteen thousand subjects. He has come to the conclusion that the way in which we explain things that happen to us is far more important than what actually happens. The person who develops a chronic pessimistic explanatory style is prone to depression and illness.

A *pessimistic explanatory style* essentially means "negative outlook on life." If you choose to interpret what happens to you in a negative, dead-end way, your very life will end up marked by these characteristics: dead-end and negative.

It may come true even if it isn't true. I share a true story with many seminar audiences about the danger of a pessimistic or cynical outlook.

Nick was a strong, healthy man who worked as a yardman for a railroad company. He was a decent worker who got along with his fellow workers and was reliable on the job. His one glaring fault was that he was a notorious worrier. He was cynical about everything, fearing the worst and explaining the world in negative terms.

One summer day the train crews were informed they could quit an hour early in honor of the foreman's birthday. Accidentally, Nick was locked in an empty isolated refrigerator boxcar that was in the yard for repairs, and the rest of the workmen left the site. Nick panicked, the fear welling up inside him.

He banged and shouted until his fists were bloody and his voice hoarse. No one paid any attention. If people heard him, they associated the sound with a playground nearby or with the noise of the trains backing in and out of the yard.

It must be 0° in here, he thought. *If I can't get out, I'll freeze to death.* He found a cardboard box, and shivering uncontrollably, he scrawled this message to his wife and family: "So cold, body is getting numb. If I could just go to sleep. These may be my last words."

The next morning the crew slid open the heavy doors of the boxcar and found Nick dead. An autopsy revealed that every physical sign in his body indicated he had frozen to death. But, ironically, the refrigeration unit was inoperative. There was plenty of fresh air in the boxcar, and the temperature inside was steady at about 61°.

Nick was a victim of his own self-fulfilling prophecy!

How you see it is how it is. One of my favorite illustrations of the extremes used by different individuals to describe and explain the same situation was told to me by successful author and friend, Reni Witt.

It seems a productivity dispatcher was sent to a building site in France during the Middle Ages to interview the laborers. The dispatcher approached the first worker on the construction site and asked, "What are you doing?"

"What, are you blind?" the worker snapped back. "I'm cutting these impossible boulders with primitive tools and putting them together the way the boss tells me. I'm sweating under this blazing sun. It's backbreaking work, and it's boring me to death!"

The dispatcher quickly backed off and retreated to a second worker. He posed the same question, "What are you doing?"

The second worker replied, "I'm shaping these boulders into usable blocks, which are then assembled according to the architect's plans. It's hard work because the building is so tall, and sometimes the work gets very repetitive. But I earn five francs a week, and that supports my family."

Somewhat encouraged, the dispatcher went on to a third worker. "And what are you doing?" he asked.

The third worker stood up, his face beaming with a smile. Lifting his arm toward the sky, he said proudly, "Why, can't you see? I'm building a magnificent cathedral."

Never think of defeat or a difficult situation as a permanent condition. Instead, view it as a postponed success. Talk about your work as an accomplishment in progress.

Turn Failure into Fertilizer

Rather than see your failure as your harvest, see it as fertilizer. Plow the information you gain from a failure back into the process. You now know what won't work, or at least you have a better idea about what won't work. Use that information to discover what will work.

How should you think of failure? Here are five ways I choose to think about it:

First, recognize that failure is a human trait, common to every member of the species.

Second, examine the mistake. Don't run from it and try to hide. Face it head-on. Don't blame others for the mistake. Confront the mistake and yourself. Analyze how and why the failure occurred. Determine what you might have done differently to avoid the mistake. Set a course of action that will lead you away from the mistake.

Third, if you can't determine what went wrong, call in an expert. Get input from someone who has had recent success in a similar situation. Find out what the person did that went "right."

Fourth, prior to trying again, visualize clearly what you will do to handle the situation affirmatively and correctly in the future.

Fifth, bury the failure. Don't frame it for continual viewing. Learn from it, discard it, and face tomorrow. Once the sun sets on the playing field, the competition of the day is over. Get ready for tomorrow rather than devote your time and energy to replaying the past.

Keep in mind that . . .

Aspiring actors and actresses who try out for parts regularly are turned down twenty-nine times out of thirty. In other words, on the average they are successful only one time in thirty as they audition for roles or commercials.

Top oil companies, even making use of consultations with and reports from expert geologists, find oil only in one well out of ten. In other words, nine out of ten wells dug turn out to be dry holes.

Winners in the stock market—no matter which way the Dow-Jones average is moving—make money on the average of only two out of five investments.

Even the best major league baseball players only make it as far as first base 40 percent of the times they come to bat, and that includes walks (which are pitching errors, not hitting successes).

Success is never directly related to genius.

It isn't related to cleverness.

It isn't related to inherited wealth. In fact, some people who seem to have everything going for them—wealthy, beautiful, talented, intelligent parents, outstanding teachers and schools, coaches and friends—turn out to be low achievers. There is an amazing historical pattern that the offspring of many of the most famous, successful, prominent people in our nation don't find personal success. Some seem unable to accept themselves. Others seem almost root-bound, with no inner drive to break out on their own. Others seem extremely frightened of independence. On the other hand, many successful leaders have come from humble, backward, and discouraging beginnings in life.

No—it's not a matter of brains, brawn, or breeding that makes for success. It's what you do with failures, and how determined you are to persevere to reach success.

Rather than give in to failures, mistakes, and temporary setbacks you may experience during the summer season of your success, choose to persevere.

Stay in for the long haul.

Success is built over time.

McDonald's didn't become a $1 billion business overnight. It took Ray Kroc and his team twenty-two years.

IBM took forty-six years to reach $1 billion in revenue.

Xerox took sixty-three years.

We look at today's corporate giants, and we tend to think that they "just happened" or that they are companies that rose up quickly. The truth is, the companies were MADE to happen. They were propelled toward success one step at a time.

Self-Discipline Is Closely Linked to Perseverance

Self-discipline is persevering in habits you have chosen to adopt. Perseverance is vitally linked to your long-range goals.

Many people think of self-discipline as meaning self-denial or self-restriction. The term is actually more appropriately aligned with self-determination, which is the process of making your own success and happiness. Self-discipline is the perseverance in action that makes self-determination possible.

Self-discipline is

- holding your ground when you'd rather run away.
- counting to ten when you'd rather lash out.
- keeping a smile on your face when you'd rather cave in.
- working hard when you'd rather give up.

Self-discipline is more than putting on a stoic front or adopting a stiff-upper-lip approach to life. Self-discipline is grounded in a genuine feeling that it's more productive to seize control of a situation than to be overwhelmed by one. Self-discipline is inner fortitude, not an outer face. It is a vital ingredient to survival through the long, hot, difficult days of the summer—indeed, more than survival, progress!

Self-discipline takes guts. It is the result of training that requires courage.

Why? Because most habits are difficult to change. Habits start off as harmless thoughts—flimsy cobwebs with very little substance. The thoughts turn into behavior. Behavior is repeated, reinforced, and repeated again. Pretty soon the flimsy cobwebs have become steel cables.

A series of fused steel cables can be either a bridge or a cage. Good habits will help you get across the chasm of changes and difficulties. Bad ones will box you in.

It takes concentrated effort to break a habit, and another word for *concentrated effort* is *work*. Not just one session of work, but repeated, periodic work. Habits are formed bit by bit. Changing them happens bit by bit. Periodic work is called by another name —*practice*.

We've all probably heard about the young violinist who gets off the bus at the Port Authority in New York City and asks a policeman for directions, "Tell me, sir, how do I get to Carnegie Hall?"

The policeman replies with one word, "Practice."

You might have heard that word a thousand times in your growing-up years. Whether it was playing the piano, throwing a football, stitching a straight seam, turning the lathe, or cooking over-easy eggs—practice was required for progress. We rarely did anything right the first time.

The concept of practice didn't end with childhood. Summer is the season for practice.

Farmers are masters of certain skills that they have learned through years of practice—driving the tractor through straight rows so as not to damage the plants, irrigating fields for an even application of water to every plant, pulling ditches, training vines, spraying trees. The processes occur again and again, year after year. The same is true for the good habits we desire to adopt in every area of our lives.

A good family relationship doesn't occur after just one evening of conversation around the barbecue pit.

In nearly all cases, a successful career comprises more than one project . . . or one hit song . . . or one best-seller.

Fitness of body requires regular exercise and a habit of good nutrition. (It's amazing to me how long it takes to get in shape compared to how quickly one can fall out of shape!)

Repeated work, repeated effort, and repeated actions become habits. There's really no shortcut.

Mental practice counts, too.

In conjunction with the 1984 Olympic Games in Los Angeles, sprinters were tested using sophisticated biofeedback equipment. Medical instruments were attached to the athletes' bodies in such a way that the activity of their muscles was measured and recorded both on and off the track. The results were nothing short of amazing. When the runners raced in their minds, their muscles contracted and expanded in the exact sequence as if they were physically running on the track.

By disciplining your mind to perform a task, you are developing the physiological patterns that will be used when you actually perform the task.

First, of course, you must learn the correct methods and form. There's no point in practicing something incorrectly. The Olympic runners tested in the study had been carefully coached through the years so that their form was not only picture perfect but maximally efficient and productive. They were rehearsing a perfect run. They knew what it felt like to run a good race. Their muscles were well trained to know how to enact the motion being imagined.

The important point to recognize is that the link is there between your ideas and behavior. Rehearse a good idea, and you develop a good physiological pattern for enacting that idea.

Let's consider a very practical example. Joe has a marketing presentation to make tomorrow morning. He knows what will be expected; he's made marketing presentations before—some more successfully than others. Tonight, Joe chooses to rehearse for his presentation in the morning rather than accept an invitation to go bowling. (That's self-discipline in action!) Joe recalls the very best presentation he's ever made. He recalls how he spoke, what he said, the feelings he had about himself, the message he was giving, and the audience seated before him. He sees his audience in his mind's eye. He envisions the room in which he will speak. He walks through every aspect of his presentation, even to picking up and setting down certain charts, overhead projections, and notes on the podium. He adopts the feelings of relaxing, confidence, and good humor that he felt during his most successful presentation in the past.

What are the chances that Joe will turn in a better performance in the morning for having rehearsed tonight?

Great!

In many ways, practice is like method acting, the technique made famous by Lee Strasberg. Actors who have trained in this method recall, or revisualize, a precise moment in their lives when they felt an emotion in its purest form—whether anger, sadness, or joy. They find that as they recall the past experience, they can re-create on cue the emotions they felt at that time. Master actors do not trust luck or the muses for a good performance. They become masters of emotional self-discipline. They practice emotions until they can portray them within seconds.

Henry David Thoreau said it this way: "What we do best or most perfectly is what we have most thoroughly learned by the longest practice, and at length it falls from us without our notice, as a leaf from a tree."

Practice may not make you perfect; it will make you many times better than you would be without it.

Perseverance Is Another Name for Summer

Overnight success is a myth. Only the lottery or a fairy godmother can grant you instant results. Every human being who has tried to accomplish something worthwhile has failed numerous times. It takes practice, patience, and persistence to build the experience needed for lasting success. This is true whether you are raising a family, learning a technical skill, closing a sale, operating heavy machinery, negotiating a business transaction, mastering a sport, or motivating people.

Anytime that you make a change in your life-style, you can anticipate a temporary drop in productivity and efficiency.

I have a friend who was a moderately successful tennis player in high school until the day he encountered a coach who taught him how to serve a tennis ball. Up to that point, he had been able to get the ball into the service court with a fairly high degree of accuracy and power—enough to win the majority of his tournaments. The coach pointed out to him, however, that his form was wrong. He would never be able to move into the ranks of A-level tennis unless he radically altered his style. Of the first hundred balls he served in practice with the new technique, only two made it across the net into the service court. The remainder slammed into the net, flew over the court, or sailed into the park next door, never to be found.

Over time, however, he became more accurate with the new technique. He was amazed to find that he had far greater power than ever before, even though he had always thought of himself as having a strong first serve. He found that he could more accurately place the ball. He also found that he was winning 90 percent of his tournaments, including a regional final.

A change meant temporary failure. Perseverance brought an even higher level of success.

Persevere in learning.

A true professional continues to learn about his profession all the days of his life. He is continually looking for the latest advance, the most recent information, the most up-to-date innovation or technique.

Are you aware that with your brain power—even if you consider yourself only of average intelligence—you have both the ability and the capacity to learn forty languages, memorize an entire set of encyclopedias from *A* to *Z,* complete the required courses at dozens of colleges, and still have used only a fraction of your ability to think, reason, and remember? If this is true, and reputable scientists have confirmed repeatedly that it is, why don't most people learn more and accomplish more in their lifetimes?

The foremost reason is that they don't continue to learn. They stop growing intellectually.

Sadly, they stop as a matter of their own choice. They think they know enough. They don't feel they are worth any more growth mentally. Some are afraid of moving "beyond" their peers. Most just settle for what will "get them by" in life.

Laziness is the number one reason we choose not to grow and develop intellectually. Studying is the only way to learn.

For many people, studying is classified in the same category as paying taxes or going to the dentist. It is something that people do not like to do and something many people will not do unless it's absolutely mandatory. The vast majority of people believe that graduation day signals the final day of studying in their lives.

The United States has the most abundant supply of free education materials in the world. The public and college libraries are bulging with enough data on every subject to make anyone who is willing to spend the equivalent of one-half hour per night both intelligent and successful.

The sad fact is that we simply do not invest in our mental

capability. We won't make the effort to study three hours a week —total.

The primary reason the Japanese are outstripping us as the top economic and scientific country in the world is that they place much higher priority on education and on a person's continuing education after formal schooling. They now produce 95 percent of the television sets viewed around the world—even though television is an American invention and the production of television sets is a market we used to corner—while a significant number of Americans spend up to 95 percent of their free time in front of the tube!

The Japanese are learning how to make the world go while we are watching the world go by.

The South Koreans, Taiwanese, Singaporeans, Malaysians, Thais, and Indonesians are standing in the wings, ready to take over from the Japanese. And the Chinese are eagerly rehearsing for their time on stage after years of pushing the plow for their shortsighted masters. The Chinese will certainly have a massive harvest for their efforts as their young people—more numerous than any other race or nation on earth—take advantage of the educational opportunities so long denied them.

Expect to get closer and closer to your goal over time.

You may not see your goal for most of the weeks during the summer season of your success. Are you aware that every sea captain who knows his next port of call usually cannot see his destination for fully 99 percent of his voyage? Nevertheless, he knows where he is going, and barring any unforeseen catastrophes, he feels confident he will reach his destination if he keeps sailing forward in that direction every day.

Expect to get better with age.

In our society, we seem to believe that life is for the young, sleek, smooth, and assertive. Older workers get little respect— except, of course, from those who work alongside them. Psychologists David Waldman and Bruce Avolio analyzed forty-three years of job performance studies on workers from eighteen to sixty-five years old—both professionals and semiskilled workers —and they found that how well people do at work depends on whom you ask and how you ask it.

If you ask a boss, older workers are frequently viewed as less productive than younger colleagues. Many times these bosses are young, and their opinions may reflect stereotypes they have learned. Ask the peers and colleagues of an older person, however, and the workers will tell you that the older workers are the most productive. Especially in manufacturing, older nonprofessionals actually produce more units per hour, delivering greater quantity and quality.

And finally . . .

Find strength in laughter.

One of the best antidotes for failure is laughter. Even when things aren't going your way, laugh!

I love to laugh—not at others' misfortunes—but at my ridiculous seriousness. I don't find contrived comedy routines or a stream of one-liners as funny as I find everyday life. I recall, for instance, the time when my skis won the ski jump competition, but I wasn't in them. I was upside down in a snowdrift right in front of the lodge in full view of an appreciative audience. They laughed. I joined them!

I remember when I was the keynote speaker for a United States congressional luncheon. A leading senator thought I was the maître d' and asked me for four rolls, butter, and a napkin. I was so flustered I went out and got them for him! We both got a good laugh out of it later.

I remember during the 1980s when I chartered a Lear jet to make a speaking engagement in Toronto in a driving snowstorm. In my business, there is no excuse for not showing up for work! At a cost of $5,000 for the plane, and after risking my life in the weather, I grabbed a cab from the airport. We slid down the highway into the city to the hotel where I was to speak to one thousand conventioneers.

There was just one problem. Not only was there no convention at the hotel, there was no hotel! It had been torn down six months earlier. The convention had moved to Vancouver, but somehow our office had missed the critical communication link.

The taxi driver thought it was the biggest hoot he had ever witnessed. As we drank hot chocolate back at the airport, waiting for the Lear jet to be refueled, the taxi driver said with a straight face, "Shouldn't you call your wife before you fly home? Maybe she moved, too!"

I remember when I had my white dinner jacket on for a formal reception and my golden retriever jumped through the open car window and gave me most of the mud that was covering his body. He monogrammed my jacket with his paw prints.

I remember a young college student coming up to me during one of my public rally speeches. He said, with a puzzling smile, "Hi, Dr. Waitley. You're a lot older in person than you are on your audiotapes!" I told him I had enrolled in a vocal cord fitness program to keep my speaking voice youthful and vital as my body withered away.

I remember when my five-year-old son came home from playing in the woodpile, smelling like a creature from the black lagoon. We had to put both him and his dog in a bathtub filled to the brim with tomato juice. A black-and-white kitty "shot" him.

I remember getting up on the roof after midnight on Christmas Eve, trying to make a noise that would sound like Santa's eight tiny reindeer. Unfortunately, I fell off the roof into the oleander bushes next to the house, yelling like Santa never did.

I remember during the movie *Earthquake*—which was shown in a theater in our town with full stereo "sense-surround"—the two elderly ladies who got up and changed their seats during the realistic-sounding rumble at the high action point of the film. One of them whispered to the other that she thought she saw a large crack beginning to appear in the theater floor under her seat. I was laughing so hard I missed the part where Ava Gardner died.

And each time I remember, I laugh.

I am thoroughly convinced that you and I will never grow old mentally and emotionally as long as we can laugh at ourselves and see the wonder of life as a child sees it. Don't take yourself too seriously during the summer season of cultivation. Chase an occasional butterfly. Dodge an angry honeybee, whose work you have interrupted. See the season for the delightful time it is. If you keep your head buried in a furrow, you won't know the joy it is to look out over the entire field before you and relish a feeling of accomplishment that the field is green and flourishing.

14

The Season for Establishing Relationships

Very few farmers in the world believe that they farm alone.

They know that without the assistance of other specialized agricultural experts, their yields would be far lower and their problems far greater.

Summer is a season for cultivating relationships even as you do the work necessary for growing success.

In summer, have a mind-set that you are going to better the lives of every person who works in your specific "field" alongside you. The more you help others who are working alongside you in your field of success, the faster you will get to your goals.

What can you do for others?

On a stormy night many years ago, an elderly couple entered a hotel lobby and asked for a room.

"I'm very sorry," responded the night clerk. "We are completely full with a convention group. Normally, I would send you to another hotel that we use for our overflow in situations like this, but I know they, too, are full."

He paused for a moment and then went on, "On a night like tonight, I can't imagine sending you out in this weather again. It may not be a luxury suite, but you can stay in my room. It's clean, and I'll stay here and finish up some book work in the office since the regular night auditor won't be coming in."

The distinguished-looking man and woman appeared uncomfortable at inconveniencing the clerk in this way but graciously accepted his offer of hospitality. When the man came down to pay his bill the next morning, the clerk was still at the desk. He said, "Oh, there will be no charge for the room. I live here full-time so I can put in as many hours as possible to earn a little extra. The room is already taken care of."

The older man said, "You're the kind of person every hotel owner dreams of having as an employee. Maybe someday I'll build a hotel for you."

The young hotel clerk was flattered, but the idea sounded so outrageous that he chuckled at the elderly man's joke after the couple had departed.

A few years passed, and one day the hotel clerk, still at the same job and place, received a registered letter from the elderly man. His comments reflected his vivid recollection of that stormy night. He invited the hotel clerk to visit him in New York and enclosed a round-trip ticket in the letter.

Arriving a few days later in Manhattan, the clerk was met by his admirer at the corner of Fifth Avenue and Thirty-Fourth Street where a magnificent new building stood.

"That," explained the elderly man, "is the hotel I have built for you to run. I told you at the time it might happen."

"You can't be serious," said the clerk. "What's the catch! Why me? Who are you anyway?" stammered the flustered young man.

The gentleman smiled, "My name is William Waldorf Astor. And there's no catch. You are the person I want to run this hotel."

That hotel was the original Waldorf-Astoria, and the young clerk who accepted the first managerial position was George C. Boldt.

No matter what endeavor you are working on—a personal goal, a financial goal, a career goal, a community goal—set yourself the ideal of helping as many people as possible to win.

If your employees win . . . you do, too. The employee who feels rewarded adequately and praised whenever possible is an employee who feels as if he or she is growing and developing. The employee who sees a boss or supervisor doing everything possible to meet his or her personal needs—from assistance during family tragedies to the establishment of an in-plant day-care facility—is an employee who is willing to give an extra effort. That extra effort directly results in increased productivity. It results also in an increase in the number of innovative ideas and suggestions that employees will be willing to make about how to improve efficiency, quality, and morale.

Consider the approach of Mo Siegel, one of the cofounders of Celestial Seasonings, a highly successful herbal tea manufacturing company in Colorado. I interviewed Siegel several years ago, and I still remember his four-pronged approach to success:

- *Develop the best possible product.* Said Siegel: "To me, it doesn't count how good our products are, but how good they can be. We constantly test our teas with thousands of people a year. We will not let anyone make a better cup of tea."
- *Love his customers and consumers.* (He used the term *customers* to refer to his distributors and *consumers* as the end-service buyers.) Siegel said, "We feel that if we can't sell benefits to the consumer, we shouldn't be in the business. We love to fill consumer needs and benefit people. We are getting over two hundred letters from consumers per week, telling us that we're on the right track."
- *Portray a love for art and beauty.* Siegel took pride in developing products that are packaged in boxes with four-color artwork.
- *Hold up the dignity of the individual.* Within his company, Siegel tried to meet that goal in several ways. Everyone is an owner at Celestial Seasonings through a stock ownership trust. Any worker on the production line has the power to pull a switch and bring the entire production to a halt if he thinks something is wrong. The company has also developed "venture" teams that work on new and innovative ideas— with rewards for those who contribute. Anyone in the company, at any level, can become part of a venture team. He said, "My people on the production line have the same dreams and aspirations that everybody else has. They think of things that are good for their families; they think of doing

something that is recognized, worthwhile. Their need for all this is no different than mine. Their need for a fair reward for a job well done is no different than mine."

Notice, if you will, the prevailing sense of *value* that Siegel has advocated for those with whom he works and does business. Mo Siegel is an executive who knows that he cannot till his garden of success by himself, and that his success is owing in part to those who work alongside him.

Celestial Seasonings has put its beliefs into written form. I believe these beliefs are among the best I've ever seen and, therefore, am happy to share them with you here:

Excellence. We believe that in order to make this world a better place in which to live, we must be totally dedicated to the endless quest for excellence in the important tasks which we endeavor to accomplish.

Our Products. We believe in marketing and selling healthful and naturally oriented products that nurture people's bodies and uplift their souls. Our products must be superior in quality, a good value, beautifully artistic, and philosophically inspiring.

Dignity of the Individual. We believe in the dignity of the individual, and we are totally committed to the fair, honest, kind, and professional treatment of all individuals and organizations with whom we work.

Our Employees. We believe that our employees develop a commitment to excellence when they are directly involved in the management of their areas of responsibility. This team effort maximizes quality results, minimizes costs, and allows our employees the opportunity to have authorship and integrity in their accomplishments, as well as sharing in the financial rewards of their individual and team efforts.

We believe in hiring above-average people who are willing to work for excellent results. In exchange, we are committed to the development of our good people by identifying, cultivating, training, rewarding, retaining, and promoting those individuals who are committed to moving our organization forward.

Our Environment. We believe in fostering an environment which promotes creativity and encourages possibility thinking throughout the organization. We plan our work to be satisfying, productive, and challenging. As such, we support an atmosphere which encourages intelligent risk-taking without the fear of failure.

Our Dream. Our role is to play an active part in making this world a better place by unselfishly serving the public. We believe we can have a significant impact on making people's lives happier and healthier through their use of our products. By dedicating our total resources to this dream, everyone profits: our customers, consumers, employees, and shareholders.*

Siegel obviously believes that if a company concentrates on helping its employees fulfill their needs for dignity, everyone will do very well.

If other members of your family win . . . you do, too. Take, for example, the situation in which a child is encouraged to dream of college, to set a goal of earning a scholarship, and to build a plan for putting herself into position to win a scholarship. The winning of that scholarship helps the child, to be sure. It also helps the entire family! Money that would have been spent toward tuition can be channeled toward other goals.

If your community wins . . . you do, too. When you work for programs that improve your community, you improve your life. Crime rates drop. Property values increase. Neighbors stay and care. Relationships develop around mutually pursued community goals.

You can take the same philosophies and put them to work in all other areas of life, too.

Can you see how you might involve those in your family as members of a venture team that comes up with new beneficial ideas for promoting your family unity, communication, and health?

Can you see how the concept of dignity might pervade your community goals?

Can you see how a commitment to excellence can be applied to every one of your goals?

---

* From Celestial Seasonings Beliefs statement. Copy provided by Mo Siegel, CEO and founder, 1985; reprinted with permission.

Summer Is the Season for Delegating Responsibility

As you work alongside various groups of others in your summertime field, you will face the challenge of delegating responsibility.

One of the most common words you will hear from people who grew up on a farm is this: *chores*. It seems every child has one or more. A chore is more than a task; it is a responsibility. The cows don't get milked if Jerry doesn't milk them. The summer squash doesn't get picked from the garden if Julie doesn't pick it. The laundry doesn't get hung on the line unless Molly does the hanging. The pigs don't get slopped unless Marv takes care of it.

Delegating responsibility is a major challenge you will face as your success grows and begins to take shape. Although you may be able to do it all in the beginning, the time will come in the growth of your success when you will need to delegate responsibility for at least one aspect of your business, your life, your career development, your community involvement, to someone else.

Summer Is the Season for Maximizing Your Communication Skills

A great joy of working is the opportunity to be with other people. Friendships with fellow workers make work flow more smoothly and productively. Getting to know customers or clients better usually results in more enjoyment in the working process. What is the key to a good working relationship? Communication.

Conversely, nothing diminishes the joy of working more than poor professional relationships or relationships in which communication is at a deadlock. One of the major complaints heard in offices and families across our land is, "We had a breakdown in communication."

Perhaps more than any other season, summer is the time for maximizing your communication skills. You need to hear what others are saying to have the feedback you need to make midcourse corrections in your plans, to recognize opportunities for what they are, and to evaluate the growth of your success field.

You need creative ideas and information from others to fertilize your ideas.

You need encouraging conversations with others to help you persevere, maintain your self-discipline, and remain enthusiastic about your goals and dreams.

Successful people know the value of sound communication skills.

Cultivate the art of listening.

Perhaps the most overlooked communication skill is that of listening. An old adage asserts, "God gave you two ears and only one mouth. Do you suppose He intended for you to listen twice as much as you speak?"

A great deal can be gained by following just that principle.

Conversations very often fall into a pattern of two people taking turns talking. One person's words may rarely relate to what the other person is saying. This happens frequently in business transactions. Both parties tend to be more concerned with manifesting power—practicing one-upmanship, impressing, winning—than with expressing and reaching a consensus. Furthermore, nothing ends a transaction more abruptly than one person showing indifference, boredom, or irritation when someone else is talking.

Poor listening skills on the part of a supervisor or boss readily result in

- reduced productivity. Employees feel that nobody really cares about them, and they translate that into a lack of care about the work they are doing, the widgets they are manufacturing, or the services they are rendering.
- high employee turnover. People don't want to work in a place where they don't feel valued. Everybody wants an honest, genuine opportunity to be heard.
- high absenteeism. People who feel as if they are voiceless cogs in the wheel don't care whether they show up or not.
- retaliation. Often a person feels that he just might be heard if he talks louder or takes actions that will force another person to listen. That can result in damage to property as well as to morale, not to mention disruption of the flow of work.
- unresolved issues. The person who isn't heard remains a per-

son who is festering inside. The problems he needs to air don't get aired, and therefore, they can't be solved.

Many people spend a hundred dollars an hour or more for a session with a psychiatrist or psychologist. The foremost reason for the majority of these visits? They have no one else who will truly listen to them!

Listening is a way to get another person's attention.

Let's assume for a moment that you desire to get another person's attention so that you can tell her about your service, a new product you've developed, or a new item you've invented. You need for her to listen to you. What's the best approach to take?

Listen to her! The biggest mistake most individuals make in communication is choosing to talk about their three favorite people: Me, Myself, and I. They are totally absorbed with: "What *I* want to say . . ."; "What *I* want to do . . ."; "What *I* want to sell . . ."; and most important, "What *I* want you to do for *me* . . ."

Turn the tables around. Place your attention on the other person. Ask, "What are *your* needs?"; "How can I help *you?*"; "What can I provide for *you* and *your* company?"

Listen closely to the answers. Zero in on her number one need, and suggest ways you might fill it. Let her feel as if she is in charge of the decision. You aren't selling her as much as you are making yourself available for her to use your abilities, draw from your advice, or buy from you.

Do you want to develop a relationship with a person? Talk about people, places, and things that are important to him.

You'll make more friends in twenty minutes of showing you are interested in another person than in twenty weeks of trying to impress that person with how interesting you are.

Above all, strive for accuracy.

Stressful communication hinges on the concept of agreement. For me to feel as if I've communicated well with you, or for you to feel that you've communicated well with me, we both must feel that we are on the same wavelength. It's a "you know that I know that you know that I know" proposition. The idea that I have in my mind is the one I trust you will have in your mind—as accurate in detail as possible.

As you work hard to achieve your goals during the summer season, you need to be able to communicate your needs, desires, and opinions to others as precisely, effectively, and efficiently as possible. You need to be able to state what you want others to do and how you want others to respond to avoid errors.

Many farmers in the central California valley order water by the acre foot. An acre foot of water is the amount of water that it takes to cover one acre of ground with twelve inches of water. Water is "owned" and regulated by water companies, who manage the dams and canal systems that carry water from the High Sierras and the mountains of northern California down to their area. Farmers arrange for water and order its delivery several days in advance.

Can you imagine this conversation?

"I need you to turn on the water."

"How much do you need?"

"Oh, I dunno. Just turn it on, and I'll tell you when to stop."

"But what if you have sufficient at 2:00 A.M.? We won't be here to get your call. You'll have too much water, and your reservoir will overflow or your crops will drown."

"Well, give me just a little then."

"How much is a little?"

"Well . . ."

You can see that such a conversation goes nowhere and accomplishes nothing. A farmer must calculate precisely what he needs and communicate it accurately.

The same holds true for all who are in the process of working their plans during the summer season of success. You need to be able to express to others

- where you are going.
- what you are doing.
- what you have to offer.
- what information you have that others don't.
- what you are hoping to accomplish.
- what methods you are using that are innovative or original.

Above all, you need to communicate your advantages. Position yourself uniquely in the market—as the best candidate for the post, the best consultant available, the best widget salesman with whom to do business (mainly because you have the best widget to sell), the best current statistics available, the best suitor, the best spouse, the best customer, and so forth.

Here are some tips for achieving better communication in the summer season:

1. Use precise language. Don't use vague generalities. Use facts, accurate figures, dates and times, and precise quotes in your communication of an idea. Be specific.

2. Use words that the other person understands. Don't speak "educationese" or "professionalese" to people unfamiliar with the jargon of your field. Talk in plain English, using concrete nouns, active verbs, and simple analogies that are readily understood. Don't overwhelm a person with your vocabulary. That's not communication; that's a show.

3. Ask for feedback from the other person. Ask, "Does this make sense to you?" "How do you see it?" "What's your interpretation or understanding of this?" "What conclusion do you draw?" Listen closely.

4. Use the person's name in your conversation. One of the most important tributes you can pay another person is to remember his or her name. If you don't catch the name during an introduction, ask, "Could you repeat your name for me? I'm glad to meet you, and I want to be able to remember your name accurately." If you have difficulty remembering names, set yourself a goal of improving your memory in this area. A number of books, techniques, and courses are available to help you develop your memory as a whole, including remembering names and faces. Avail yourself of the opportunity to grow in this area.

Then when you speak to the person, include the name periodically in your conversation: "Thanks for your opinion, Bill." "What do you think, Jane?" "How's it going, George?" "It's been good talking with you, Betty."

5. Make eye contact. When someone else is talking, look directly in his eyes. You'll learn more! Eye contact also communicates to the other person that you are both confident and interested in what he is saying.

6. Go into a conversation with the attitude, "I'm going to make this person happy she talked with me." Be generous in giving genuine compliments or praising the achievements of the other person. Help draw out the other person with questions.

7. Introduce yourself at the beginning of a phone conversation or in making a personal visit. Do so with a firm handshake if you are speaking to the person face-to-face. Say, "I'm happy to meet you. My name is _____." Or say, "Hello, this is _____ speaking." You may want, or need, to remind the person of your last conversation or a previous encounter. If you are calling on behalf of a company, state its name very directly and slowly. Nothing can be more disconcerting than to have a person say several minutes into a conversation, "Who is this?" or "What company did you say you're representing?"

8. Speak positively about projects and other people. Negativism not only drags people down, it grinds conversation to a halt and is unproductive to reaching conclusions, making decisions, propelling ideas forward, or energizing projects. Don't complain or gripe, even if you feel you have cause. Above all, don't gossip about others whom you both know. The person with whom you are talking will wonder later, "What is he saying about me?" or "What rumors might she be spreading about me?" Don't repeat information shared with you in confidence. Be discreet.

9. Make certain that you understand what the other person is saying. If you aren't sure you understand a directive or a concept, ask clarifying questions. Say, "If I'm hearing you correctly, you would like . . ."

10. Don't waste the other person's time. Don't drag on a meeting, appointment, or encounter with the thought that if you spend more time in the person's presence, he will think better of you. The exact opposite may be true! In business encounters, state what you need to state, get the information you need to get, make the suggestions you have to offer, and be prepared to leave.

11. Treat the other person with respect. See the other person as a brother or sister, not as an object and certainly not as a sex object. Neither worship nor degrade the person. Respect the humanity and the boundaries. Be courteous and polite—no matter where the person is on the corporate ladder. Don't order people around. State your requests in terms of "please" and "thank you."

12. Put yourself in the other person's shoes. Empathize. Try to see the world from his vantage point. Ask yourself, How would I like working for me? How does my supervisor like my performance? How would I like being married to me?

Take full responsibility for the success of the communication process. As a listener, take full responsibility for hearing what others are saying. As a talker, take full responsibility for being certain that others understand you. Never meet anyone halfway in your relationships or your communication. Give 100 percent.

Good communication is a must if you are going to engage in one of summer's most important activities . . . negotiation.

Summer Is the Season for Negotiation

The art of negotiation belongs to those who have mastered the skills of effective communication. If you find yourself on the losing side of negotiations, back up and evaluate your communication skills.

The best negotiators are truly able to put themselves in another person's shoes. Bullies make the poorest communicators, primarily because they see only their own point of view.

In addition to communication skills, you must have a general attitude of cooperation before you will succeed in negotiations. Skills in communication are something that only *you* can improve and enact. An attitude of cooperation is something that only *you* can choose to have.

Negotiation requires vulnerability.

Psychiatrist Bernard Holland has pointed out that although juvenile delinquents appear to be very independent, have a reputation as braggarts, and strongly denounce authority, underneath their hard exterior shell, they are often very soft, vulnerable, quiet people who want to be dependent upon others. What keeps them from doing so? Fear. They are afraid of being hurt—very often because they have already been hurt one or more times in their lives and they felt that wound more deeply because they were sensitive in nature. The defensive posture they adopt is one rooted and grounded in fear.

Many people are hurt. A good negotiator must recognize this without exploiting it. Do what you can to allay the fears of another person.

Negotiation requires empathy.

Negotiation also requires empathy. A woman took her five-year-old son to a large department store. It was near Christmas, and the store was packed with people. She thought it would be fun for him to see all the decorations, window displays, and toys, and have a visit with Santa Claus. As she dragged him by the hand, about twice as fast as his little legs could move, he began to fuss and cry, clinging to his mother's coat. She said, "Good heavens, what on earth is the matter with you? I brought you with me to get in the Christmas spirit. Santa doesn't bring toys to little crybabies."

She finally looked down and realized her young son's shoelaces were untied. "Maybe you're upset because your shoes are untied," she said, kneeling down in the aisle to tie his shoes. As she knelt, she looked up. For the first time, she saw the department store through the eyes of her child. From that position one could see no baubles, bangles, beads, presents, gaily decorated display tables, animated toys, or decorations. All one could see were huge posteriors and giant stovepipe legs—all jostling and rushing and crushing. The scene was terrifying!

Empathy often requires little more than kindness and a willingness to recognize the pressures that another person is under.

Ronnie L. found the TWA ticket office in midtown Manhattan to be crowded with travelers as she made her way through the revolving doors from the sticky 95° summer heat outside. She then waited in line behind a chain-smoking, somewhat overweight man who became more and more agitated during the wait. When he finally began to converse with the agent behind the counter, he barked out commands with such a loud voice that the entire travel office looked up to see what was going on. He wanted his flight now. He wanted it cheaper. He couldn't understand why first class was sold out. On and on. The woman behind the counter looked as if she could burst into tears at any time if she didn't strangle him first.

At last the man stomped away. Ronnie knew she needed to arrange a rather complex flight schedule with several stopovers, and it would take both time and effort on the part of the reservations clerk. She paused for a moment until the agent asked curtly, "Yes?"

"You look as though you've had a very tiring day," Ronnie said.

The clerk looked up at her. That was the first time someone had actually paid attention to her as a human being rather than an extension of her computer. "Why, yes, I have, actually. We've been swamped. And I've got a summer cold. I feel really miserable, and the air conditioning in here is freezing."

Ronnie commiserated with the clerk and empathized with her condition. "In spite of all that," she said, "you seem to be handling the situation very well. That last customer was particularly difficult, yet you dealt with him very professionally. What a great skill to have."

The clerk smiled, "Oh, he wasn't so bad. We all try to do a good job. Now, how can I help you?"

Ronnie got the flights she wanted at the lowest possible fare. She also got a surge of joy at feeling that she'd helped turn around another person's day. The clerk also felt rewarded and had the satisfaction that she had helped a customer.

Anticipate the other person's position.

Before you enter a negotiation, anticipate the points that the other person will bring up. Mentally rehearse the encounter. Abraham Lincoln gave this advice: "When I'm getting ready to reason with a man, I spend one-third of my time thinking about myself and what I'm going to say—and two-thirds thinking about him and what he is going to say."

· What are the grievances of the other person?
· Which of them may be valid?
· Do you truly want to be in a cooperative relationship with this person or this company?
· Do you want to find middle ground on which you both can live peacefully?

Imagine the farmer in a border dispute. Perhaps he sees his land overlapping that of his neighbors by just a few feet. How would you go about preparing for a negotiation? Several conclusions are possible.

You might both avoid the area—leaving it barren and unproductive. (That, of course, is a waste of good soil.)

You might farm the area in turns—one cultivating it as a part of his field one year, the other person the next season.

You might call in the surveyors and settle the issue decisively based on facts.

You might split the difference, and each farm get half the disputed area.

Virtually all of these solutions will work. Which one brings greatest benefit to both farmers in your opinion? Which one results in a good ongoing relationship between the farmers?

There is more than one solution.

Go into a negotiation realizing that more than one solution is possible. In fact, several solutions are likely to resolve the issue. Aim for the one that brings the greatest "win" to both parties. If both people walk away from the negotiation feeling positive about the future and about the person on the other side of the table, progress has truly been made!

Avoid insults and affronts.

Avoid emotionally charged accusations.

Be prepared to give as much as you receive.

Choose to respect the other person, who has ideas, opinions, motivations, reasons, hurts, past experiences, goals, and dreams. They are not necessarily invalid just because they have collided with yours.

Consider your negotiation to be a triangle, with each side being equal. You are at one point. Your boss, client, spouse, associate, or competitor is at another point. Find a mutually agreed upon third point to balance your negotiations. It may be your children, the people who work in both companies, the community, the work load.

Make an agreement to work together to reach a decision that will benefit all three parties equally—you, the other person, and the mutually recognized third party or issue.

Here are several additional points to consider as you negotiate during your summer season of success:

1. Stick to the subject. Don't wander to stray issues. Don't bring up issues from the past unless they directly relate to the current situation.

2. Avoid absolute words and phrases. Don't use words such as *never, always,* or *typical behavior.*

3. Don't feel that you need to destroy the other person to reach a satisfactory conclusion to the problem. Work for a win-win result.

4. Avoid sarcasm, insults, and phrases that intimidate. There's no point in bloodying your opponent or the person with whom you are trying to reach consensus. Anyone in emotional pain will be less inclined to pursue a line of reasonable and conciliatory negotiation.

5. Don't allow any insults hurled at you to lodge in your mind. Let them fly right on by. Keep your cool. Don't take all of the comments you hear personally.

6. Be prepared to give some concessions. Negotiation is a give-and-take game. Recognize going into a negotiation that you won't get everything you want. Prioritize what you hope to gain. Analyze what you can live with and what you can't live without.

7. Don't give away something absolutely essential to you. Have a bottom line beyond which you cannot be moved, especially when a negotiation involves behavior that nudges up against your most basic values. If you give beyond the point of your value system, you will walk away with a bitter taste in your mouth. That will lead only to a deep inner frustration that can lead to disease, depression, or destructive behavior.

8. Periodically pause to reflect on the process. Take time periodically in the negotiation to draw closure and to reflect on what you have just agreed to. Make sure you both have a clear understanding of what you are saying and preparing to do.

9. Project your decision into the future. Spend a portion of your time discussing what the consequences will be if you don't solve the problem now, reach consensus now, or make decisions now. Play out various scenarios. What might be the consequences of various decisions and plans?

10. Keep an open, positive mind. Be willing to learn something. Be willing to grow. See the positive result that might come from your negotiation. In fact, stay firmly focused on it!

Recognize, always, in your negotiations that there is no such thing as winning an argument—only winning an AGREEMENT.

Negotiation is a two-letter word: WE.

Agreements are essential if you are to have others working successfully alongside you in the field of your success. Keep the idea at the forefront of your mind that you cannot achieve the success you want by yourself. You can't realize your dreams totally on your own. You can't reach your goals totally by yourself. You can't work your plan in isolation from others.

If you are selling a product . . . you must have a customer. You will certainly have a competitor. You're likely to have an employer (or stockholders). And as you become successful, you are likely to have employees to supervise. Your product will affect your community. Your job will have an impact on your family. And you'll eventually need to be in touch with, or be aware of, the vendors who produce the raw components for your product.

If you are working toward a goal of greater community service . . . you'll be in contact with those you serve . . . those who are working alongside you . . . and those who control funds or resources that you need to tap. You may run directly into others who have opposing political or social agendas. You'll likely be in competition with others who are seeking to draw from the same sources of funding you are tapping.

If you are cultivating a field of improved family relationships . . . each person in your family is someone with whom you will be in near constant negotiation—whether it's who gets to use the shower first or who gets to control the family budget.

The principles are equally true—

Nobody can grow your garden of success but you.

You can't grow a successful garden on your own.

Negotiation is a must. Agreements are the bases for moving forward toward reaching your goals.

The Big Three for Good "Field" Morale

Delegating.
Communicating.
Negotiating.

Acquiring these big three skills is a must if you are to arrive in autumn with happy workers willing to give extra effort to gleaning the harvest . . . *and* if you are to enjoy the summertime work season together!

Don't downplay their value. They are of utmost importance to your success.

15

The Season for Optimism

How do you stay up during the long, hot summer season?
How do you keep going?
Where do you find the motivation for persevering?
Where do you find the inner strength to develop self-discipline when times are tough, the hours are long, the work is intense, the summer work is before you?
The cool, soothing "waters" bubbling forth for the summer season are to be found in one word: *optimism*.

Water Your Growing Field with Optimism

Many people say, "I'm so exhausted by the daily grind of giving my best effort to developing new habits and cultivating new projects, how do you expect me to have enough energy to be enthusiastic, too?"

They are making an assumption that enthusiasm requires energy. The converse is more nearly true. Optimism yields energy.

Michael Scheier, from Carnegie-Mellon University in Pittsburgh, and Charles Carver, from the University of Miami, developed a scale for evaluating pessimism and optimism. The two then used the scale for evaluating the relationship between a person's attitude and his ability to cope with difficulties. They discovered that people with general optimism handled stress better, recovered faster following surgery, and were more successful in completing treatment for alcoholism.

In a study with college students, Scheier and Carver found optimistic students reported fewer symptoms of stress (such as muscle soreness, fatigue, dizziness, coughs) during final-exam week than did pessimistic students. Jay Hill, a Dartmouth College psychology professor, studied 160 students who were taking a test, and he found that optimists had a lower heart rate and blood pressure than pessimists.

When one evaluates these studies and many others that are similar, the conclusion is readily drawn: Optimists are more likely to obtain a good outcome than pessimists.

Positive thoughts alone, of course, don't make this happen. Optimists—because they believe for a good result—are more likely to find ways, try methods, and formulate plans of action that lead to good results. Pessimists, on the other hand, are more likely to work on coping with emotions related to a problem than to work at solving the problem itself.

Optimism can be a lifesaver—literally!

Physicians and psychiatrists now agree that most fatigue is of mental origin rather than physical dysfunction. Boredom, irritability, resentment, frustration, feelings of haste, anxiety, worry, futility, and tension are all emotions that leave you drained. They are emotions that snuff out energy and leave you bone tired.

Pep pills won't pick you up and keep you up for the duration of the summer season. Neither will sleeping twelve hours a night. To get energy, you've got to give out enthusiasm. It's the best thing that you can do to keep yourself "up and at 'em" during the long, hot months of summer.

How do you turn on enthusiasm when you feel lifeless? Here are some ideas to incorporate into your daily life:

1. Smile more: Scientists have discovered that the physical act of smiling actually relaxes facial tension while producing a subtle chemical change in your body. Put a smile in your voice, too.

2. Maintain good posture. Stand up straight, chest out, stomach in, shoulders back. You'll feel a lift to your spirit even as you improve your posture. Depressed, unconfident, cynical people tend to walk with a marked slump. Confident people stand tall, sit tall, and walk tall. Send a message to your mind, as well as to others, that you are capable of striding strongly into tomorrow. It actually takes no more energy to stand up straight, sit up straight, or walk tall than it does to slouch.

3. Speak in a clear, audible voice. Mumbling does not generate enthusiasm; it drains it. Very often a mumbler is asked to repeat himself. It takes twice the energy to say something twice!

4. Don't see tasks as interruptions; rather, see each task as a new activity. Let's suppose for a moment that the doorbell rings while you are in the middle of mixing a cake or typing a memo. Don't sigh in disgust that you have been interrupted. Consider the ringing doorbell to be a separate task awaiting your quality response. Go to the door with confidence and a smile on your face, looking for what opportunity may be there. Even if it's a person selling something that you don't desire to buy, count it an opportunity to give that person an encouraging word that will keep him motivated to continue his quest for success. Return to your cake or your memo as if you are coming to a new task. See it with fresh eyes.

5. Avoid clock watching. If you are feeling under the pressure of a deadline, don't look at the clock every few minutes. You'll only add to the tension, and your enthusiasm will drain away from you; the time will seem to go by much faster than you want it to. If you are feeling bored, looking at the clock several times an hour will also drain your enthusiasm and make you feel frustrated; time will seem to stand still. The truth of the matter is that the clock is ticking at the same speed in both instances. It's your concept of time that is resulting in tension. Focus, instead, on the task at hand. Give it your concentration, and let time take care of itself. You'll find it much easier to stay enthused about the job in front of you.

6. Look for the creative twist. If you are facing a task that is dull or repetitious, find a way to make it interesting. Make your work a game. Try to surpass a self-imposed quota; attempt to do each portion of the task with greater skill; use your imagination to set up a scenario that may be light years away from the present moment. Choose to enjoy your work by seeing it in a new light.

The comic strip "Calvin and Hobbes," by Bill Watterson, provides wonderful examples of how a young boy uses his imagination to turn everything from undesirable foods (as far as he is concerned) and difficult school situations into far-reaching fantasies in which he is always the superhero. We could all use a little more of the Calvin spirit when it comes to our routine chores.

Are you running for exercise? Imagine yourself in the New York City Marathon entering Central Park ahead of the pack.

Are you washing the car? Imagine that you are preparing your car for the Indianapolis 500.

Are you tallying the figures from last month's sales? Imagine earning the salesperson of the year award at the national convention.

7. Think and speak well of your health. Don't dwell on your ailments, or they will reward you by staying with you longer and visiting your house more often. Focus on your well-being and the well family.

8. Read, listen to, and watch the news for "need to know" information in improving your professional and personal growth. Resist the temptation to waste time and pollute your mind with the sordid details of someone else's tragedies. You'll become jaded and cynical if you get hooked on tabloid exposés.

9. Select more friends and associates who are optimists. The mutual attraction should not be the sharing of common problems as much as the sharing of solutions and goals.

10. Learn to stay relaxed and friendly. No matter how much pressure you're under, be constructively helpful.

11. Greet others with a hearty hello. Give enthusiasm to others, even if you don't feel much energy in yourself. The more you attempt to lift up others and praise their work, the more you'll feel energized. Try it!

12. Sing! In the shower. In your car on the way to work. (You may get a few weird stares but only from sour grumps. Others will actually smile and may begin to sing themselves!) Sing at the top of your lungs. You'll be amazed at how your attitude changes the longer you keep the melody flowing! You'll come away energized.

13. Concentrate on a joyful thought before you go to sleep. Don't attempt to go to sleep imagining the worst-case scenario, dwelling on the tragedies of the day, worrying about what may happen a year from now, or concentrating on a mistake in the past. Make your last conscious thought of the day a joyful one. Your dreams will be more pleasant, and you'll awaken more refreshed.

The wonderful thing about enthusiasm is that it's infectious. Your enthusiasm will rub off on others. In turn, their enthusiasm will influence you. Get a cycle of enthusiasm started in the place where you work, the place where you work out, and the place where you rest from your work.

Seek to develop a family that's enthusiastic, a company department that's enthusiastic, a team that's enthusiastic, an entire corporation that's enthusiastic!

The more enthusiasm builds around you, the easier it is to maintain a personal level of high optimism.

Summer Is the Season for Applying Positive Self-Talk to Your Field of Success

When the hot rays of discouragement and the long hours begin to deplete your field of the nutrients it needs, it's time for positive self-talk.

Self-talk is an extension of your goal statements. Summer is the season for revising those statements to put them in the present tense.

Perhaps your goal was "I will establish a regular and enjoyable habit of jogging three miles a day."

Summer is the time for restating that goal—again writing it on an index card that you can carry with you everywhere. Say on it: "I enjoy jogging three miles every day."

Perhaps your goal was "I will gain control of my habits and quit smoking."

Summer is the time for rewriting that goal onto a card that reads, "I am enjoying the control I feel and am delighted that I am not smoking today."

Perhaps your goal was to "be more patient and loving with my children."

Rewrite your goal in the summertime of your success so that you are reading several times throughout the day: "I am patient and loving with my children today."

Again, as when you were making your initial goal statements . . .

1. Keep your statements personal. Rather than put, "A raise in salary is desirable" . . . write, "I am enjoying my job and am doing the high-quality work necessary to earn a raise."

2. Keep your self-talk in the present tense. Rather than say, "Someday I'll visit the Grand Canyon" . . . write, "I am inspired by the Grand Canyon." Rather than write, "I want to be the director of my department" . . . write, "I enjoy gaining the skills and the experience that I need to become director of this department."

3. Keep your goal statements short and concise. It shouldn't take you more than four or five seconds to say your goal. Don't write, "After I've saved five thousand dollars and have added an office to my house and have finished a course in computers, I hope to go into business for myself and grow that business into a major corporation." Instead, write, "My own business is beginning to take more shape each day."

4. State your goals positively. Rather than write, "I will lose 20 pounds by Christmas" . . . write, "I am on my way to being a slim, trim 125 pounds." Rather than say, "I won't be late for appointments" . . . write, "I enjoy arriving a few minutes early for my appointments."

5. Keep your goals noncompetitive, avoiding comparison with others. Rather than write, "I'll do a better job than she" . . . write, "I am doing the best I can at my job." Rather than write, "I'll drive him out of business" . . . write, "I'm doing what I know to do to develop a highly successful business." Instead of saying, "I'm the best sales executive in the company, making the most money" . . . write, "I'm having my best year, producing 20 percent more than last year."

Consult your cards several times a day. If you are carrying eight cards with you (one for each of the major goal areas of your life, as discussed in chapter 5), you should be able to voice your goal statements to yourself in under thirty seconds. That's the time of an average radio commercial!

Indeed, you might want to think of those self-talk times as commercial breaks in which you are selling yourself on *yourself!*

Create your own self-talk tape.

You may also want to make a cassette tape of some of your self-talk statements to play to yourself as you drive your automobile to work or perhaps as you sit back and relax in the quiet of your study at home. You don't need to go to a recording studio for this production. Simply take a blank tape and a portable cassette recorder, go to a quiet place, and record your positive statements about yourself as you envision yourself to be.

Here are some self-talk statements that I have recorded, in my own voice, to play back to myself in relaxed moments:

- My breathing is relaxed and effortless.
- My heartbeat is slow and regular.
- My muscles are relaxed and warm.
- I feel at peace.
- I'm aware that I am a unique and special person.
- I'd rather be me than anyone else in the world.
- Now is the best time to be alive.
- I give the best of myself in everything I undertake.
- I keep the commitment I make.
- I earn the respect of others.
- I give as much as I can to those around me.
- I am reaching my financial goals.
- I have a deep sense of joy.
- My world is opening and expanding.

- I see new opportunities each day.
- I take time to enjoy sunsets and flowers.
- I visit older people and enjoy being with them.
- I am gentle.
- I take time to play like a child.
- I am strong.
- I'm a winner.
- Today is the best day of my life thus far.
- I thank God for His many gifts to me.

And so forth! When you record your self-talk, which may be very different from my examples, speak in a normal voice level. Keep the statements short, only about four or five seconds long. Repeat them several times. With each repetition, speak with a different tone, such as soothing, affirming, commanding, inspiring.

You can listen to your tape even as you listen to relaxing music in the background. As you listen, you will be hearing your voice and forming a mental picture of yourself as the way you WANT to be. That's the most positive form of influence and motivation you will ever receive—hearing from *your* lips the image of *you* in the future.

Self-talk is a form of positive feedback.

The primary function of positive self-talk is to reinforce a positive self-image. A positive self-image, in turn, becomes the template against which positive action is drawn. In today's terms, a positive self-image is like the programming system for a personal computer. Software programs put into the system seem to run "automatically" because they are readable by the programming system. Conversely, the programming system makes the development and use of new software programs possible.

Your actions and your image of yourself are inextricably linked. They *cannot* be separated. You are what you do. You do what you are. As much as you might try to mask who you are or portray a certain image to the world, what you are will eventually reveal itself through what you do—the words you speak, the things you do, the activities in which you engage, the choices you make, the decisions you reach, the people with whom you align yourself, the work you produce. Equally true, the words you hear, the experiences you take into your life, the consequences of your choices, the work you pursue, the relationships you have—all create who you are.

Laboratory experiments have proved that our attitudes—the way we think and the way we desire to grow—can be put under our conscious control. They are not automatic givens unless we choose to let them be. With practice, a new set of attitudes can be developed that will result in an automatic unconscious reflex of behavior.

In other words, your attitudes will direct your behavior whether you recognize them as the source of your actions or not. The successful person recognizes the process and takes charge of it. He or she chooses to have attitudes that will yield positive behavior. Giving oneself positive feedback is a way of saying, "This is who you are. Therefore, act this way—make decisions based on this self-image, choose relationships in keeping with this self-image, make choices and decisions according to who you are, engage in work that is in keeping with the values and beliefs you hold. And in turn, reap all of the positive benefits of being this person."

If you continually project to yourself an image of yourself that says you are slovenly, lazy, and worthless, and you have no purpose in life, you'll act out that characterization. You'll BE that person and DO what a slovenly, lazy, low-self-esteem, directionless person will do.

On the other hand, if you project to yourself an image of yourself that says you are a winner—a person with value, purpose, direction, plans, goals, dreams, and a willingness to pursue your future with energy, ideas, and creativity—you'll BE that person. You'll begin to act as a person who not only aims at success but is successful. You'll work harder, create more, think faster, become more involved with others, and achieve goals.

Successful individuals tell themselves over and over again— with words, pictures, concepts, and emotions—that they are in the process of winning personal victories and achieving important life goals. When you are positive and constructive in your self-talk, your self-image expands. It grows to maturity.

When should you engage in positive self-talk?

It's especially important after each performance or project. Confirm to yourself that you have completed a task, and affirm to yourself that you are a doer, a person on the way to achieving your goals. Evaluate your performance, and applaud the things that you did well. Be aware of mistakes you made, but don't dwell on them. Use them as "instructional" feedback; see your mistakes as things not to do next time. In that way, you'll engage in positive, constructive self-evaluation—not negative, damaging, pull-you-down, destructive self-criticism.

Are you aware that you can literally talk yourself out of repeated successes by saying such things as, "Oh, I was just lucky," or "Wasn't that a fluke?" or "I'm amazed I could do that"? Don't discount your ability. Don't attribute your achievement to an external circumstance. Don't give in to feelings that you don't have a "right" to win; that signifies a level of guilt, and unresolved guilt can be one of the most damaging of all feelings to the human personality. At the same time, don't become arrogant in assuming that you will always maintain and sustain the same high level of achievement in the future, as if it's an automatic given. Strike a balance. Recognize that you reached your goal and won the victory because of your effort, your well-developed skills, your experience, and your attitude. Enjoy winning. Realize that you need to continue to exert effort, develop your skills, add to your experience, and maintain a positive attitude to continue to grow and achieve.

I have observed many sales executives who earned more in a single month of brilliant performance than they did in the entire previous year. Too often they are not able to sustain the success. Some take a vacation. Others stay in the office doing busywork or misuse their time while in the field. The month following their top performance becomes a disaster. Then they relax and get back to work. In talking with them, I have found that many such salespeople feel that the lower level of performance is their norm. They weren't really expecting to be successful and certainly not to be successful on an ongoing basis.

Every now and then, I encounter a salesman or saleswoman who follows one month of outstanding achievement with another and yet another month. These men and women have succeeded in reinforcing their self-image and have internalized their desire for, their willingness to pursue, and their ability to accept success. They didn't write off one month of brilliant sales as a fluke or view it as something they didn't really deserve. Quite the contrary! They saw their one month of brilliant sales as the new norm they wanted to set for their lives. They saw a high sales record as something that was not only achievable but repeatable. These men and women say to themselves in self-talk, "I was salesperson of the month. I'll be salesperson of the year. This past month's success will someday be the number of my lowest month in the year, not my highest."

Self-talk helps you adjust your goals ever upward.

Self-talk isn't magical.

Self-talk is like more sunshine, peat moss, and water on a flower bed in early summer. It's the creation and development of an internal environment that yields external results.

Self-talk sounds like this:

- · "Thank you very much."
- · "I feel good about the result."
- · "That's more like it."
- · "Now we're getting somewhere."
- · "Keep going. You're even better than this effort."

To the person who has fallen short of a desired achievement, self-talk takes the form of encouragement and reinforces the possibility of achievement in the future:

- · "Next time I'll get it right."
- · "Let's review the situation and find a solution that will work even better."
- · "Let's roll up our sleeves and try again."

Almost without exception, the real achievers in business, family life, and any other activity have accepted their uniqueness, feel comfortable with their self-image, and are willing to know and accept their God-given traits, abilities, and personalities. As a result, they more readily affirm and encourage the accomplishments, traits, and abilities they see in others.

When you hold yourself in high regard, it's much easier to hold others in high regard.

When you are able to applaud yourself, it's much easier to applaud others.

When you see yourself as a winner, it's much easier to recognize and encourage others who win.

It's no surprise that such people naturally attract friends and supporters. Individuals who give to others from the security of positive reinforcement never stand alone. They are confident in who they are and what they're worth, and they are able to give unflinchingly of that confidence to others. They draw successful others to them like magnets and encourage others to come up to their level by affirming their abilities, desires, and victories.

In Summer . . . Take Time to Enjoy the Beauty of the Season

Don't become so busy living life that you don't take time to build one.

Don't become so busy living with a spouse that you don't take time to build a marriage.

Don't become so busy living with your children that you fail to raise up successful men or women.

Don't become so busy working at a job that you fail to build a career.

Are you aware that Olympic athletes practice and train physically and mentally for twelve hundred days, six days a week, up to twelve hours a day for a sporting event that on the average lasts less than three minutes?

Each of us is involved in an Olympic event of sorts. It's called life. It requires all of our energy, focus, and commitment to go for the gold medals. Still, every game I know has time-outs, seventh-inning stretches, or half-time breaks. Even individual events in the Olympics occur in rounds, trials, and related events that are subsets of competition with breaks for rest in between.

Constant focus is possible.

Constant exertion is not.

When should you take a break? When you see some of these telltale signs of stress:

- Insomnia and frequent sleep interruption
- An inability to concentrate
- Low productivity and poor decision-making skills
- A decline in sexual responsiveness and ability to perform
- Frequent headaches, backaches, muscle spasms, or tiredness
- Frequent indigestion, diarrhea, or urination
- Frequent colds or infections
- Cold hands, especially when coupled by shortness of breath

- Frequent accidents and minor injuries
- Chronically hostile or angry feelings
- A recognition that you are overly frustrated with minor annoyances
- Neglect of self—in terms of leisure, rest, exercise, or diet

Pace yourself.

Live to see your success.

As a first step, see a physician. Also learn self-relaxation techniques, including deep breathing and muscle relaxation exercises. Engage in contemplation. Learn what it truly means to relax with slow music and to spend time imagining and contemplating.

Take regular vacations. Exercise regularly. Spend time with friends and laugh with them!

Eat meals high in fiber and protein and low in fat, cholesterol, and sugar.

Above all, treat people the way you want to be treated. Choose to have a home filled with goodwill.

Don't let summer stress keep you from an autumn harvest.

Enjoy the beauty of the season along the way.

Let enthusiasm energize your efforts.

Look forward to harvest with eagerness and joy. The next season in your success is . . .

AUTUMN!

Final Words as the Summer Season of Your Success Draws to a Close . . .

Effort at maximum levels.
Evaluations continuous, resulting in adaptations.
Endurance as a fixed mind-set.
Established relationships, growing and joyous.
Enthusiasm—high!

It's time for an exciting, rewarding HARVEST of your success!

So get ready . . .

AUTUMN is coming!

Set for the Harvest

🍃 *Does your internal and external feedback tell you that your optimism for success is warranted?*

🍃 *Do your associates and loved ones concur that your efforts are ripe for rewards?*

🍃 *Have you anticipated unexpected roadblocks and changes in the market and made the necessary provisions and corrections?*

🍃 *Are you absolutely honest with yourself that you are reaching goals that you have set and ones that will benefit others around you?*

🍃 *If life were a Broadway play, would ticket sales and audience response match your own "gut feeling" that your play is a hit?*

🍃 *Are you excited about your progress?*

🍃 *Do you have plenty of "weedkiller" in store to curb the growth of envy, jealousy, and criticism that may accompany your success?*

🍃 *Can you handle success without being overly impressed with yourself?*

If your answers are yes, you are ready for AUTUMN.

Autumn

THE SEASON FORECAST

 To the unsuccessful person: Autumn is the time for natural harvest, for facing the end of one's job, career, or life. It is the time for dreading yet another winter. It is the time for watching the trees lose their leaves and feeling a sense of loss, the passing of time. Autumn is a wistful time for wishing things might have been different. Autumn brings a harvest of regret.

To the successful person: Autumn is the time for reaping the rewards of success! It is the season for enjoying the fullness of life—partaking of the harvest, sharing the harvest with others, and reinvesting and saving portions of the harvest for yet another season of growth. Autumn is the time for feeling a sense of accomplishment, for recognizing that life must be enjoyed as it is lived.

*To the successful person,
autumn is the fourth season
of an abundant success.*

16

The Season for Harvest

We look forward to harvest all year, each year.

That's when the crops are brought in.

There's food on the table and in the pantry.

The prevailing attitude is one of celebration.

Satisfaction and a sense of accomplishment permeate the atmosphere.

The backbreaking work has been done. The setbacks, the unforeseen obstacles, and hindering external forces have been conquered or overcome.

After a winter of dreaming, goal setting, and planning . . . a spring of tilling and planting . . . a summer of nurturing, cultivating, weeding, and tending . . . we are ready to reach those goals and move into our dreams.

One has a feeling of completion and accomplishment and, with that, joy.

The lesson of harvesttime is a simple one. Through goal setting, knowledge, hard work, and persistence, it is possible to get what you want out of life.

Can You Enjoy Your Harvest?

One of the foremost challenges of the autumn season of your success is to enjoy yourself once you have accomplished your goals.

Many executives with corner offices overlooking magnificent city skylines never seem to look out their windows. They remain caught up in a real game of monopoly, trying to figure out how much is enough and how to stay on top. I know several successful business executives who own fabulous homes in the country or near the ocean, but they go home only to eat and sleep. They rarely enjoy the views they have worked hard to have outside their windows.

Consider those who work six days a week to provide a better life for their children. Many work so long and hard at the task that they awaken to find that their children are gone and now have children of their own.

Others go for thirty years without taking a real vacation, only to discover that when they do go, they are no longer able to water ski, scuba dive, mountain climb, or hang glide—all of which they had hoped to be able to do once they reached their goals.

One can be so busy playing king of the mountain that he loses the sense of joy in climbing. For others, the mountains only seem to grow greater.

There's even a dark side to the Japanese economic miracle. As the undisputed world leader in consumer electronics, automobile quality, and many other high-tech industries, Japan has a per capita income among the highest in the world.

But what about the quality of life?

A popular Japanese song recites the days of the week as, "Monday, Monday, Tuesday, Wednesday, Thursday, Friday, Friday." This parody mocks the custom of working seven days a week with no real pleasure.

Rush hour traffic in Tokyo makes Los Angeles freeways look like open roads. Many who commute by car in Japan leave home at 5:00 A.M. and park in front of their offices, sleeping for an hour or so in their automobiles so they will have a parking space during the workday.

To compensate for all this stress, they have a new "pep-up" beverage called Regain. Its ingredients include caffeine, a nicotine derivative, and vitamin B_1. Take a sip and it's like having a cup of coffee, a cigarette, and a dose of vitamins all in one bottle.

The Japanese call their living conditions *manuke,* which means "we lack three things"—time, space, and private lives.

The secret of reaping the greatest benefits in the harvest season is to be able to enjoy the rewards you have earned.

Part of that ability must be cultivated during the spring and summer seasons. If you haven't learned to stop and smell the roses along the path of your journey, you aren't likely to stop and smell them once you arrive at your destination.

Three great tragedies are these:

- · Never to have a dream worth striving for.
- · Never to endure until you reach that dream.
- · Never to be able to experience the joy of your dream once it is in hand.

In the autumn of a professional career, the wise individual looks back and reflects, "I've enjoyed every mile and every day of the journey to this point." The unsuccessful individual bitterly complains, "I worked myself to the bone, and now I'm too tired and don't have enough time or money to enjoy the fruits of my labors. Is this all there is?"

Avoid the great harvest trap.

Perhaps the greatest failure of our time is to equate harvests—and success—solely with material possessions.

Success is a very personal thing. It is what you define it to be. Too often, we mold our ideas about success to fit the popular definition. We spend our time and effort, and invest our resources, in an attempt to gain the outward trappings of what we believe others will regard as success—the vehicles, mansions, adornments, memberships, and travel stickers. What is the meaning behind this posturing? Why try so hard to prove something to someone else, or even try to prove something to ourselves, with a display of toys, gadgets, bay windows, and luxuries?

The so-called me generation often glorifies and encourages a display of worldly goodies to a great extent because it views these accoutrements as saying to the world, "I've arrived." Actually, a concentration of status symbols is more likely to say to others that the owner may be slightly lacking in self-esteem. With the easy credit of our times and a plethora of plastic credit cards, almost anyone with a steady job can display a foreign sports car, a power boat, or a camper in the driveway—whether or not it is paid for.

Please do not misunderstand me. I am all for purchasing items of quality and fine workmanship because they endure and function properly and safely. But I see little point in purchasing items with high price tags simply because they are expensive or I might impress someone by wearing or displaying them. That's not how I define success.

Some of the most successful people in the world project a modest image. If they have a great deal of money, you wouldn't notice it by what they wear or drive. In fact, you will likely discover their wealth only when a worthy cause needs a sponsor. Even then, there's usually little fanfare.

The truly successful person projects by the unassuming way he lives, plays, and works with others that he has dreamed dreams, set goals, made plans . . . and met them.

The real harvesters of genuine success don't brag. They are neither blowhards nor showboats.

Value is something quite apart from price tag. The toys and trappings of affluence tell nothing about how important a person truly is. The true value of a person is measured by other scales: the integrity, generosity, contributions, and work of that person. The truly successful person inspires others to do more than they have thought possible of themselves.

Spend your life-force wisely.

One of the most meaningful relationships in my life has been my friendship with the late Dr. Hans Selye. Dr. Selye, who died in 1982, is the acknowledged father of the concept of stress. He believed that each of us has a stress savings account deposited in our bodies as our life-force. The object before us, in his terms, is to spend this account wisely over the longest time span possible.

The difference between a stress savings account and a normal bank account is that we cannot make any deposits into the life-force account. We can make only withdrawals. The reason that most people age at different rates, according to his theories, is that they spend at varying rates. Big spenders age more quickly.

What does it mean to be a big spender of one's life-force? To a great extent, it means to overreact to petty circumstances as if they were life-or-death matters. We frequently see that spending in progress on our freeways, in our airports, in our offices, in restaurants, and at home with our children.

Are you aware that more than 90 percent of our confrontations in life are with *imaginary* predators and demons? We aren't facing real enemies or real problems—only the fear of them or imagined projection of them. In other words, we define problems where none exist. As a result, we frequently choose to stew in our own juices and do battle with ourselves rather than flee the scene or fight the enemy. Emotionally upset individuals literally withdraw all of their energy reserves ahead of schedule and run out of life too soon.

Ask yourself today,

- How fast am I spending my life-force?
- On what am I spending it?
- Is this a good use of my energy?
- What happens if I do nothing in this circumstance?

In other words . . .

- Will the problem I'm perceiving go away or resolve itself without my action?

  If so, let it!
- Will this really matter fifty years from now?

  If not, question how much time and energy you should devote to it.
- Is this something that directly affects my value system about which I must take a stand to be true to myself?

  If so, fight on. If not, let the matter rest.
- Will anyone be hurt if I do nothing?

  Include yourself in that appraisal. Don't stand by and allow yourself or others to be wounded or put down. On the other hand, if there's no harm, consider it to be a "no foul" situation.
- Is this a nuisance or an issue?

  Nuisances can be ignored. Issues require action.

Harvest Is a Time for
People to Gather Together

We all look forward to the harvest season in part because that's usually a time of family togetherness.

Harvest requires all hands to be busy. Look at our farmer once again. Harvest is the time when farmers help one another to get the crops in before the weather changes and while the harvest is ripe.

The full push of work together usually erupts in joyful celebrations . . . together.

How sad it is when people arrive at their goals and look around only to find they are alone.

That won't happen if you modify your natural self-centeredness along the way. The more you accept others and value them, the more they will accept you and value you. The more you associate with others—both to give to them and to receive from them, freely and generously—the less likely you are to be isolated.

Loneliness bears its own stresses. One of Dr. Selye's wise observations is this: *"One of the most effective keys to living is to persuade others to share our natural desire for our own well-being."*

According to Dr. Selye, this can be accomplished only by making a constant effort to earn the respect and gratitude of our business associates, family members, community friends, and neighbors. Dr. Selye suggested that rather than attempt to accumulate money or power, we attempt to accumulate goodwill. This is possible only when we do things that will help our neighbors. Horde goodwill, Dr. Selye advised, and your house will be a storehouse of happiness. "Anyone can attract the curiosity and the attention of crowds," he believed, "but the blessing is to earn the trust and respect of one child."

On your way to success, have you made plans to

- grow friendships . . . not only bank accounts?
- grow good neighbors . . . not only an investment portfolio?
- grow relationships with those whom you would like to spend time when you retire . . . not only a retirement account?
- grow loving bonds with your family members . . . not only bonds from which to clip coupons?

If you are growing a life-style that is pleasing and inspiring to yourself, and if your efforts are setting a healthy example for those who look to you for guidance and encouragement, you are indeed becoming a wealthy person.

Please do not get a wrong impression about my opinions on financial success. I am very much in favor of becoming extremely financially successful, and I see nothing wrong with it. In fact, I believe that's what free enterprise is all about, and I'm grateful that I was born in and continue to live in a nation based on capitalism and the opportunity to own property, start a business, and prosper. I believe strongly that we should have the right to earn as much as we're willing to work for by providing products or services that benefit as many people as we can. The key, as far as I'm concerned, is to work, create, and provide for the BENEFIT of others—not to exploit them, cater to their fears, play on their insecurities, titillate their sexual perversions, or feed their obsessions.

Plant a service that actually improves the quality of others' lives.

Grow a garden of products that you would gladly share with your innocent young grandchildren.

Till a crop that improves the quality of life for others.

And you will reap a harvest that is both tangible and intangible.

Both are good. The intangible harvest will be the more valuable to you when you enter the autumn of your life and not only the autumn season of your success.

Wealth is a condition of being.

Having money is only one aspect of wealth. The concept of wealth again relates directly to value and to the definitions that you personally place on value.

To the sick person . . . wealth is health.

To the lonely person . . . wealth is someone to talk to and share life with.

To the estranged person . . . wealth is hearing words of love and forgiveness.

Some people with the Midas touch are impoverished in spirit and in happiness. Some people who can just barely put food on the table are filled with joy.

Harvest Is a Time for Pulling Out Any Remaining Weeds

Much of a farmer's efforts throughout the growing season is aimed at eliminating weeds from the field. Weeds soak up nutrients better directed toward plants that will bear fruit. Weeds can choke out, overshadow, or strangle fruit-bearing plants, vines, and even trees.

Have you witnessed the kudzu plants that are growing without restraint in many areas of our southern states? This rapidly growing vine is presently spreading without control, engulfing entire trees, fences, and buildings in its path—completely overtaking them to create near magical shapes of green in untilled fields.

Weeds—such as kudzu, which yields no positive by-product or fruit that I know of—destroy and kill.

In our lives, many activities soak up our time, energy, and resources and fail to bear lasting fruit. In many cases, they also destroy and kill. Harvest is the time to clear the field of the weeds as well as to bring in the fruit.

As far as I am concerned, real poverty lies in these weeds:

- Cruelty and abuse of others
- Dishonesty
- Insensitivity
- Gluttony
- Sloppiness or laziness of effort
- Anger
- Self-criticism
- Guilt

Just as important as gathering the rewards associated with our goals is eliminating the weeds that rob our lives of resources and destroy inner character.

Sort the grain.

One of the most famous stories in the New Testament deals with a farmer who grows both wheat and tares—a type of darnel grass in the Middle East that looks very much like the real thing in its formative stages. Even an experienced farmer is unable to tell the darnel grass from the good wheat in the early stages when pulling out the darnel would be possible. As the plants grow, the darnel intertwines its roots with those of the wheat. To pull out the darnel as the plants mature would then mean to pull out the good wheat along with it. The Old Testament advises to leave both alone to maturity . . . and then in the harvest to separate the wheat from the darnel. It is more than a matter of separating the plants. The grain of the darnel is mildly poisonous. It has a bitter taste and can result in nausea.

You may not be able to tell a weed from a good plant as you till your garden of success. They may look very similar to you until you near harvesttime. Eventually, however, you need to separate the weeds from the plants bearing good fruit. Otherwise, they will poison your success.

Let me give you a practical example. Let's assume that you have been given an assignment from the president of your company to put together a special team to undertake an important project. You target certain people within the company for your special task force—based on the skills they can bring to your area and their reputation for working hard, meeting deadlines on time, and generating quality ideas and contributions.

As the project develops, you note that a couple of your team members always seem to have a negative attitude. They seem to dwell continually on why certain things won't work, on the mistakes being made, and on the impossibility of getting so much done in so little time. Eventually, you feel as if you are driving the project with its hand brakes set.

Despite your conversations with them—intended to boost their morale, lift their spirits, and praise their work—these two people continue to drag down the group. Still, the deadline is approaching. You need the skills of these two individuals. You plow ahead. Tempers flare. Some voice concern; others threaten to quit. You realize that you should have dismissed the two negative thinkers on your team, but by now, you have no time left to bring new people up to speed. Somehow you hold it all together and arrive at your deadline with a finished project that receives high praise from the company president.

Success has been achieved. Rewards are harvested. Praise-laden memos, promotions, and pats on the back are distributed all around. You bask in the joy of a job well done.

The company president, impressed with your success, asks your team to take on a second challenge. He intimates that he'd like your team to become a special projects unit within the company. Now is the time to separate weeds from wheat. Now is the time to separate the poisonous grain from the good grain.

What can you do? Ask for permission to reorganize your team before undertaking the second task. Ask, further, for the privilege to do that prior to each new challenge assigned by the president!

At the end of each sport season, coaches and managers review their rosters, make changes, recruit new players, and retire jerseys.

At the end of a harvest season, a farmer checks over his equipment, retires some of it, and puts new equipment into next year's budget.

Harvest is a time for

· appraising all assets (as well as liabilities).
· objectively analyzing what worked and what didn't.
· making decisions about what to do with your harvest.

The Four Bins of Your Harvest

A harvest, in the natural world, has at least four ideal—and historically traditional—bins, places in which to store what you have produced.

Bin 1: A place for storing a portion to eat now.
Bin 2: A place for storing a portion to save for future eating or emergencies.
Bin 3: A place for storing a portion to take to market—for reinvesting in your field and for purchasing future seed, equipment, and more acreage!
Bin 4: A place to put the portion of your harvest that you will give away.

Let's look at each bin of harvest more closely . . .

A Portion of Your Harvest Should Be Enjoyed Now

A harvest is laden with rewards. Select a few choice ones and enjoy them today.

Many people spend their entire lives waiting for life to happen: when they're old enough to leave home . . . when they graduate from college . . . after they get married . . . when the bills are paid . . . after the children are out of college . . . when they retire.

Some people never partake of the rewards they have earned. That happens, to a great extent, because they don't see themselves as worthy of enjoying the success they've created. Don't be among them!

Others let the national economy, world politics, or faraway natural disasters keep them from enjoying the fruits of their labors. They feel guilty for having, when others don't.

If people follow this line of reasoning perpetually, they will never enjoy success. They may achieve it, but it will bring them no joy.

A preoccupation with instant gratification and a policy of forever delaying gratification are at the extreme opposite ends of the success continuum. The truly successful person finds a happy medium.

You cannot base your ability to enjoy life on uncertain events or possible occurrences. Another problem or crisis situation will come along just as you prepare to partake of your harvest, forcing you to stall your experience of rewards until yet another time, which also never arises.

Learn to partake of your success as you achieve it, regardless of the national debt or the name of the person just elected president. The only time for happiness is now. Happiness should always be in season. I've encouraged you through this book to enjoy each season—to be happy as you dream, set goals, and make plans . . . to be happy as you till the soil and plant your seeds . . . to be happy as you cultivate, weed, and fertilize your field of success. I now encourage you to be happy in your harvest.

You will note, of course, that I suggest you only partake personally of a portion of your harvest. To partake of your entire harvest creates an attitude of self-centeredness and negates a major percentage of your potential to plan for, plant for, and reap future successes.

Sample a portion of your reward.

Delight in it.

Enjoy it to the max.

And don't feel guilty about it.

As you enjoy a portion of your harvest, include your family and friends in that time of celebration. Let them bask in the glow of your awards. Take them to award dinners that may be in your honor, and recognize them publicly as having a stake in any honor you receive.

Let your spouse and family share in your financial rewards. Plan purchases or trips that will be mutually enjoyed by all.

As you set spiritually based goals for yourself and reach them, be generous in sharing with your family and friends the experiences you have had and the changes you sense occurring in your inner person. They'll be encouraged and inspired—perhaps, most of all, by your willingness to share with them your experiences at that deepest emotional level of your life.

If you choose to enjoy your harvest along the way, you'll always be assured of enjoying your harvest on your last day of life. After all, you never really know which day may be your last day to enjoy a harvest.

I will never forget one Friday in the Chicago O'Hare Airport. I had just finished speaking and was anxious to get home to my family in California, so I could spend another day, another week, another month on the road. I seemed to be chasing life at that time. I hurried to the gate from which my plane was scheduled to depart, but by the time I arrived, the door had closed, and the airplane was pulling back from the gate. It was a DC-10. Flight 191.

In a little over an hour later, a broken bolt would give way on that plane. The wing pod would fall off, and the plane would crash, with great loss of life.

To this day, I keep that invalidated ticket on Flight 191 to remind me to enjoy a portion of all life's harvests as they are reaped. When I get angry or frustrated from time to time, my wife will pull out that ticket and ask simply, "What are you grousing about today?" I look at my ticket, I look at my life, and I must conclude, "Nothing." Every day is Christmas and every day is Easter to me.

A good question to ask yourself today is this: *How do I plan to enjoy my achieved success?*

George Sand, the nineteenth-century French novelist, described success as having these five necessary ingredients:

1. Simple taste.
2. A certain degree of courage.
3. Self-denial to a point.

4. Love of work.
5. A clear conscience.

In my opinion, the fifth ingredient she listed—a clear conscience—is absolutely essential. A wealthy, successful, and happy Manhattan real estate broker once said, "I could have made a lot more money in my life, but I preferred to sleep well at night." Virtually all success must be defined and built from the inside out.

Sleeping well after a good day at earnest work is one joy of life. Thousands of people in our nation—perhaps even millions— would give anything to be able to fall asleep easily tonight and stay restfully and peacefully asleep without awakening to worry.

Even as you enjoy your success with a good conscience, don't feel as if you need to apologize to anyone for having your success, for desiring to be a success, or for trying to succeed. Life is more than a gift to you; it is a gift that comes with a responsibility to use your abilities to the fullest. Anything that you can achieve through honest, genuine effort is inherently good, especially as it spills over to benefit others along the way.

A Portion of Your Harvest Should Be Saved

In many ways, barns and silos are a farmer's savings banks for hay and grain. A pantry lined with canned goods and a freezer filled with produce are a gardener's savings banks.

A portion of any harvest you reap should be set aside and saved, with an eye toward withstanding future emergencies or pursuing unanticipated opportunities.

Are you aware that only three out of every one hundred Americans who reach the age of sixty-five have any degree of financial security? Most people live out their lives under the delusion that they are immortal. They live for today, buying on impulse and overextending their credit. Most of the money they earn in their lives—which for the average full-time laborer is likely to be well in excess of $750,000—is spent along the way.* They arrive at retire-

---

* Stop to consider the mathematics. A person who works from age twenty-two (just out of college) until age sixty-five, earns an overall "average" of $23,250 per year, will earn $1 million.

ment with few resources upon which to draw and frequently settle for a standard of living *lower* than what they experienced when they first began their careers!

The successful person chooses not to be a part of that process. How can you avoid this fate?

1. Pay yourself at the first of each month. Pay yourself as if you were a phone or utility company. Set aside a definite sum of money, and deposit it into a savings account from which you refuse to draw unless the emergency is dire. Saving $20 a month, with compounded interest at 5 percent, can give you a sizable nest egg after twenty years—more than $15,000. The good news is that virtually *all* Americans in the work force can save that amount.

2. Invest in yourself. Invest in knowledge and training so that you might upgrade your life in *all* ways—staying abreast of current trends and developing the skills that will keep you flexible and adaptable in today's changing marketplace.

3. Develop an appreciation for and a delight in activities that cost very little or nothing. A walk in the park or along neighborhood sidewalks. A ride on the bus to a free zoo or gallery. Conversations with friends. Visits to a playground with a child you love—a son or daughter, a niece or nephew, a grandchild, or perhaps the child of a friend or neighbor. Playtimes with your friends and family. It takes *no* money to toss around a football on the front lawn for an afternoon . . . to ride bikes in a family-designed scavenger hunt . . . or to sit around on the patio telling stories. No football? Imagine you have one! Charade football can be even more fun than the real thing. No bicycles? Conduct your treasure hunt on foot.

Life is made up of small pleasures that cost nothing—and yet are priceless. Good eye contact over the breakfast table. Watching a child take the first awkward steps. A grandparent's touch. A baby's smiles. A child's delight in a finger painting. The loving gaze of a spouse. A father's encouraging clasp of a shoulder.

4. Don't feed your greed. If you find yourself becoming preoccupied with "things," turn off the source of that stimulation. Steer your conversations away from discussing things, and direct them toward discussing ideas. Avoid wandering around the mall or shopping as a recreational pastime. Turn off commercial television. You'll be amazed to discover how your thoughts turn away from material objects to people, goals, and projects that have lasting merit.

5. Map out a plan for the financial resources you will need during your retirement years. And then start to work on that plan this month. Determine at what point in your future you would like to be able to live without depending on day-to-day income from your job. How much in liquid assets will you need to maintain a life-style that you will find comfortable? How much will you need to save *now* on a monthly basis to have that much available by the year you desire to retire? You may want to consult a licensed financial planner to help you develop your personal plan. The most important aspect of a plan, of course, is working it—sticking with it and abiding by it month after month and year after year.

A Portion of Your Harvest Is Best Plowed Back into Your Field

Reinvestment should claim a part of every harvest you reap. A farmer understands this principle clearly.

I recently drove through the San Joaquin Valley in central California. This valley is one of the foremost cotton-producing areas in the United States, along with Texas and the states in the Deep South. The cotton harvest was in its final stages, and a number of farmers were already engaged in a practice that is now mandated by law: They were shredding the depleted cotton plants and plowing them back into the earth—returning to the soil the plants from which the wisps of white cotton had already been sucked away by giant cotton-picking machines.

Gardeners acknowledge this principle when they take the stalks and vines that have yielded vegetables and fruits and recycle them into compost.

In growing our gardens of success, we must make provision for putting a portion of the harvest back into the endeavors in which we have worked.

It seems obvious to everyone but us that we Americans are

disposing of our past rewards at a greater pace than we are replenishing our investment today for future harvesting.

Japanese workers save an estimated 20 to 30 percent of their spendable incomes—more than triple that of Americans. In Japan, what's left over after bills are paid is called discretionary income, which means one has a choice to spend it or save it. Most choose to spend it with discretion—both saving and investing a considerable portion. In America, we call this after-expenses money disposable income. When most Americans get their hands on disposable income, they hasten to dispose of it. For many, what is earned on Friday at quitting time is nowhere to be found by Monday morning's starting whistle.

In 1960, the United States held 25 percent of the world market share in manufacturing and was the dominant leader in the world marketplace. By 1979, however, our share of world manufacturing was down to 17 percent—a drop of nearly 8 percentage points in less than two decades!

In 1960, American companies produced 95 percent of the autos, steel, and consumer electronics purchased on the U.S. market. In 1980, American companies produced only 79 percent of the autos and 86 percent of the steel—hefty declines. An even greater decline, however, came in consumer electronics. The share of the U.S. market for American companies plummeted from 95 to 50 percent!

That trend has continued. As we prepare to enter the twenty-first century, our market share is being whittled more and more each year. We should wake up and remember that ancient Oriental proverb, "He who rests on laurels gets knocked on rear end."

The Japanese learned from their failure in World War II that you reap what you sow. They resolved to plow the fields of technology with dedication and hard work. They stayed lean and hungry as a nation. In the fifties, sixties, seventies, and eighties, the Japanese worked on quality control, shared responsibility, employment incentives, and the development of nonadversarial relationships between customers and companies as well as between management and employees. Meanwhile, American companies became fat and sedentary. Confrontations between labor and management grew. Our products became shoddier. We developed a general malaise and began to expect to reap rewards without real effort. We now are reaping what we sowed—little input has yielded less output.

Still, I sense a new season of planting beginning across our nation. We are beginning to awaken to the values that made us a truly great nation in the first place. We are renewing that half-forgotten art of reinvesting some of our profit into the fields that yield our harvest. We are beginning to plow new ground of self- and collective-awareness of interdependency. We are starting to put the nutrients back into the soil, to revitalize and sustain our growth in coming seasons. The search for excellence is real.

I speak every week, often several times a week, in a corporate or institutional setting. All across this nation I hear a new corporate voice: "Our first responsibility is quality of product and service to our customer." I'm encouraged.

One top executive said at a meeting I attended: "The successful people I know aren't obsessed with beating out the other person and stepping on others' heads to get to the top. Their motivation, instead, is to do such a good job at their assigned task that they come to be regarded as first in a fast field of excellent talent. In fact, the better your competitors do, the better it makes you look if you win first place. And the ultimate goal of any business is to assemble the best-trained, most highly motivated team in the industry so that as a group you can all become first in the marketplace."

Refreshing words, aren't they? In the free market system of business, which I still believe is the most healthy for all concerned, we seem to be joining ourselves together in an interdependent team moving ahead to reach a mutual goal—being the best we can be.

Keep the benefits of competition in perspective.

This mutuality of spirit does not, of course, negate the benefits of competition. Competition, when tempered by cooperation, is a safeguard of quality, reasonable prices, and fair play in the marketplace. It is a prime motivator for personal excellence.

Through the years, I've met a number of individuals who do not seek to use all of their talents because they believe it is wrong to be competitive. As a result, many of their inner abilities go untested. Many of their innate talents are not turned into finely honed skills.

Competition has merit. It compels us to test ourselves and to discover new things about ourselves.

Competition within a broader framework of competition is very healthy. It results in the bonding together of teams, which are essential for any building process.

Don't overlook the benefits of competition as you reinvest a portion of your harvest. Use your harvest dividends as an incentive for helpful, constructive competition.

This can be done on an individual level as well as a corporate one. Reinvest in your education, training, or skill development. And challenge yourself to compete against your personal best! Just as a factory needs to retool periodically, so do we as individuals need to keep our minds retooled. Otherwise, our skills become obsolete, our knowledge old, and our ability to think, write, and remember rusty. School is never out for the successful professional.

Extend this opportunity for personal professional development to others in your firm. Make it an incentive. Offer it as a prize. Your employees will not only consider it a great benefit, but your company will gain by the new information and higher level of skills they bring back into your workplace.

Within your family, consider setting aside a portion of your income to create prizes. You may desire for each person to have an equal opportunity to gain a portion of the prize, or you may choose to set aside one prize for which all children have the opportunity to compete equally. For example, you may feel the need for more space in your house. Consider letting the new room-to-yourself "prize" go to the child who completes a designated set of chores over a six-month period with the greatest regularity, highest performance level, and least amount of reminding.

Setting up such a competition, of course, does not mean that you favor one child over the other. In fact, it results in quite the contrary. A new room, generally speaking, tends to be awarded to the oldest child. That may not be the fairest division of space. Younger children rarely get to compete for the opportunity to have privacy, although their need for it is no less than that of older children.

Competition should never become an excuse for allowing your family to become divisive. Friendly competition is fun, challenging, and rewarding . . . and afterward, all parties shake hands!

The world at large is a place of competition. Letting your children experience that is not a hindrance to their growth but an opportunity to learn how to compete—and still end the race as friends.

Reinvest in the spirit of individuality.

With our free enterprise system, we have a unique right shared by only a few other nations with whom we compete economically. A person in our society has a right to think differently, act differently, and be different. Resident in that right is the right to create differently—to innovate, to experiment, to start a new business, to try something that has never been done before.

A portion of what we reinvest in ourselves should be what causes us to create or renews a creative spirit within us.

For you personally, it may be

- season tickets to the symphony.
- a weekend retreat to a place of beauty.
- a week at a spa.
- a trip abroad.
- an entire afternoon off to visit a local gallery or museum, viewing the treasures there in reflective solitude.
- an entire Saturday alone to read and relax while the rest of the family runs errands.

You may think of these pleasant activities as rewards. In many cases, however, they also rejuvenate your ability to lead, to create, to innovate, to motivate, to generate, to inspire. As such, these activities are investments in your field of success. They give you pleasure and build you up so that you can give of yourself again in a future season of tilling, planting, and cultivating a successful harvest.

Reinvest in a way that leads to greater environmental wholeness.

It's important to note in our farming analogy that what a farmer tills back into the soil, or what a gardener turns into compost, is good for the natural environment. The farmer gives back to nature.

We can give a portion of all our harvest in life back to nature. Let me note several practical examples.

Perhaps one of your goals is to adopt a more nutritious way of eating. Invariably, you will be drawn to fresh foods as you enact your plan. Dispose of the waste of fresh foods in an ecologically sound manner. Even an apartment dweller can create a compost bin on the balcony. Should you not desire to do so, recognize that by purchasing more fresh foods, you will be purchasing fewer processed foods, which will cut down on the amount of packaging you purchase. That, too, has ecological benefit because it lessens the need for landfill. As you become more healthy, the environment will, also.

Perhaps one of your professional goals is to involve yourself more with coworkers—to build a network of colleagues, each person highly supportive of the others. One project that you might undertake together—as a means of forging camaraderie and of developing friendships away from the workplace—might be planting trees in a local reclamation project or developing an inner city garden. As you reach your professional goal, the environment benefits!

Consider family projects based on helping to clean up our polluted world. Unless we all cherish the natural environment we have inherited from ancestors long ago, and take cues from animals such as the snow leopard, the condor, and the whale, we may well find New York becoming the *Tyrannosaurus rex* of modern society, and Los Angeles, the mastodon. What a sad world it will be if all the animals our children know are the rubberized and polyester foam images on stage at Disney World.

Reinvest in things that last.

In a recent Gallup Poll, participants were asked to rate twelve factors of success, such as unlimited money, luxury car, good job, happy family, and so forth. I found the results very interesting. At the top of the list were these five treasures: good health, happy family, enjoyable job, good education, and peace of mind. At the low end of the list were expensive possessions, luck, talent, and inherited wealth.

I encourage you to spend a few minutes contemplating those top five definers of success:

· Good health. That's certainly a harvest you can enjoy!
· Happy family. That's another harvest from which you can partake without any pangs of guilt.
· Enjoyable job. Delight in it. You can openly express your joy at having a job you like. It's a harvest! Partake of it.

- Good education. Again, you can partake freely in your delight at what you know, have learned, and enjoy thinking about or imagining.
- Peace of mind. Consume all you want! It's a harvest of incredible value that has unending rewards.

Now, ask yourself several key questions related to each of these harvests:

How might I reinvest in the garden of success that yielded this wonderful harvest? For example, ask, What resulted in my having peace of mind? What can I do to reinvest in that activity, enterprise, or relationship so that I and others might have peace of mind in the future?

How might I share this harvest with others? Ask, How did I gain my good education? Who helped me? What I might do to help others?

How might I save a portion for future use? Ask, What can I do to sustain these good harvests? How might I lose what I have gained? How can I AVOID losing this harvest? In not losing a good harvest, you are "saving" it!

A Portion of Your Harvest is Best Given Away

In ancient days, farmers left a corner of their fields unharvested so that the poor might glean them. The practice ensured that everybody in a community had sufficient to eat. It's a principle we still have at the core of our national ethic.

One great benefit of acquiring financial wealth is the joy that comes with giving a portion of it away for the benefit of the world in which you live.

Financial resource is behind every great invention, every scientific breakthrough, every innovation of medical technology, every educational institution, and every new corporation or business (and the jobs and products it represents).

Farmland must be financed so that we can have food.

Factories must be retooled so that we can remain competitive in the world market.

Needy students must be given scholarships so that we can make maximum use of our greatest national resource: brain power.

Laboratories must be funded so that one day we can benefit from vaccines, medications, and technical systems that will not extend life but enrich life.

The successful person looks beyond himself and realizes that just as he could not have tilled his garden of success alone, he is part of a larger garden that requires his tilling efforts.

Others have helped and will help you reach your goals. It is your responsibility to help others.

What are the consequences if we do not share generously of what we have harvested?

The communities in which we live—our immediate neighborhoods, our nation and, ultimately, the entire world—begin to decay.

What could be repaired . . . is left to crumble.

What could be built . . . goes unbuilt.

What could be healed . . . continues to become sicker and eventually to die or decay.

What could be reused . . . is left to rust, pollute, contaminate, or occupy in an unbeneficial way.

What could give life . . . is denied.

We must give to move life forward.

Giving Holds Its Own Treasures Within

I heard a story about a wealthy man who lost his wife when their only child was young. The widower hired a governess to serve as a nanny for his son and as a general housekeeper. When the boy reached his teens, he became ill and died. Heartbroken from this second tragic loss of a loved one, the father passed away a short time later.

No will could be located, and since there were no known surviving relatives, the state began the process of confiscating the deceased executive's fortune. The man's personal belongings were put up for auction.

The old housekeeper had very little money, but she was determined to buy one family keepsake. It was a painting that had hung on a stairway wall in the house for many years—a large oil portrait of the young boy she had loved and nurtured for fifteen years.

When the items of the home were auctioned, no one wanted the painting so the housekeeper was able to buy it for just a few dollars. Once she had the painting in her home, she began to clean it and polish the frame, cherishing the memories the painting evoked within her.

As she took the frame apart to repair it, a paper fell out from behind the cardboard backing. It was her former employer's will. In it he stated that all of his wealth should go to the one who loved his son enough to claim the portrait.

The woman had no material reward in mind when she bought the painting. All she wanted was a reminder of her love and concern for the family to whom she had devoted many years of service.

It's not what you accumulate that counts. It's how you give away yourself. Life isn't a collection. It's a celebration.

The By-Products of Your Harvest of Success

No matter what area of your life you are harvesting, you will no doubt find that you are reaping several automatic dividends that come with accomplishing a task.

The first is a sense of accomplishment. You performed well. You achieved a goal. You are a winner.

Self-empowerment.

With a sense of accomplishment comes a certain degree of self-empowerment. Make certain that your new dividend of power yields for you . . .

> **P**—purpose. Let your feelings of power energize your greater purposes in life.
>
> **O**—open-mindedness. Don't allow your new feelings of power to make you dictatorial. Stay open to new ideas. Don't shield yourself from people.
>
> **W**—wisdom that is tempered by good judgment, common sense, and knowledge.
>
> **E**—energy. A feeling of self-empowerment, when focused

toward a still higher goal in life, can be the energy that motivates you forward.

R—responsibility. With accomplishment comes added responsibility for making this world a better place. Power without responsibility invariably leads to corruption and evil.

Don't let your feelings of accomplishment, and the resulting self-empowerment, go to your head. It's easy to become authoritarian, dogmatic, and arrogant—insulting or demeaning in one's attitude, words, and actions toward others. British nobleman Lord Acton stated wisely, "Power tends to corrupt and absolute power corrupts absolutely."

Power is actually a neutral substance. It can be used for good or evil. In the right hands, power can be used to help others, create new jobs, establish new business enterprises, build communities, extend faith, improve health, and enrich relationships.

The joy of self-empowerment comes when one is able to say, "No matter how successful or wealthy I may become, my values and relationships will remain constant."

Wisdom

A second by-product of success is wisdom, which I define as . . .

- having good judgment.
- being informed.
- acting sharp in practical affairs.
- building on the experience of others.
- knowing how to use knowledge appropriately and for the good of others.

No one is born with wisdom. It is a quality that develops slowly over the years, season after season, cycle of success after cycle of success. Wisdom cannot be inherited. It must be learned, nurtured, and practiced.

Wisdom can be summed up as "adapting to new information and situations while incorporating past experiences." That, frequently, is the feeling people have as they enter their harvest season of success. They realize they have been required to adapt and change, to grow and develop, as they moved through the seasons in a cycle of success. They can now look back—"older and wiser" as the saying goes—and see their past seasons with greater clarity.

Wisdom is a sifting process. Take time during your autumn season of success to reflect on what you did right, did wrong, and why.

Have you injured people along the way? What must you do to make amends?

Did you take shortcuts? They will eventually catch up with you.

What do you need to review?

What would you like to repeat?

What do you hope never to encounter, experience, or endure again?

Take time during your harvest season to reflect on how you have changed. Think back over this season . . . as well as other cycles of success in the past.

Autumn is the time for gaining perspective on the whole of your life, for seeing the big picture.

During World War II, parachutes were being constructed by the thousands. From the worker's point of view, the job was tedious. It involved crouching over a sewing machine for eight to ten hours a day, stitching what seemed to be endless lengths of colorless fabric until one had a formless heap of cloth on the floor under the machine. The job could easily have been regarded as a menial, thankless, boring job—its best harvest being a moderate paycheck.

The workers who stitched the parachutes rarely held that opinion, however. Each morning, they were reminded that every stitch they made was part of a lifesaving operation. They were challenged to imagine, as they sewed, that the parachute they were stitching would eventually be worn by a husband, a brother, or a son.

That's a good perspective for each of us to have about our work and about the successes we achieve. Ask yourself,

· How does this fit into the overall purpose of my life?
· How does this affect my life as a whole?
· How might my past be redeemed by this success?
· Who benefits by this success other than myself?

To a great extent, a portion of every success we achieve belongs to someone else. Perhaps it's a favorite teacher in elementary school; a coach; a parent; a loving aunt, uncle, or grandparent; a Sunday school teacher; a rabbi or pastor; a best friend; an encouraging counselor. Wisdom is the perspective in which we recognize that we are not a product solely of our own creation, although we are solely responsible for what we do with the contributions others have made to our lives.

Take time during the harvest season of your success to count not only the immediate blessing but *all* your blessings. An old gospel song goes,

> Count your blessings, name them one by one.
> Count your blessings, see what God has done.

That's a good theme song for the autumn season of your success.

As you recall and recognize your bounties in life, you'll gain added strength to press forward.

Applause

A third by-product of your harvest of success is usually applause. For some people, that's the most difficult aspect of success to handle.

You might interpret applause as recognition. Sometimes that recognition isn't voiced; rather, it is manifested in a seemingly different way that people treat you or speak about you, or the tone of voice they use in speaking to you.

Ray Kroc, McDonald's founder, said most people have difficulty associating applause with their careers since they can't actually hear any applause per se, such as that an entertainer receives on stage. In Kroc's opinion, the real applause is the inner feeling of a faster heartbeat, the pride of accomplishment, and personal satisfaction. For younger people, a compliment on a job well done is the most resounding applause. If they never hear it, they're missing something special. If they love what they are doing enough, he said, their natural enthusiasm will coax the applause from others.

Sometimes jealousy manifests itself as a rather warped, twisted version of applause. We must recognize that people are very rarely jealous of something unless they admire it, wish they had it or were like it, or want it.

Handling the applause of others is a challenge you face as a successful person. The best way I know to do that is to applaud back.

Time and time again I've found myself a member of audiences in which an actor, a musician, or a speaker gave a truly outstanding performance. You can feel the energy in the air as the audience leap to their feet in thundering ovation. Many times, these performers—at the top of their field and at the peak of their skills—graciously turn to applaud the orchestra behind them and then turn to applaud the audience before them. You see, they know they couldn't have performed as well as they did by themselves.

An excellent performer—a truly successful person—knows that he or she is defined as a successful performer only by an appreciative audience. A successful performer also knows that a good audience actually compels a better performance.

In all my years of conducting inspirational seminars and presenting motivational speeches, I've become something of an expert on audiences. I've discovered many truths about them. One is that every audience is different. No matter how many times I speak, I have yet to speak to an identical audience. For one thing, it's rare for two audiences to be made up of exactly the same people, and even if they are, the people tend to sit in different places. And even if they sit in the same places, the time of day is different, the level of experience we all have is different, and our motivational level is different!

Another thing I've learned about audiences is that each has a different temperament. A lazy, relaxed audience can sometimes be almost impossible to motivate. An audience composed of people who are required to be present sends forth signals that are very different from those from an audience in which the people have enthusiastically waited an hour to get in the door.

The enthusiastic audience actually draws more out of a speaker than a lukewarm audience. The speaker's message may be the same for both groups. His or her personal motivational level may be high. And yet, the presentation to the enthusiastic audience will be a much stronger, livelier, and more meaningful one.

Don't be surprised if you get one level of applause from one audience in your life and another level from another audience. Your family may be ecstatic about your promotion. Your coworkers may be only mildly appreciative of your achievement. You may be exhilarated at the number you finally see on the bathroom scale as you weigh yourself in the morning. Nobody else may care.

Ultimately, you must play to an audience of one: yourself. You must evaluate your performance in light of your dreams, goals, plans, inner sense of values, and beliefs.

As you achieve success, recognize that the response you receive will vary from person to person and from group to group. Those who are enthusiastically for you will compel you to pursue even loftier goals.

That's one reason I'm so committed to surrounding myself with successful, motivated people. They encourage me to be more than I am, to do more than I have done, and to set higher goals than I've yet imagined.

As you celebrate in your autumn season of success, choose carefully people with whom to celebrate. Invite those who have contributed to your success, those who will appreciate it and you, and those with whom you can truly rejoice in the fact that life is wonderful, full of purpose, and well worth the living with gusto and joy.

Which brings us to a final by-product of a successful harvest . . .

Joy

Rare is the farmer who brings in a harvest without having a great deal of deep inner satisfaction and joy.

Henry Fonda once said, "There is joy in work. All that money can do is buy us someone else's work in exchange for our own. There is no happiness except in the realization that we have accomplished something."

Joy is having the deep-down pervasive sense of pleasure and satisfaction that comes from knowing you are surrounded by those who love you and appreciate your work.

Joy is from within.

Joy is lasting. It is not a "happy hour" feeling of escapism, a TGIF party, or a moment of ecstasy. Joy is rooted in having a purpose for being and knowing that you are fulfilling it.

Allow yourself to feel joy in your success!

FINAL WORDS IN THE HARVEST SEASON OF AUTUMN

- *Relishing achievement*
- *Sharing the bounty*
- *Saving for a rainy day*
- *Replenishing the soil*
- *Renewing*

Beyond the Harvest

♦ *Is that all there is?*

♦ *What do I do for an encore?*

♦ *What's the next step?*

♦ *How do we go from theory into reality?*

♦ *Life is not like a book which is finished when it's read. Life is like a garden. It changes every day. The need to tend it is constant.*

♦ *The next step in this book, as in a garden, is to take a specific time frame and start digging in the soil. Inspiration, when combined with dedication and perspiration, leads to graduation.*

Let's take what we have shared and put it to work, for 90 days, the length of a season.

A 90-Day
Cycle
of Success

THE SEASON FORECAST

 To the unsuccessful person: Time doesn't matter. Life moves according to chance. What comes, comes. What doesn't, doesn't.

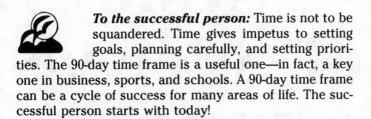 ***To the successful person:*** Time is not to be squandered. Time gives impetus to setting goals, planning carefully, and setting priorities. The 90-day time frame is a useful one—in fact, a key one in business, sports, and schools. A 90-day time frame can be a cycle of success for many areas of life. The successful person starts with today!

*To the successful person,
greater success is only
90 days away!*

17

Putting the Seasons to Work

A farmer knows from experience that different crops take different lengths of time to grow. Beans can be harvested within several weeks. Apricots take years.

In many areas of life, 90 days is regarded as an appropriate growing cycle.

The business world operates on a quarterly basis—"earnings are up during the third quarter," "sales are slightly down in the first quarter report," "analysts are expecting a fourth-quarter upturn."

The sports world to a great extent operates on a "seasonal" basis in which the majority of games are played during a 90-day cycle—not counting postseason play-offs. To be certain, the sports seasons of today have a great tendency to overlap. In years past, one could move from basketball to the first half of the baseball season (the All-Star Game) to the second half of the baseball season to the football season in a rhythm that very closely matched that of the business world.

The academic world, in many universities and colleges, is set up on a quarterly basis—the fourth quarter usually being summer. Even academic institutions that operate on the semester schedule usually have nine-month terms, or "three quarters" worth of time.

I personally have found a 90-day cycle of success to be a wonderful unit of time. It's a time period that is long enough for me to plan for, begin, work hard at, and accomplish certain objectives. At the same time, it isn't forever. It's a short enough time to generate a sense of urgency for me. I can also encompass in my mind a starting date and an ending date.

If time were not a factor . . .

It would take a hundred lifetimes for any one of us to accomplish all that we are capable of doing. However, we are given only one life span to do our best and be all that we can be. If we had forever, we'd have no real need for setting goals, planning carefully, setting priorities, or even working hard at any task. We could squander time and still manage to accomplish something—if only by chance.

Time, however, is a ruler. It requires discipline. It forces us to take stock of our reason for being and to take action.

Ultimately, time is the master equal opportunity employer. Each person has exactly 168 hours per week, 24 hours per day, 60 minutes per hour.

A 90-day cycle of success is always that—90 days, 2,160 hours, 129,600 minutes. Nothing you can do, invent, say, or think will add another minute to those days. Unfortunately, while you cannot give birth to more time, you *can* kill time. You can choose to waste it or spend it wisely. Therefore . . . use your hours to maximum advantage!

The Winter Season of Your
90-Day Cycle of Success

Begin your 90-day cycle of success by taking an evening to do the following twelve exercises. Or you may want to set aside a weekend or a Sunday afternoon for this activity. All twelve of the exercises, taken as a whole, will take you about four hours.

I find it helpful to do these exercises alone on a quiet Saturday afternoon of one week and then set aside my goals until the following weekend. Then I return to them to review them, make adjustments, and add additional items—or in some cases, subtract items if I feel that I have overextended myself. I then discuss the ideas with my wife and get her input. I make sure that my goals mesh with hers, and that we are both on the same wavelength, especially when it comes to planning any specific goals in which she has a part (which are virtually all of them, by the way).

Exercise 1

Take five minutes and grade yourself on a scale of 1 to 5 as you answer these questions (1 = I'm reacting and feeling guilty for a lack of balance or accomplishment in this area; 5 = I'm consistently accomplishing and actively managing my goals and objectives).

My professional life—job or career   _____

My family relationships   _____

My mental growth and development (including learning new things, reading books and magazines, taking courses, acquiring new skills)   _____

My friendships and relationships with business and professional colleagues   _____

My financial picture (including positive cash flow, assets, level of debt)   _____

My physical being (health, fitness)   _____

My spiritual life   _____

My involvement with the community   _____

Note areas in which you score low. Circle them.

Exercise 2

Take ten minutes and list everything you *need* to do in the next 90 days. These are obligations that you have already made. Include events for which you already have tickets, projects that you are already assigned to complete, and so forth. Divide your list into eight sections: *Personal, Family, Social, Financial, Physical, Spiritual, Community,* and *Professional.*

Exercise 3

Now review your list and spend another ten minutes adding things you *want* to do. Identify things you can do in areas where you scored low in Exercise 1 to improve your satisfaction level about your overall success.

Here's a sample list to give you some ideas:

Personal

Read one book:

Attend a class on:

Listen to an audiocassette program on:

Family

Go out on a date with my spouse (alone) six times (an average of twice a month).

Go on one minivacation with my family to:

Work with my children at least twice a week to help them develop their skills at:

Play with each of my children at least ten minutes a day.

Social

Attend one dramatic production.

Attend one concert.

Get together with each of these five friends at least once during this time period:

Meet this acquaintance for breakfast or lunch to get to know him or her better:

Call each one of my ten best friends and ask, "Of all your friends that I don't know, which three should I meet and why?"

Schedule at least two appointments with people recommended to me by my friends:

Financial

Save at least 5 percent of my income during this time.

Develop a monthly budget.

Invest in:

Physical

Work out twice a week.

Join an organized sport or take lessons in a sporting activity:

Enroll in an exercise class:

Spiritual

Read the Bible five days a week.

Have a daily quiet time for contemplation and reflection.

Attend church consistently.

Attend a Bible study on:

Meet with someone to discuss spiritual concepts:

Community

Work on an environmental project:

Write a letter expressing one of my opinions to a person in elected office:

Send a thank-you note to a leader affirming the job the person is doing:

Professional

Reach this quota:

Develop these projects:

Meet with these colleagues:

Finish these reports:

Write these documents or memos:

Prepare these presentations:

Plan each day on the day before.

Keep my calendar up to date.

Exercise 4

Take five minutes to record three things that tend to slip through the cracks in your professional life. Do the same for your personal life. Take a look at your list completed in Exercise 3 and note whether you have addressed these concerns by setting specific, well-defined goals.

Exercise 5

Spend about thirty minutes relaxing and reflecting on some of your long-range goals. (I suggest you limit yourself to the next five years.)

Make notes to yourself along these lines:

This is where I would like to be professionally and financially:

These are the terms that I would like to be able to use to describe my family:

These are the skills I would like to acquire or the courses of instruction I would like to complete:

These are the people I would like to have met:

These are the hallmarks I would like to see established in my spiritual life:

These are associations, affiliations, or memberships I would like to have:

These are projects I would like to have completed:

This is the way I would like to be able to describe my physical life:

These are the experiences I would like to have had or to have on a regular basis (including places to visit, habits to acquire):

Exercise 6

Spend about twenty minutes comparing, side by side, your list of long-range goals and your list of 90-day goals. Make adjustments.

- Will the items on your 90-day list help you achieve your long-range goals?
- Are some of your long-range goals unmatched to short-term goals? If so, you may want to spend a few extra minutes evaluating what to add to (or subtract from) your short-term list of goals that will enable you to reach your long-range goals.

Exercise 7

Take about ten minutes to reflect on and make notes regarding these questions:

- When and where do I do my best creative thinking?
- What is my most productive time of day?
- How much time a day do I seem to waste? When during the day do these times seem to occur most frequently or for the longest periods?
- Do I have a twelve-month calendar? Is it current, with all my appointments and obligations listed on it?

Exercise 8

Based on the information in Exercise 7, take about five minutes to write down how you will attempt to block out your days into units of time that will allow you to accomplish the most. List what your foremost priorities will be for each of these time blocks:

6:00 A.M. *to 9:00* A.M.
9:00 A.M. *to noon*
Noon to 3:00 P.M.
3:00 P.M. *to 6:00* P.M.
6:00 P.M. *to 9:00* P.M.

You may want to adjust these time blocks to more accurately reflect your schedule. Here's a sample:

6:00 A.M. *to 8:30* A.M.
Jog or exercise twenty minutes.
  Read newspapers.
  Have a good breakfast.
  Go over day's schedule with family members.
  Listen to instructional audiocassette on way to work.

8:30 A.M. *to noon*
Write.
  Work on creative projects.
  Work on projects that require intense concentration.

Noon hour
Have lunch with professional colleague two days a week.
  Work out at nearby gym three days a week.

1:00 P.M. to end of workday
Meet with colleagues.
   Make phone calls.
   Schedule meetings.
   Work on routine tasks.
   Go over mail/write memos.
   Go over following day's agenda with secretary or
   coworkers.

6:00 P.M. to bedtime
Listen to inspirational audiocassette on way home.
   Spend time with each child in play, conversation.
   Spend time with spouse in quiet, focused conversation.
   Read at least one hour.
   Once a week, schedule cultural event, movie, or dinner out
   with family.

Exercise 9

If you do not have a twelve-month calendar, as mentioned in
Exercise 7, develop one. You can buy blank monthly calendar
sheets at a local stationer and make your own calendar. I like a
calendar with large empty blocks so that I can tailor-make them to
suit my plans and goals.

Once you have made a calendar . . .

Spend about thirty minutes identifying key days through the year
when you will

- have an annual physical (including any specialty exams, such
  as a Pap smear or mammogram, prostate exam, or ultrasonic
  scan of carotid arteries).
- see the dentist.
- meet with your attorney.
- conduct a home-safety, home-repairs survey.
- meet with your financial consultant (or tax accountant, book-
  keeper, or CPA).
- host your pastor (or rabbi, priest, or spiritual mentor) for
  lunch.
- spend a weekend away with your spouse.
- go away on a family vacation.

Exercise 10

Focus on the next 90 days on your calendar. Consult your goals from Exercise 3. Put due dates related to them on your calendar. If you have set goals of meeting with certain individuals, going out on dates with your spouse, and so forth, write in those events.

If you have set a goal of completing a major project, presentation, document, or course of study, set aside blocks of time (even entire days) for working exclusively on those tasks.

Exercise 11

Take five minutes to write down your foremost goal from each of the categories, and using suggestions offered in chapter 5, prepare positive self-talk statements on index cards. Remember to keep the statements succinct, positive, personal, and in the present tense.

Exercise 12

Finally, spend about ten minutes writing down a motivational statement at the beginning of each week of the next 90-day cycle. Make a commitment within yourself to read this phrase each time you consult your daily schedule. By the end of the week you should have it memorized. These motivational thoughts will be like water for your garden in which you are growing success.

As you encounter motivational ideas, phrases, or quotes, keep a page in the back of your planning journal for them. Use this source of ideas from which to draw your weekly motivational concepts.

If you do not already have a log of such ideas, let me share with you twenty of my favorite concepts:

- Time is the ultimate equal opportunity employer.
- If you don't know where you are going, any old road will take you there.
- Most people live their entire lives on a fantasy island called Someday Isle.
- If it is to be, it's up to me.
- Most people spend more effort and time planning a party than planning their whole lives.

- I would rather fail trying than succeed in doing nothing.
- You never break a habit; you replace it with a new one.
- Crisis is opportunity riding on a dangerous wind.
- The two greatest fear busters are knowledge and action.
- Success is a process, not a status.
- The road to success is always under construction.
- Real success comes in small portions, day by day.
- If you think you can, you can.
- LUCK is Laboring Under Correct Knowledge.
- The most important opinion you have is the one you hold of yourself.
- Our rewards in life will depend on the quality and amount of contribution we make.
- Losers let it happen. Winners make it happen!
- Winners work at doing things the majority of the population is not willing to do.
- The reason so many individuals fail to achieve their goals in life is that they never really set them in the first place.
- What you get is what you set.

Once you have completed these exercises the first time through, you should be able to plan future 90-day periods in approximately an hour and a half. Make this an enjoyable time. Perhaps you'll want to go with your spouse for brunch to set your personal goals. Make your professional goals during a workday several days in advance of the next 90-day period.

The Spring Season of Your 90-Day Cycle of Success

Spring is the time to get specific as you initiate your coming season of success.

Focus on your coming week.

Map out a specific plan for your coming week before Monday morning. I know many people who enjoy doing this on Friday afternoon so they can enjoy a carefree weekend. I personally enjoy making my weekly plans on Sunday afternoon. Be prepared to start Monday morning with both feet running.

- Detail what you hope to accomplish at home and at work.
- Double-check your calendar to make certain that all of your appointments are on it as well as deadlines for certain goals.
- Block off segments of time that you will need for completing the coming week's work goals or for working on long-range projects.
- Make luncheon appointments in advance.
- Make a special note of two or three major items you need to accomplish during the coming week.
- List two or three people you would like to contact during the week, either by making a phone call or by dropping them a short note.

Don't forget to consult your spouse as you project your coming week. You may well have forgotten a key event or appointment made on your behalf!

Planning your coming week should take you no more than thirty minutes and may take as little as five minutes. It will be some of the most valuable time you spend toward accomplishing your short-term and long-term goals.

If you are the manager of a group of people, make a list of the key items you are expecting from each person during the coming week. (That way, you will be on top of what you are expecting of your entire department at a glance.)

You can plan your week more easily if you adopt a habit of writing down every commitment at the time you make it. For example, don't say to someone, "I'll call you next week." Instead, say, "I'll call you next Thursday. What would be a good time?" Then write your commitment on your calendar. If you tell someone that you will follow up with a memo or report, write down your commitment to do that as part of the things you plan to do the following day.

You may want to keep a separate list handy of items that you need to do on a weekly basis: standing meetings and appointments, deadlines for turning in time reports or expense accounts, and so forth. Having this list handy will save you time as you plan your week. Schedule routine activities first on your calendar so that you can assign the remainder of your time to projects, appointments, or meetings that are flexible.

I suggest that you leave open a couple of hours toward the end of your work week. Assign them as such. That way, should unforeseen circumstances keep you from accomplishing all of your goals or prohibit you from following the schedule you have mapped out, you'll still have time set aside for completing those tasks. If you don't need the time at the end of the week, you can always use it to enhance your long-range goals—for example, by catching up on your journal and professional magazine reading, conducting additional research, holding impromptu meetings with your staff members (for morale building), working on a long-range project, or beginning a project scheduled for the coming week.

Zero in on your next day

Before you leave work in the evening, map out your agenda for the following day. Put items in priority. Know what you are going to do first when you walk into your office the following morning.

If you have fully planned your week, planning a specific day should take only a couple of minutes.

- Include habits that you are attempting to form. Nothing is too insignificant to put on your daily list; after all, this list is intended to help you and is FYEO—For Your Eyes Only. I know a person who even put "floss" on his daily list of things to do; he had not developed that habit as a child and was determined to do so as an adult.
- Highlight items that are "must do's."
- You may want to add several items in an in-case-I-still-have-time category. These should be items that, for the most part, appear elsewhere on your *weekly* list.
- Set aside time that is isolated. This should be considered not-to-be-interrupted-unless-the-emergency-is-truly-great time. In my studies of top performers I have found that most truly successful people tend to work on their key projects and priorities *before* 8:00 A.M. or *after* 5:00 P.M. simply because those are times when they can totally block out meetings, urgent phone calls, and other distracting interruptions. Top performers usually require one to two hours a day of "isolation time."

I believe, of course, that you can schedule this time during a regular workday. You need to make it a priority. Shut your door. Ask your secretary to take messages and guard your door. Alert

your colleagues, as well as your employees or those you supervise, about your need for this time. If your supervisor has a regular isolation time, you may want to adopt that time frame as your
own. (That way you will know that you are less likely to be interrupted by the boss for emergencies or consultations.)

The key to making successful daily and weekly plans is fitting
as many activities as possible into blocks of time.

The Summer Season of Your 90-Day Cycle of Success

During the summer season of your success, you should refer
frequently to the lists that you have made for yourself. This is the
season for working your plan. To work your plan, you need to
keep it at the forefront of your mind.

Carry your plan with you.

Not only should you keep your set of positive self-talk cards
with you, you should always have your calendar, including your
daily and weekly agendas, no farther than a briefcase away.

Are you aware that up to 90 percent of your best ideas will
come to you while you are away from your office? At these moments of inspiration, you need to be able to record your ideas
quickly and easily. Make certain that you always have a few blank
sheets of paper in your planner or clipped to your calendar and
agendas.

When you hear interesting statistics, quotes, or ideas, make a
note to yourself. Writing down these motivational and creative
ideas will stimulate you to continue your forward progress, even
as they add to your storehouse of knowledge.

Chart your progress

Keep track of your efforts. You may want to . . .

- keep a graph or chart for your jogging or exercise routines.
- make a graph to chart your progress as you lose weight.
- consider making bar graphs to display to yourself the number of times that you perform a task in the course of developing a new habit.

Keep lists of your accomplishments.

You'll find it helpful to keep a running list of "things done" as a companion to your list of "things to do." Looking at a list of things done—and done well—will keep you motivated.

Set your alarm for an hour earlier . . . tomorrow.

Get a jump on the day. Over a year, you'd gain about 260 hours by getting up an hour earlier than you are presently, and still you'd be able to sleep in on weekends. That's the equivalent of six and a half full work weeks! There's no time like the present to get started.

Periodically look through your "idea file."

Thumb through the lists or cards of ideas that you have gathered. You may be surprised as you rediscover some real gems. You may even find the exact idea that you need to get your plan moving forward toward your goals.

As you gather ideas, make QUANTITY a goal. Get as many ideas as you can get. If you are facing a tough problem or decision, try to come up with as many ideas—good, bad, or off the wall—as you can. When you run out of ideas, ask others to submit some. Make lists of all possible solutions, alternatives, possibilities. Let your mind expand all the way to the edge of the impossible.

Later, after the ideas have had a little time to cool, evaluate them. Choose among them. Take the approach that seems most in line with your goals, your values, your budget, and your ability to marshal resources and team players.

Do *not* attempt to create ideas and evaluate them at the same time. Go for QUANTITY in creating ideas. Go for QUALITY in evaluating them.

Make summer your time for seeking out idea-oriented people.

Ideally, encounters with these people should already be on your schedule. If they aren't, add them to your schedule as you

- sense the need for more ideas in a particular area of concern or need.
- meet idea-oriented people.
- become aware of idea-based seminars, lectures, meetings, books, or tapes.

Avail yourself of the opportunity to spend time in what I call expansive discussion with people who are wealthy in ideas and willing to share them generously. Adjust your schedule to accommodate such people. If you can't extend one particular conversation because of prior time commitments, reschedule an encounter. Go into such a session with lots of questions.

You can get opinions, information, and creative ideas from idea-oriented people if you are willing to listen rather than talk. Ask the person, "What do you know about this?" "Have you ever had this type of experience?" "What would you recommend to a person in this situation?" "What have you done?"

Idea people get excited when you express your ideas, and they enjoy talking about their own. They get fired up during a conversation. Best of all, they're the most likely people to fire up *you.* You will likely go away from such encounters with dozens of new possibilities to think about, new ideas to consider, new approaches to weigh.

Here are some items to keep in mind as you stay open and tuned in to the possibility of further growth and expansion during the summer season of your success:

1. Be aware that not all of the appointments that you desire to make at the beginning of a 90-day cycle, or even a work week, are likely to be known to you at the outset of your planning. Stay flexible as the days roll by. Find ways to schedule in worthy appointments, and make conversations with idea people a priority.
2. Don't limit yourself to ideas only in your discipline. You may be amazed to discover innovations in a field very different from the one in which you are planting and cultivating your success. Cross-pollinate whenever you can!
3. Write down ideas as soon as you leave conversations with idea-oriented people. A note pad and pen may be disruptive to a conversation. Be sure, however, to note the key ideas of a conversation as quickly as possible after it's over. Don't let ideas flutter away before you can net them.
4. Robert Hazard of Quality Inns divides ideas into two categories: lifters and poppers. Lifters are those he borrows from others. Poppers are those that come out of his own thinking process. Record the ideas of others and the ones that you contributed to a conversation or the ones that

spin off as you dwell on the ideas of another person. You're likely to find that lifters can start a chain reaction of poppers.

5. Find a way of keeping track of ideas that is comfortable for you. For some, carrying a packet of index cards may be the best way to go. For others, a pocket dictation machine or tape recorder may be the ideal method. Taking notes in a small loose-leaf notebook and transferring them to a more permanent format later may be the best method.

Give yourself a monthly checkup.

Review your goals and lists. Make adjustments you may need to make. Consider them to be midcourse corrections. Also . . .

- Monitor your stress level.
- Review ways in which you are feeding your willpower with motivating, inspiring "food."
- Double-check your practice of positive self-talk. Are you sticking with it?

The Autumn Season of Your 90-Day Cycle of Success

When harvests come, recognize them. Herald their arrival to yourself!

Enjoy the process of sharing your rewards with others. You may want to designate a portion of each paycheck or bonus check for specific charities. Enjoy mailing the checks.

You may want to purchase something and deliver it in person to a homeless shelter, Salvation Army collection center, or a program that gathers and delivers toys for needy children during the holidays. Make your giving count. Focus it just as you would an investment. Anticipate a good return.

And . . .

Reward yourself. Enjoy what you have accomplished. Relax in the pleasure of a job well done . . . a conscience clear . . . a means of helping others. And celebrate!

18

A Parting Word to Successful Life-Farmers

Just as the seasons roll around, so, too, the message of this book must be taken as a whole.

Life *is* a magnificent fertile garden plot given you to till, to plant, to nurture, and to reap from. What you grow in your garden *is* your choice. How you choose to enjoy the process along the way *is* also your choice.

Your garden will never be in a state of perfection. It will always be in transition.

With the end of each season is the anticipation of the next. No one season is the best, not even harvest. It has its special joys and its special challenges, just as each of the other seasons.

The end of a harvest brings a farmer to yet another winter season.

Again, there's a time to . . . Dream new dreams. Set new, and even higher, goals. Make new, and even better, plans.

At the conclusion of your harvest season—with your larder full for the winter, your friends sharing in your joy, others blessed by your generosity—step back to view the landscape of your garden. See its fertile soil of knowledge, role models, dreams, energy with which to put forth effort, creativity, resources. Use the final moments of your harvest season to ask yourself several questions before you move inside for the coming winter season . . .

· What about this harvest gives me greatest pleasure?
· Have I reaped the harvest I intended to reap?
· How might I have improved my yield?
· What would I like to grow next in this garden?

To everything there is a season and place under heaven.
There is a magnificent rhythm and cycle to life. Seed to sprout,
   Sprout to bloom,
        Bloom to blossom,
             Blossom to fruit,
                  Fruit to seed.
Success is a process. It cycles again and again. How you use the cycle to produce what benefits your life and the lives of others is up to you.
Enjoy your growth.
Be a man or woman . . .

                                    for all seasons!